90
calories

TODAY'S
All-Purpose
Cookbook

Favorite Recipes® *of Home Economics Teachers*

© Favorite Recipes Press/Nashville EMS MCMLXXXII
P. O. Box 77, Nashville, Tennessee 37202

Library of Congress Cataloging in Publication Data
Main entry under title:
Todays all-purpose cookbook.
Includes index.
1. Cookery.   I. Favorite Recipes Press.
TX715.T628   641.5   81-17244
ISBN 0-87197-136-4   AACR2

Dear Homemaker:

In the 1980s more women than ever before must integrate the roles of career person, mother and spouse into one frantic nonstop life-style. For you, time and efficiency are important. But so are the satisfaction of cooking and the anticipation of trying new recipes. That's why we feel you will enjoy this new Favorite Recipes Press cookbook so much.

Not only does it contain a brand new selection of favorite recipes of Home Economics teachers across the land, but abounds with kitchen tricks to save time and money; convenient charts and cooking hints. It's the kind of cookbook that everyone will enjoy using . . . from ingenues to cooking wizards.

The *TODAY'S All-Purpose Cookbook* is written especially for the all-purpose you!

Cordially,

Mary Jane Blount

Mary Jane Blount
FAVORITE RECIPES PRESS

Board of Advisors

Favorite Recipes Press wants to recognize the following who graciously serve on our Home Economics Teachers' Advisory Board:

Frances Rudd
Supervisor, Home Economics
   Education
Arkansas Department of Education

C. Janet Latham
Supervisor, Home Economics
   Education
Idaho State Board of Vocational
   Education

Catherine A. Carter
Head Consultant, Consumer
   Homemaking Education
Illinois Division of Vocational
   and Technical Education

Barbara Gaylor
Supervisor, Home Economics
   Education Unit
Michigan Department of Education

Louann Heinrichs
Home Economics Teacher
Greenville High School
Greenville, Ohio

Roberta Looper
1982 President, National
   Association of Vocational
   Home Economics Teachers
Livingston, Tennessee

Phyllis L. Barton
Past President, National Association of
Vocational Home Economics Teachers
Alexandria, Virginia

Contents

Introducing:
Your Every Day Cookbook

Now you can easily plan your menus every day with this innovative all-purpose cookbook. It's sure to be your most basic kitchen tool . . . a guidebook of cooking know-how . . . and a fast reference for practical advice . . . all rolled into one handy book!

TODAY'S All-Purpose Cookbook includes recipes to fit every budget, plus photos to help you serve finished dishes with a flair. But right now, thumb through the pages and become familiar with all the kitchen tricks and cooking information. Sensational ideas in every chapter! You'll be able to prepare for all occasions — from family snacks to a dinner party for 12 — with the ease and efficiency of an all-purpose homemaker!

Kitchen Tricks...

. . . FOR UTENSILS

- Use a pizza cutter to slice warm brownies easier.
- When your rubber spatula gets battered, trim the edges and continue using. Even as it narrows in size, it's ideal for scraping the contents of narrow-necked bottles.
- To freshen a sponge, soak overnight in water mixed with a small amount of salt or baking soda — or place in the washing machine with your next load of clothes.

. . . FOR SAVING ENERGY

- Turn the oven off the last few minutes of baking. The retained heat will continue baking without extra energy expense.
- To prevent heat from escaping, select pots with tight-fitting lids.
- For even cooking and less heat loss, choose pans with flat bottoms.
- Use a double boiler to heat two foods at the same time.

. . . FOR COOKING

- Scoop out a stray piece of eggshell easier with an empty eggshell half.
- Cottage cheese stored upside down keeps twice as long.
- Heat your pan first before adding butter or oil; foods won't stick.
- Revive the flavor and texture of nuts by heating in a 100° oven for ten minutes.
- When you buy fresh parsley or chives, quickly wrap and freeze unused portions to prevent withering.

Leftovers...What To Do Next

One of the biggest challenges for today's cook is how to "love those leftovers!" Whether it's a second night casserole or a dab of vegetables too small to serve, leftovers always seem to be there. Transform those tidbits into delicious meals the second time around using the following guidelines. Who knows? They may even taste better than the first time you served them!

LEFTOVER

Vegetables

SURVIVAL TRICKS

- Mix with a fresh vegetable salad for a meal-in-a-hurry.
- Save small dabs in the freezer until a container is full . . . then use with vegetable soup stock for a garden-fresh taste any time of the year.
- Make into a casserole by contrasting colors and texture for a gourmet delight.
- Slice baked potatoes and mix with salad dressing for a quick addition to an easy supper, picnic or cookout.
- Freeze tomato paste in small portions; then use when needed to create savory sauces in just the right quantity.

Meat, Poultry, Fish

- Bite-sized bits of roast beef, ham or turkey turn a plain green salad into a complete meal — fit for the most discriminating guests.
- Use your imagination and create a casserole you've never tried before by adding rice or noodles to a variety of meats in a sauce spiced to perfection.
- Invent your own soup! Blend with a creamy sauce and serve as an appetizer for your next dinner party.
- Try this for a lunch box treat . . . mix with celery and mayonnaise, cream cheese or sour cream and create a tasty sandwich spread.

Fruit

- Top your favorite pudding, ice cream or pound cake with warm fruit cooked until soft and delicious!
- Serve dabs of fruit with grated cheese, nuts or flaked coconut for a snack that's as tasty as it is nutritious.
- Add sour cream and a new spice or two to warm fruit. An easy gourmet treat.

Making Sauces Simple

Miraculously transform meat, fish or poultry into a masterpiece just by adding a simple sauce! Basic savory sauces are few in number, but their variations are almost limitless when spices, herbs or seasonings are added. (See the Spice/Herb Chart on pages 12 and 13 for ideas to combine new flavors!) Here are some quick sauces using creamed soups as a base — so easy for today's busy cooks.

JIFFY SAUCE	SOUP BASE	HOW TO DO IT
Cheese	Cream of celery, chicken or mushroom	Mix 3 tbsp. milk with 1/2 cup Cheddar cheese; season to taste.
Mock Hollandaise	Cream of celery, chicken or mushroom	Mix 1/4 cup mayonnaise with 3 tbsp. water and 3 tsp. lemon juice; season to taste.
Mushroom	Cream of Mushroom	Mix with chopped, fresh mushrooms; season to taste.
Peppery Cheese	Cheddar Cheese	Mix with cayenne pepper and Tabasco sauce to taste.
Sour Cream	Cream of celery, chicken or mushroom	Mix with 1/2 cup sour cream. Add milk, if needed; season to taste.
Tomato	Tomato	Saute onions and green peppers. Add a dash of Worcestershire sauce for extra flavor; season to taste.

Flavor Makers ...

SPICE/HERB	MEAT/DAIRY	FISH/EGGS/ POULTRY	VEGETABLES	FRUIT	BREADS/ SWEETS
Allspice	Ground beef Ham Roasts Sausage Stews	Clam chowder Oysters	Beets Red cabbage Spinach Sweet potatoes Tomatoes	Apples Bananas Cherries Citrus fruit Peaches	Cookies Fruit pies Mincemeat Pumpkin pie Spice cake
Basil	Beef Cheese dishes Liver Pork Veal	Duck Egg dishes Goose Seafood Turkey	Carrots Green beans Peas Summer Squash Tomatoes		
Caraway Seed	Cheese dip Cottage cheese Liver Pork	Fish salads Stuffed eggs Tuna casserole	Cauliflower Cucumbers Potatoes Sauerkraut	Apples Applesauce	Biscuits Corn bread Rye bread

Celery (seed salt, flakes)	Cheese mixtures
	Ham spread
	Meat loaf
	Roasts
	Stews
		Chicken
		  casseroles
		Chowders
		Deviled eggs
		Seafood
			Coleslaw
			Corn
			Potatoes
			Sauerkraut
			Tomatoes
				Fruit salads
				Fruit salad
				  dressings
					Bread

Cinnamon	Ham Lamb Pork	Chicken Duck Fish	Artichokes Beans Beets Carrots Pumpkin Sweet potatoes	Apples Cranberries Dates Grapefruit Peaches Pineapple	Cakes Cheesecake Chocolate Cookies Pies Waffles
Cloves	Beef Ham Pork Sausage	Chicken Duck Fish	Beans Beets Onions Sweet potatoes Tomatoes Winter squash	Apples Bananas Citrus fruit Cranberries Peaches Pears	Cookies Fruitcake Gingerbread Mincemeat Steamed pudding Sweet breads
Cumin	Beef Cheese dishes Chicken Indian dishes Mexican dishes	Chicken soup Chili powder Curry powder Deviled eggs Fish	Beans Cabbage Pea soup Rice Sauerkraut	Chutney	Rye bread
Curry	Beef Veal	Chicken Clam chowder Egg dishes Seafood	Carrots Lentils Rice Tomatoes	Apples Bananas Pineapple	Biscuits
Ginger	Barbeque Corned beef Meat loaf Pot roast Veal	Chicken Poultry stews Turkey	Beets Carrots Pumpkin Sweet potatoes Winter squash	Apples Bananas Figs Pears Pineapple	Cookies Gingerbread Indian pudding Pies Spice cake

Herbs and Spices

SPICE/HERB	MEAT/DAIRY	FISH/EGGS/POULTRY	VEGETABLES	FRUIT	BREADS/SWEETS
Marjoram	Beef Cheese dishes Game Ham	Chicken Creamed eggs Goose Seafood	Mushrooms Peas Salad Greens Zucchini		

Mustard	Beef and Veal
	Cheese spread
	Ham and Pork
	Sausage
		Chicken
		Deviled eggs
		Omelets
		Seafood
			Any vegetable,
			  when mixed
			  in butter or
			  sauce
				Fruit salad
				  dressings
					Biscuits

Nutmeg	Cheese fondue Ground meat Sausage	Chicken Oysters	Carrots Cauliflower Chinese peas Green beans Spinach Summer squash	Bananas Cherries Peaches Pears Prunes Rhubarb	Cakes Cookies Custard pie Doughnuts Muffins Puddings
Oregano	Beef and veal Italian dishes Mexican dishes Pork	Eggs Fish Game birds Turkey	Bean salads Green beans Guacamole Mushrooms		

Paprika	Beef
	Cheese mixture
	Pork
	Sour cream
	  mixes
	Veal
		Fish
		Omelets
		Poultry
			Beans
			Cabbage
			Cauliflower
			Corn
			Potatoes
				Fruit salads
				Fruit salad
				  dressings	

Rosemary	Beef Italian dishes Pork Veal	Chicken Rabbit Salmon	Broccoli Brussels sprouts Cabbage Potatoes	Fruit cocktail Jam Jelly	Ham biscuits
Saffron	Sausage Veal	Chicken Curry Seafood Spanish dishes	Rice		Cakes Fancy rolls

Tarragon	Game
	Meat marinades
	Steak
	Sweetbreads
	Veal
		Chicken
		Duck
		Eggs
		Squab
		Turkey
			Marinades for:
			  Cauliflower
			  Artichokes
			  Asparagus		

Thyme	All meats Cheese mixtures Game Liver	Duck Poultry Scrambled eggs Shellfish	Beans Spinach Tomatoes Zucchini		

Appetizers and Accompaniments

Appetizers are versatile! They cover the gamut from charming tidbits for nibbling on before dinner, to an evening's entire repast. Best of all, serving them is a clever way to use up leftovers!

In addition to appetizers, this useful chapter offers many fine recipes for accompaniments. From tempting jelly, jam and relishes, you'll want to try this fall harvest season, to chunky soups and chowders — just right for cold winter nights. Your all-purpose cookbook will come in handy year-round!

TRICKS OF THE TRADE

- Use skewered fruit for colorful drink stirrers.
- Keep the season in mind . . . use bright in-season vegetables with dips.
- To avoid sogginess, spread bread, cut in fancy shapes, with a thin coating of butter before adding spreads or fillings.
- Freeze bread for easier cutting into fancy shapes.
- Serve cheese at room temperature.
- When serving appetizers on a silver tray, protect the tray from food acids with lettuce or grape leaves as an undergarnish.
- Make "pincushions" of an apple or half a grapefruit, pineapple or orange by studding with delicacies, such as cubes of cheese, meat or fruit, on toothpicks.
- For a large party, arrange several small attractive plates of appetizers, which can be refilled easily, rather than a large one which loses its attractiveness as guests enjoy it.

CHEESE CANAPES

1 c. shredded med. Cheddar cheese
1 c. shredded Monterey Jack cheese
1 c. chopped green onions with stems
1 c. chopped mushrooms
1 c. chopped ripe olives
1 c. mayonnaise
1 loaf cocktail rye bread

Mix . . . . . first 6 ingredients together in large
bowl.
Spread . . . on cocktail rye bread.
Bake . . . . . at 375 degrees for 10 minutes.
Note . . . . . May be frozen before baking.

Mary Alsteens
Tomahawk H. S., Tomahawk, Wisconsin

CHEESE PUFFS

1 loaf unsliced white bread
1   3-oz. package cream cheese
1/4 lb. sharp cheese, shredded
1/2 c. butter
2 egg whites, stiffly beaten

Trim . . . . . crusts from bread and cut into 1-
inch cubes.
Melt . . . . . cheeses and butter in top of double
boiler, stirring until smooth and
creamy.
Remove . . from heat.
Fold . . . . . in egg whites.
Dip . . . . . . bread cubes into cheese mixture to
coat.
Place . . . . on baking sheet.
Chill . . . . . in refrigerator overnight.
Bake . . . . . at 400 degrees for 12 to 15 minutes
or until golden brown.

Marie W. Davis
Grenada H. S., Grenada, Mississippi

CHEESE ROLL

1 lb. Velveeta cheese
1 8-oz. package cream cheese, softened
1 c. chopped nuts
Chili powder

Mix . . . . . first three ingredients together.
Shape . . . . into a log by rolling between waxed
paper.

Roll . . . . . log in chili powder until coated.
Wrap . . . . in waxed paper.
Chill . . . . . for several hours or overnight.

Flora Hoybook
DeSoto H. S., DeSoto, Texas

CHEESE STRAWS

4 c. sifted flour
1/4 tsp. soda
1 tsp. salt
1/2 tsp. red pepper
3/4 c. Wesson oil
1 lb. sharp cheese, shredded

Sift . . . . . . dry ingredients together and set
aside.
Cream . . . oil and cheese in bowl until
blended.
Combine . dry ingredients and cheese mixture,
adding additional oil if necessary.
Press . . . . . through cookie press onto baking
sheet.
Bake . . . . . at 350 degrees for 12 minutes.
Yields . . . . 250 Cheese Straws/about 10 calories each.

Rita Marable
Crawford County H. S., Roberta, Georgia

HAWAIIAN CHICKEN WINGS

1/2 c. cornstarch
1/2 c. flour
1 egg, beaten
2 lb. chicken wings, disjointed
1 tbsp. soy sauce
1/2 tsp. monosodium glutamate
3/4 c. sugar
3 to 4 tbsp. catsup
1/4 c. chicken broth
1/2 c. vinegar
1/2 c. light corn syrup
1/2 c. crushed pineapple, drained

Combine . cornstarch and flour in bowl.
Beat . . . . . egg with 1/2 tablespoon water in
small bowl.
Dip . . . . . . wings in flour mixture, then into
egg mixture.
Fry . . . . . . in hot oil until brown, turning
once.

Place .... in baking dish.
Combine . all remaining ingredients in sauce-
pan, blending well.
Bring .... to a boil.
Pour ..... over chicken wings.
Bake ..... at 350 degrees for 1 1/2 hours.

Edith G. Gray
Cottonwood H. S., Salt Lake City, Utah

DRIED BEEF LOG

2 sm. jars dried beef
1 8-oz. package cream cheese, softened
2 tbsp. mayonnaise
1 tbsp. grated onion
1 tbsp. prepared horseradish
Chopped parsley

Place .... dried beef in blender container.
Process ... until finely chopped.
Combine . beef with remaining ingredients ex-
cept parsley in bowl, mixing
thoroughly.
Shape .... into 6 x 12-inch log.
Roll ..... in chopped parsley.
Serve .... with crackers.

Viola B. Farner
Central H. S., Louisville, Kentucky

GROUND BEEF
HORS D'OEUVRES

1 lb. ground beef
1 med. onion, chopped
Salt and pepper to taste
1 can refried beans
1 sm. can chopped green chilies
2 c. grated Cheddar cheese
3/4 c. taco sauce
2 green onions, chopped
1 sm. tomato
1/2 sm. bell pepper

Brown ... ground beef and onion in oil in skillet, stirring until crumbly.
Season ... with salt and pepper.
Spread ... refried beans in bottom of small
casserole.
Layer .... ground beef and remaining ingredients over beans in order given.

Bake ..... at 400 degrees for 25 minutes.
Serve .... with sour cream and tostados.

Eileen Beauregard
Sequoyah H. S., Doraville, Georgia

PRETEND PATE

1 env. unflavored gelatin
1 10-oz. can beef consomme
1 8-oz. package cream cheese
1 8-oz. tube fine liver sausage
1/2 tsp. horseradish
1 1/2 tsp. Worcestershire sauce
1/2 tsp. Tabasco sauce
Salt and pepper to taste

Dissolve .. gelatin in consomme in saucepan
over low heat.
Pour ..... half the consomme into 4-cup
mold.
Chill ..... in refrigerator until firm.
Combine . remaining ingredients and remain-
ing liquid consomme in food pro-
cessor container.
Process ... until smooth.
Pour ..... over first layer in mold.
Chill ..... in refrigerator until firm.
Unmold .. and serve with dark rye bread.

Mrs. B. Williams
Crescent Heights H. S., Calgary, Alberta, Canada

CRAB MEAT APPETIZERS

1 stick butter, softened
6 to 7 oz. crab meat, flaked
1/2 tbsp. mayonnaise
1/2 tsp. garlic salt
1 8-oz. jar Cheese Whiz
6 English muffins, halved

Combine . first 5 ingredients in bowl, mixing
well.
Spread ... on English muffins.
Place .... on cookie sheet and freeze.
Cut ...... each half into quarters.
Broil ..... until golden.
Yields .... 49 servings/about 55 calories each.

Sally A. Goode
Norwayne H. S., Creston, Ohio

SAUSAGE SQUARES

1 lb. hot sausage
1/2 c. chopped onion
1/4 c. grated Parmesan cheese
1 egg, beaten
1/4 tsp. Tabasco sauce
1 1/2 tsp. salt
2 tbsp. chopped parsley
2 c. Bisquick
2/3 c. milk
1/4 c. mayonnaise
1 egg yolk, beaten

Brown ... sausage and onion in skillet over low heat, stirring until crumbly.
Drain .... sausage well.
Add ..... next 5 ingredients, mixing well.
Mix ..... Bisquick, milk and mayonnaise in bowl.
Spread ... half the dough over bottom of greased 8-inch baking pan.
Cover .... with sausage mixture.
Spread ... remaining dough over top.
Brush .... with beaten egg yolk.
Bake ..... at 400 degrees for 25 to 30 minutes.
Cut ...... into squares.
Serve .... hot or cold.

Deborah L. Vana
Varina H. S., Richmond, Virginia

TUNA ROLL

6 tbsp. chopped parsley
1 can tuna, drained
1/4 tsp. Tabasco sauce
1 sm. onion, minced
1/2 c. chopped cashews
1 8-oz. package cream cheese, softened

Mix ..... 4 tablespoons parsley and remaining ingredients in bowl.
Shape .... into a roll and chill until firm.
Roll ..... in remaining 2 tablespoons parsley.
Serve .... with crackers.

Judy Sandlin
Del Crest Jr. H. S., Del City, Oklahoma

POTATO SKINS

4 sm. baked potatoes
Peanut oil for deep frying

1 c. grated cheese
12 slices crisp-cooked bacon, crumbled
1/2 c. sour cream and chives

Cut ...... potatoes in half lengthwise.
Scoop .... out potatoes leaving shells.
Fry ...... shells in hot deep fat until crisp.
Drain .... well on paper towels.
Arrange .. shells on cookie sheet.
Sprinkle .. with cheese and bacon.
Broil ..... until cheese melts.
Serve .... with sour cream and chives.

Becky Minson
Duncan H. S., Duncan, Oklahoma

VEGETABLE SANDWICHES

2 cucumbers, grated
1 sm. onion, grated
1 sm. bell pepper, chopped
2 tomatoes, chopped
1 pkg. unflavored gelatin
1 pt. mayonnaise

Drain .... vegetables thoroughly.
Soften ... gelatin in 1/4 cup cold water in medium bowl.
Add ..... 1/4 cup boiling water, stirring until dissolved.
Stir ...... vegetables into gelatin.
Add ..... mayonnaise, stirring to mix.
Chill ..... in airtight container overnight.
Serve .... as spread on bread or crackers.

Linda W. Skelton
Walterboro Sr. H. S., Walterboro, South Carolina

STUFFED MUSHROOM CAPS

2 doz. large mushrooms
1/2 c. soy sauce
1/2 lb. ground beef
1/4 c. minced green pepper
2 tbsp. bread crumbs
1 egg yolk
1 tbsp. minced onion
1/2 clove of garlic
1/4 tsp. each pepper, salt

Remove .. stems from mushrooms.
Marinate .. caps for 1 hour in soy sauce.
Chop .... stems finely.
Combine . stems with remaining ingredients in bowl, mixing well.

Drain . . . . mushrooms caps.
Stuff . . . . caps with meat mixture.
Brush . . . . tops with soy sauce.
Broil . . . . . for 8 to 10 minutes.
Note . . . . . stuffed mushrooms may be frozen before baking. Thaw before baking.
Yields . . . . 24 servings/about 40 calories each.

Sandra J. Lau
Lockport Sr. H. S., Lockport, New York

VEGETABLE FONDUE CURRY

1 green onion, minced
1/4 c. butter
2 tbsp. flour
1 tsp. minced ginger root
1/2 c. chopped apple
1 to 2 tsp. curry powder
1 tsp. salt
1 tsp. sugar
4 whole cloves
Dash of cayenne pepper
2 c. milk
1/2 c. moist shredded coconut
1/4 c. lemon juice
Thin cream

Saute . . . . onion in butter in electric skillet until transparent.
Blend . . . . in flour.

Add . . . . . next 7 ingredients, mixing well.
Add . . . . . milk gradually, stirring to blend.
Cook . . . . until thick, stirring constantly.
Reduce . . . temperature to very low.
Cook . . . . covered, for 30 minutes longer, stirring occasionally.
Remove . . cloves; stir in coconut.
Add . . . . . lemon juice gradually, blending well.
Place . . . . in fondue pot or casserole with warmer.
Serve . . . . with fresh vegetables.
Add . . . . . cream as needed to thin fondue.

Photograph for this recipe on page 14.

ZIPPY BEAN AND BACON DIP

1 11 1/2-oz. can bean with bacon soup
1 3-oz. package cream cheese, softened
1/2 c. minced ham
2 tsp. horseradish
1 tsp. prepared mustard
1 lg. green pepper

Beat . . . . . soup and cream cheese together in bowl.
Stir . . . . . . in ham, horseradish and mustard.
Remove . . top and seed from pepper.
Fill . . . . . . with dip.
Chill . . . . . in refrigerator until serving time.
Serve . . . . with celery sticks and crackers.

Photograph for this recipe on this page.

CHEDDAR CHEESE DIP

2 c. sour cream
1 1/2 c. shredded sharp Cheddar cheese
1 med. green pepper, finely chopped
1 sm. onion, minced
1/2 c. chopped stuffed green olives
2 tbsp. lemon juice
1 tsp. salt
1/4 tsp. paprika
1 tsp. Worcestershire sauce
Dash of Tabasco sauce

Combine . all ingredients in bowl, mixing thoroughly; cover.
Chill . . . . . for several hours.
Serve . . . . with crackers or chips.

Connie Schlimgen
Washington Sr. H. S., Sioux Falls, South Dakota

SNAPPY HAM AND CHEESE SNACKS

1/4 c. chopped onion
2 tbsp. catsup
1 tbsp. prepared mustard
1/4 c. butter, melted
1 8-oz. can Pillsbury Refrigerated Quick
   Crescent Rolls
8 thin slices boiled ham
Sesame seed (opt.)

Combine . first   3   ingredients   with   3
             tablespoons butter in small bowl,
             mixing well.
Separate .. roll   dough   into   4   rectangles,
             pressing to seal perforations.
Cut . . . . . . each   rectangle   in   half;   stretch
             dough to form eight 4 x 4-inch
             squares.
Spread . . . with catsup mixture; top with ham.
Roll . . . . . up tightly, sealing edges.
Cut . . . . . . each roll into 3 pieces.
Place . . . . seam side down on baking sheet.
Spread . . . with remaining 1 tablespoon butter.
Sprinkle .. with sesame seed.
Bake . . . . . at 375 degrees for 18 to 22 minutes
             until brown.

Photograph for this recipe above.

CHEESY DIP

1 1/2 c. grated Cheddar cheese
3/4 c. mayonnaise
1/3 c. bacon bits
1 tbsp. minced onion
1/2 c. slivered almonds

Mix . . . . . all ingredients together in bowl.
Serve . . . . with a variety of crackers and raw
             vegetables.

Janet K. Alvord
Gilmanton H.S., Gilmanton, Wisconsin

EVERLASTING BRANDIED CHEESE SPREAD

1 lb. sharp Cheddar cheese, grated
4 oz. cream cheese, softened
3 tbsp. olive oil
1 tsp. caraway seed
1 tsp. dry mustard
1 1/2 oz. Brandy

Combine . cheese, cream cheese and olive oil
             in bowl.
Add . . . . . caraway seed, mustard and Brandy,
             mixing well.
Store . . . . in sealed crock in refrigerator.
Serve . . . . at room temperature.
Note . . . . . As spread is used, add grated
             cheese, mustard and Brandy as
             desired.

Beverly W. Wisner
Maitland Jr. H. S., Maitland, Florida

CHILI CON QUESO

1 tsp. chopped onion
1/4 stick margarine, melted
Dash of garlic powder
Tabasco sauce to taste
1 jar hot taco sauce
1 lg. package Velveeta cheese, cubed

Saute . . . . onion in margarine in skillet.
Add . . . . . garlic powder, Tabasco and taco
             sauce, mixing well.
Add . . . . . cheese gradually, stirring constantly
             until melted.
Serve . . . . warm with tostados.

Gloria Walsh
Hoffman Estates H. S., Hoffman Estates, Illinois

CRAB MEAT DIP

1 8-oz. package cream cheese, softened
2 tbsp. finely chopped onions
1/2 tsp. creamy horseradish
Dash of pepper
1 can crab meat, flaked
1 tbsp. milk
1/4 tsp. salt

Cream ... all ingredients together in bowl.
Spoon ... into casserole.
Bake ..... at 375 degrees for 15 minutes.
Serve .... hot with assorted raw vegetables.

Kay F. Poole
Friendly Sr. H. S., Silver Spring, Maryland

PIZZA DIP

1 8-oz. package cream cheese, softened
1 bottle of cocktail sauce
3/4 c. diced cooked shrimp
3/4 c. chopped green onions
3/4 c. chopped bell pepper
3/4 c. diced tomatoes
3/4 c. chopped ripe olives
3/4 c. diced mozzarella cheese

Spread ... cream cheese to cover bottom of
            pizza pan.
Pour ..... cocktail sauce over cream cheese.
Combine . remaining ingredients in bowl, mix-
            ing well.
Spread ... over cocktail sauce.
Chill ..... for 2 hours.
Serve ... with Ritz crackers.

Patricia Moore
Hot Springs H. S., Hot Springs, Arkansas

PIZZA FONDUE

1 lb. mozzarella cheese, grated
1/2 c. milk
1/2 c. Parmesan cheese
1 4-oz. package sliced pepperoni, chopped
1 8-oz. can tomato sauce
1/4 tsp. garlic powder
1/2 tsp. oregano
1/2 tsp. Italian seasoning
1 loaf Italian bread, cut into 1-inch cubes

Combine . all ingredients except bread cubes
            in fondue pot.
Cook .... over medium heat until cheese is
            melted, stirring constantly.
Serve .... warm with bread cubes for dipping.

Diane Intoccio
Reynoldsburg Jr. H. S., Reynoldsburg, Ohio

SUMMER DELIGHT FRUIT DIP

1 8-oz. package cream cheese, softened
1 jar marshmallow creme
1 tbsp. orange juice
Dash of ginger
1 tbsp. orange rind

Combine . all ingredients in bowl, mixing well.
Chill ..... in refrigerator overnight.
Serve .... with variety of fresh fruit chunks.

Kathleen Hammer
Cradock H. S., Portsmouth, Virginia

ARTICHOKE DIP

2 14-oz. cans artichoke hearts, drained,
    chopped
2 c. Hellman's mayonnaise
1 pkg. Good Seasons Italian dressing mix

Combine . artichoke hearts, mayonnaise and
            Italian dressing mix in bowl.
Chill ..... in refrigerator until serving time.
Serve .... with bread sticks or thin wheat
            crackers.

Pamela Truhett
Woodland H. S., Woodland, Mississippi

NANCY'S ARTICHOKE DIP

1 1/4 c. mayonnaise
Parmesan cheese
1 15 1/2-oz. can artichoke hearts, chopped

Combine . mayonnaise and 1 cup Parmesan
            cheese in casserole.
Fold in ... artichoke hearts.
Bake ..... at 350 degrees for 20 minutes.
Sprinkle .. with additional Parmesan cheese.
Serve .... warm with crackers.

Nancy Burky
Osborne H. S., Marietta, Georgia

BROCCOLI DIP

1 med. onion, chopped
1 sm. jar sliced mushrooms
1/2 stick margarine
3 pkg. frozen chopped broccoli, cooked,
    drained
1 can cream of mushroom soup
1 roll garlic cheese, sliced
1 roll jalapeno cheese, sliced
1 pkg. chopped blanched almonds

Saute .... onion and mushrooms in margarine
            in skillet.
Add ..... broccoli and soup, mixing well.
Reduce ... heat and add cheeses.
Cook .... over low heat until cheese melts,
            stirring constantly.
Add ..... almonds, mixing well.
Serve .... warm with party crackers.

Lucy Ray
Hambrick Jr. H. S., Houston, Texas

CALEEN'S MEXICAN DIP

1 lg. can refried beans
8 to 10 green onions, chopped
1 lg. tomato, chopped
1 4-oz. can diced green chiles
1 sm. can sliced black olives
1 pt. sour cream
1 c. grated Cheddar cheese

Layer .... ingredients in order given in 8 x
            12-inch serving dish.
Chill ..... for several hours.
Serve .... with corn chips and Salsa Cruda.

Salsa Cruda

4 med. tomatoes, peeled, chopped
1/2 c. each finely chopped onion, celery
1/4 c. finely chopped green bell pepper
1/4 c. olive oil
2 to 3 tbsp. finely chopped green chiles
2 tbsp. red wine vinegar
1 tsp. mustard seed
1 tsp. crushed coriander
1 tsp. salt
Dash of pepper

Combine . all ingredients in large bowl.

Chill ..... covered, for several hours, stirring
            occasionally.
Serve .... as relish or sauce.

Bette Jahrmarkt
Chaparral H. S., Scottsdale, Arizona

LEEK DIP IN A LOAF

1 c. sour cream
1 c. mayonnaise
1 pkg. Knorr leek soup
1 pkg. chopped spinach, cooked, drained
1 bunch green onion tops, chopped
1 can water chestnuts, drained, chopped
1 lg. round loaf French bread

Mix ..... all ingredients except bread to-
            gether in bowl.
Hollow ... out French loaf, cutting bread into
            bite-sized cubes.
Spoon ... dip into French bread bowl.
Serve .... by spreading dip on French bread
            cubes.

Sheila D. Walker
Ygnacio Valley H. S., Concord, California

HOT SPINACH DIP

1 pkg. frozen chopped spinach, drained well
1 8-oz. package cream cheese, softened
1/2 c. mayonnaise
1/3 c. Parmesan cheese
2 tbsp. lemon juice
6 slices crisp-cooked bacon, crumbled
2 tbsp. chopped green onion

Combine . all ingredients in microwave serving
            dish, mixing well.
Microwave on Medium for 3 to 4 minutes, stir-
            ring several times.
Serve .... warm with crackers.

Martha Dunlap
Corsicana H. S., Corsicana, Texas

SPINACH DIP

2 10-oz. packages frozen chopped spinach,
    cooked, drained
1 c. grated Cheddar cheese

3 hard-boiled eggs, chopped
1/2 c. celery, chopped
1/2 c. onions, chopped
1 1/2 c. mayonnaise
1 1/2 tsp. salad vinegar
2 tsp. horseradish
1/2 tsp. Tabasco sauce (opt.)
1/2 tsp. salt

Combine . all ingredients in large bowl, mixing well.
Chill . . . . . well before serving.

Betsy Gustwick
Congress Jr. H. S., Denton, Texas

DILL PICKLES

Cucumbers
2 c. vinegar
4 tsp. salt
2 tbsp. sugar
1 tsp. pickle spice
Fresh dillweed
Chopped garlic

Pack . . . . . cucumbers solidly into clean jars.
Combine . next 4 ingredients with 6 cups water in saucepan.
Heat . . . . . to boiling point.
Pour . . . . . over cucumbers, leaving 3/4-inch headspace.
Add . . . . . dill and garlic.
Place . . . . lids on jars loosely.
Place . . . . in 200-degree oven until cucumbers change color.
Remove . . from oven.
Seal . . . . . jars tightly.

Geralyn Sue Knill
Bunker Jr. H. S., Muskegon, Michigan

CILE'S DILL PICKLES

1 qt. vinegar
3/4 c. salt
Cucumbers
14 med. heads dill
Garlic
Powdered alum

Combine . vinegar, salt and 2 quarts water in large kettle.
Pack . . . . . cucumbers in sterilized jars.

Add . . . . . 2 heads dill, 2 thin slices garlic and 1/4 teaspoon alum to each quart.
Cover . . . . cucumbers with hot vinegar mixture leaving 1/2-inch headspace.
Seal . . . . . jars with sterilized lids.
Yields . . . . 7 quarts.

Jane J. McFerrin
Shamrock H. S., Decatur, Georgia

PEPPER JELLY

1 c. chopped green peppers
1/4 c. jalapeno peppers, chopped
1 1/2 c. cider vinegar
6 1/2 c. sugar
4 or 5 drops of green food coloring
1 bottle of Certo

Process . . . peppers and 1/3 cup vinegar in blender container.
Combine . with sugar and remaining vinegar in saucepan.
Boil . . . . . mixture for 5 minutes.
Stir . . . . . . in food coloring and Certo.
Pour . . . . . into hot sterilized jars leaving 1/2-inch headspace.
Seal . . . . . with paraffin.
Serve . . . . over cream cheese with crackers.
Yields . . . . 3 pints.

Mrs. Nancy Weis
Glasgow H. S., Glasgow, Kentucky

SOUR CHERRY JAM

5 c. fresh sour cherries, pitted
5 c. sugar
2 tbsp. lemon juice

Heat . . . . . cherries slowly in covered saucepan until skins soften slightly.
Add . . . . . sugar and lemon juice, mixing well.
Cook . . . . briskly for 15 minutes or to 218 degrees on thermometer.
Chill . . . . . in refrigerator overnight.
Bring . . . . jam to a boil.
Boil . . . . . for 1 minute.
Pour . . . . . into hot sterilized jars leaving 1/2-inch headspace; seal.
Process . . . in boiling water bath for 5 minutes.
Yields . . . . four to five 8-ounce jars.

Linda A. Lee
Lewiston-Porter Sr. H. S., Youngstown, New York

SEASONED SALT

1 box salt
1 1/2 oz. pepper
2 oz. cayenne pepper
1 oz. chili powder
1 oz. garlic powder
1 oz. Accent

Combine . all ingredients in large bowl, mixing well.
Store . . . . in airtight container.

Brenda Simmons
Dayton H. S., Dayton, Texas

SQUASH RELISH

2/3 c. salt
2 c. chopped onion
2 c. chopped bell pepper
1 lg. jar pimento, chopped
8 c. chopped squash
2 tsp. celery seed
2 c. white vinegar
2 tsp. mustard seed
3 c. sugar

Dissolve . . salt in 3 quarts water in large kettle.
Soak . . . . . next 4 ingredients in salted water for 1 hour.
Bring . . . . remaining ingredients to a boil in large kettle.
Add . . . . . drained vegetables to syrup mixture.
Bring . . . . to a boil.
Pour . . . . . into hot sterilized jars leaving 1/2-inch headspace.
Seal . . . . . with sterilized lids.
Yields . . . . 6 quarts.

Julie E. Browning
Mabank H. S., Mabank, Texas

BARBECUE SAUCE

1 c. chopped celery
1/3 c. catsup
1 tsp. hot sauce
1 tbsp. dry mustard
1/2 c. packed brown sugar
1 c. chopped onion
1 tsp. salt
1 tsp. chili powder
1/4 c. vinegar

Combine . all ingredients and 1 cup water in saucepan, mixing well.
Cook . . . . for 45 minutes.
Braise . . . . chops or ribs in sauce in usual manner.

Anne P. Barrett
Dixon Jr. H. S., Provo, Utah

SOOTER'S BARBECUE SAUCE

1 onion, chopped
1/2 c. chopped celery (opt.)
2 tbsp. butter
2 tbsp. vinegar
1 1/4 c. packed brown sugar
1/4 tsp. liquid smoke
2 c. catsup
3 tbsp. Worcestershire sauce
Salt and pepper to taste
1/2 tsp. mustard
1/2 tsp. cinnamon

Brown . . . onion and celery in butter in skillet.
Add . . . . . 1/2 cup water and remaining ingredients, mixing well.
Simmer . . for 30 minutes.
Serve . . . . over brisket.

Donna McGivern
Deer Creek H. S., Edmond, Oklahoma

GRANDMA'S CHILI SAUCE

18 tomatoes, cored, quartered
3 green peppers, chopped
1 c. sugar
1 1/2 c. vinegar
2 tsp. salt
1 tsp. each cloves, cinnamon and allspice
2 onions, diced

Combine . all ingredients in heavy saucepan.
Simmer . . until thick.
Pour . . . . . into hot sterilized jars.
Seal . . . . . immediately.

Anne E. Shadwick
Seneca H. S., Seneca, Missouri

HOT-SWEET MUSTARD SAUCE

1/4 c. dry mustard
2 tbsp. vegetable oil

1/4 c. sugar
1 tbsp. cornstarch
1/2 tsp. salt
1/4 c. white vinegar

Combine . mustard and oil in small bowl, stirring to blend well.
Add ..... 2 tablespoons water gradually, stirring constantly.
Combine . sugar, cornstarch and salt in small saucepan.
Add ..... 1/2 cup water and vinegar gradually, stirring constantly.
Cook .... over medium heat for 10 minutes or until thick, stirring constantly.
Add ..... to mustard mixture gradually, stirring constantly to blend.
Store .... covered, in refrigerator, stirring before serving.

Dianna Roller
Mountain Home Sr. H. S., Mountain Home, Arkansas

ALL-PURPOSE MEXICAN HOT SAUCE

2   16-oz. cans tomatoes
2 med. canned jalapeno peppers, peeled
1 tsp. garlic salt
1/4 c. white vinegar
1   4-oz. can diced green chiles
2 tsp. dried minced onion

Drain .... tomatoes into blender container, setting tomatoes aside.
Add ..... peppers, garlic salt and vinegar.
Process ... to blend well.
Add ..... chiles, onion and reserved tomatoes.
Process ... 1 to 2 seconds.
Store .... covered, in refrigerator.
Keeps .... for several weeks.

Von Esther Squires
Fort Morgan H. S., Ft. Morgan, Colorado

GERMAN MUSTARD BUTTER

1 lb. margarine, softened
1 1/2 to 2 c. mayonnaise
1 sm. jar creole mustard
2 tbsp. Worcestershire sauce

2 tsp. Season-All
1 tbsp. Tabasco sauce

Combine . all ingredients in bowl, mixing well.
Store .... covered, in refrigerator up to 1 week.
Serve .... with smoked meats as sandwich spread.

Diana K. Dukes
Marion H. S., Marion, Texas

ASPARAGUS SOUP MARSEILLES

1 lb. chopped asparagus spears, cooked, drained
2 1/2 c. milk
1 tsp. instant minced onion
1 tsp. each salt, dry mustard
1/2 tsp. capers
1/2 tsp. capers juice
Dash of pepper

Place .... all ingredients in blender container.
Process ... at high speed until thoroughly combined.
Pour ..... into 2-quart saucepan.
Heat ..... to serving temperature.
Garnish .. with chopped hard-cooked egg and pimento strips.
Yields .... 4 servings/about 117 calories each.

Photograph for this recipe below.

BROCCOLI CHOWDER

1 med. onion, finely chopped
1 lb. broccoli, chopped
3/4 c. celery, chopped
3 potatoes, peeled, sliced
2 carrots, sliced
1 tsp. dillweed
1 tsp. salt
1/2 tsp. pepper
1 qt. milk
1 c. grated Cheddar cheese
1/2 lb. crisp-cooked bacon, crumbled

Saute .... onion in bacon drippings in skillet until lightly browned.
Add ..... remaining vegetables, seasonings and 1 cup water.
Simmer .. covered, for 30 minutes.
Stir ...... in milk and continue cooking.
Add ..... cheese just before soup reaches boiling point, stirring until cheese melts.
Garnish .. with crumbled bacon.
Serve .... with hard crusted bread.
Yields .... 6 servings/about 505 calories each.

Carole Roth
Clear Lake Sr. H. S., Clear Lake, Iowa

CREAM OF BROCCOLI SOUP

1 c. finely chopped broccoli
1 sm. onion, chopped
1 1/2 tbsp. dry parsley flakes
1 can chicken broth
Salt and pepper to taste
1 c. cream
2 tbsp. cornstarch
Milk

Combine . broccoli, onion and parsley with broth and enough water to measure 2 cups liquid in saucepan.
Cook .... until broccoli is tender.
Puree .... vegetables and broth.
Add ..... seasoning and cream and continue cooking over low heat.
Blend .... cornstarch and a small amount of milk until smooth.
Add ..... to soup, blending thoroughly.
Cook .... until soup thickens, stirring constantly.
Garnish .. with parsley and pimento.

Note ..... recipe may be used with nearly any vegetable substituted for broccoli.
Yields .... 4 servings/about 295 calories each.

Margaret Ann Dover
Concord H. S., Concord, North Carolina

CREOLE BEAN SOUP

2 c. navy beans
1 hambone
2 c. shredded carrots
1/2 c. chopped onion
1/2 c. chopped celery
1/4 c. chopped green pepper
1 tsp. salt
2 c. canned tomatoes

Soak ..... beans overnight in 6 cups water in large saucepan.
Add ..... remaining ingredients except tomatoes.
Simmer .. for 2 1/2 hours or until beans are very tender.
Remove .. hambone.
Cut ...... ham from bone and add to soup.
Mash .... beans.
Stir ...... in tomatoes.
Simmer .. until hot.

Dorothy G. Rothermel
Pasadena H. S., Pasadena, Texas

CHEESY CHOWDER

1 c. chopped potato
1/2 c. chopped carrot
1/2 c. chopped celery
1/2 c. chopped green pepper
4 tbsp. butter
3 c. chicken broth
Dash of pepper
2 c. milk
1/2 c. flour
3 c. shredded sharp process American cheese
1 tbsp. snipped parsley

Cook .... vegetables in butter in Dutch oven until tender but not brown.
Add ..... broth and pepper.
Simmer .. covered, for 30 minutes.
Blend .... milk and flour in bowl until smooth.

Stir . . . . . . in cheese and parsley.
Add . . . . . to chowder, stirring to mix well.
Cook . . . . until thick and bubbly, stirring constantly.
Yields . . . . 8 servings/about 300 calories each.

Cynthia Kolberg
Fairfield Jr.-Sr. H. S., Goshen, Indiana

HAMBURGER SOUP

2 lb. ground beef
5 3/4 c. tomato juice
1 c. stewed tomatoes
2 tsp. basil
2 tsp. oregano
2 tbsp. dried onion flakes
1 bay leaf
1 tbsp. Worcestershire sauce
1 tbsp. garlic powder
2 c. chopped celery
1 c. sliced carrots
2 c. shredded cabbage
2 c. French-style green beans
Salt and pepper to taste

Brown . . . ground beef in soup pot.
Drain . . . . pan drippings.
Add . . . . . remaining ingredients, mixing well.
Cover . . . . bring to a boil and reduce heat.
Simmer . . for 2 hours.
Yields . . . . 10 servings/about 200 calories each.

Debra A. H. Bean
Rule H. S., Knoxville, Tennessee

CREAM OF POTATO SOUP WITH RIVVELS

1 lg. potato, cubed
Milk
Salt to taste
Butter to taste
1 egg
2 to 3 c. flour

Cook . . . . potato in water to cover in large saucepan until tender.
Add . . . . . 1 quart milk, salt and butter to potato and water.
Heat . . . . . slowly. Do not boil.
Combine . egg and flour in bowl, working with fingers into very small lumps.

Shake . . . . off excess flour and allow rivvels to dry briefly.
Drop . . . . into hot soup.
Cook . . . . until rivvels are done and soup is thickened, stirring occasionally.
Add . . . . . additional milk if needed.
Yields . . . . 4 servings/about 605 calories each.

Rosemary Harwood
North Stanly H. S., New London, North Carolina

CLAM CHOWDER

1/4 lb. salt pork, diced
1 c. sliced onions
1/2 c. chopped celery
1/2 c. chopped green pepper
1 c. sliced carrots
2 c. cubed potatoes
1 16-oz. can tomatoes
1 tsp. salt
1/4 tsp. pepper
1/2 bay leaf
1/2 tsp. thyme
1 tbsp. chopped parsley
2 8-oz. cans minced clams

Brown . . . salt pork in soup pot.
Add . . . . . vegetables, seasonings and 5 cups hot water.
Drain . . . . clam liquid into soup, reserving clams.
Cook . . . . covered, for 3 hours.
Remove . . bay leaf and add clams just before serving.

Kay Caskey
Manogue H. S., Reno, Nevada

SUPER V-8 SOUP

1 lb. ground beef
1 med. onion, chopped
1 lg. can V-8 juice
3 c. mixed vegetables
Salt and pepper to taste

Brown . . . ground beef and onion in skillet, stirring until crumbly.
Add . . . . . remaining ingredients, mixing well.
Simmer . . until vegetables are tender.
Yields . . . . 4 servings/about 415 calories each.

Marie L. Bristol
Park Sr. H. S., Cottage Grove, Minnesota

Salads

Today's all-purpose cook knows there's more to creative salad making than a toss of a lettuce leaf. In addition to traditional recipes, this chapter has specialties of seafood, fresh fruit, gelatins, vegetables and more.

As a main course, "do it yourself" salad bars are fun to have at home. Such a colorful party buffet too! Once you've mastered the basics of salad making, there's no end to the variety of combinations you can create!

TRICKS OF THE TRADE

- A muffin tin is a clever double for individual gelatin molds.
- Bring wilted greens back to life by dipping into hot water; then into ice water mixed with a little vinegar or lemon juice.
- Separate lettuce leaves easily by removing the core and holding the head upside down under cold water.
- Thin honey with bottled lime juice to taste for an easy, tasty fruit salad dressing.
- Fluff up gelatin desserts or salads by beating slightly-thickened gelatin until light. Fold in remaining ingredients; chill until firm.
- To prevent soggy vegetable salads, place a saucer upside down in the bottom of the salad bowl so moisture runs underneath.
- Keep salad greens looking fresher longer by sprinkling with lemon or lime juice.
- Don't overlook your herb and spice shelf for distinctively different salad flavors.

BANANA SPLIT SALAD

1 lg. carton Cool Whip
1 can sweetened condensed milk
1 can cherry pie filling
1 8-oz. can crushed pineapple, well drained
3 bananas, chopped
1/2 c. chopped nuts

Combine . Cool Whip and condensed milk in
bowl, beating well.
Fold in ... remaining ingredients.
Chill ..... in refrigerator until serving time.

Rochelle Buttress
Panama H. S., Panama, Oklahoma

BLUEBERRY SALAD

1 6-oz. package raspberry Jell-O
1 tbsp. vinegar
1 can blueberries in syrup
1 sm. can crushed pineapple
1 8-oz. carton sour cream
1 8-oz. package cream cheese, softened
1/2 c. sugar
1/2 tsp. vanilla extract
Pecans, chopped (opt.)

Dissolve .. Jell-O in 2 cups boiling water and
vinegar.
Add ..... fruit, mixing well.
Pour ..... into serving dish.
Chill ..... until firm.
Combine . remaining ingredients in bowl.
Spread ... over Jell-O mixture.

Jean Pearson
Robert E. Lee H. S., San Antonio, Texas

CAN OPENER SALAD

1 21-oz. can peach pie filling
1 11-oz. can mandarin oranges, drained
1 c. miniature marshmallows
1 20-oz. can pineapple tidbits, drained
2 apples, diced

Combine . all ingredients in bowl.
Chill ..... overnight.
Yields .... 10 servings/about 275 calories each.

Judy Baldridge
Douglass H. S., Douglass, Kansas

CRANBERRY SALAD

1 env. unflavored gelatin
1/4 c. sugar
1 3/4 c. cranberry juice cocktail
2 tbsp. lemon juice
1 c. chopped unpeeled apple
1/2 c. chopped celery
1 3-oz. package cream cheese, softened
1/2 c. finely chopped pecans
1/2 c. applesauce
1/2 c. sour cream
1/2 c. salad dressing
1 tsp. celery seed

Combine . gelatin, sugar and 3/4 cup cranberry
juice in large saucepan.
Cook .... over low heat until gelatin dissolves,
stirring constantly.
Stir ...... in lemon juice and remaining 1 cup
cranberry juice.
Chill ..... until partially set.
Add ..... apple and celery.
Cut ...... cream cheese into 1/2-inch cubes
and shape into balls.
Roll ..... in pecans.
Fold ..... into gelatin mixture.
Pour ..... into 3-cup mold.
Chill ..... until firm.
Unmold .. on serving platter lined with salad
greens.
Combine . remaining ingredients in small bowl.
Chill ..... until serving time.
Serve .... over gelatin mold.

Photograph for this recipe below.

CHERRY-PISTACHIO SALAD

1 sm. package pistachio instant pudding mix
1 sm. carton Cool Whip, thawed
1 15-oz. can crushed pineapple
1 sm. jar maraschino cherries, chopped
1 c. chopped pecans

Sprinkle .. pudding mix over Cool Whip in bowl, mixing well.
Add ..... remaining ingredients, mixing well.
Chill ..... for at least 2 hours.

Beverly Burton
Skiatook H. S., Skiatook, Oklahoma

CONGEALED PINEAPPLE-CARROT SALAD

1 3-oz. package lemon gelatin
1 No. 2 can crushed pineapple
1 3-oz. package cream cheese, softened
1/3 c. mayonnaise
1 med. carrot, grated
1 c. finely chopped celery
1/2 c. chopped nuts

Dissolve .. gelatin in 1 cup boiling water in bowl.
Drain .... pineapple, reserving juice.
Add ..... reserved juice and enough water to measure 1 cup liquid to gelatin.
Chill ..... gelatin until partially set .
Blend .... cream cheese and mayonnaise in small bowl.
Combine . with gelatin, mixing well.
Stir ...... in remaining ingredients.
Pour ..... into mold.
Chill ..... until firm.
Yields .... 10 servings/about 200 calories each.

Rosemary R. Sutton
Berea Community School, Berea, Kentucky

DUMP, STIR AND CHILL SALAD

1 can sweetened condensed milk
1 can strawberry pie filling
1 lg. can crushed pineapple, drained
1 12-oz. carton Cool Whip

Combine . condensed milk, pie filling and pineapple in bowl.
Fold in . . Cool Whip.

Pour ..... into 9 x 13-inch pan.
Freeze ... for at least 5 hours.

Mary Jo Jackson
Central H. S., Switz City, Indiana

FROZEN STRAWBERRY SALAD

1 sm. container Cool Whip
1 pt. frozen strawberries, partially thawed
1/2 c. mayonnaise
3/4 c. miniature marshmallows

Combine . all ingredients in bowl, mixing well.
Pour ..... into 8 x 12 x 2-inch pan.
Freeze ... until firm.
Cut ...... into squares.

Linda Mottley
Lee-Davis H. S., Mechanicsville, Virginia

LEMON FIZZ SALAD

1 lg. package lemon Jell-O
1 med. can crushed pineapple, drained
12 oz. 7-Up
4 bananas, sliced
2 c. miniature marshmallows
1/2 c. sugar
1 tbsp. flour
1 egg, well beaten
1/2 c. pineapple juice
2 tbsp. butter
1 c. whipping cream, whipped
Chopped nuts (opt.)

Dissolve .. Jell-O in 2 cups boiling water in bowl.
Add ..... pineapple.
Chill ..... until partially set.
Add ..... next 3 ingredients and pour into 9 x 12-inch pan.
Chill ..... until firm.
Combine . sugar, flour, egg and juice in saucepan, mixing well.
Add ..... butter.
Cook .... over medium heat until thick, stirring constantly; cool.
Fold ..... whipped cream into cooled mixture.
Spread ... over congealed layer.
Sprinkle .. with nuts.

Anita Craven
Farrer Jr. H. S., Provo, Utah

JELLIED WALDORF SALAD

1 3-oz. package lemon gelatin
1/8 tsp. salt
1/2 c. mayonnaise
1 c. diced celery
1 1/2 c. diced apples
1/2 c. chopped nuts
1 c. Cool Whip

Dissolve .. gelatin in 1 cup hot water in large
bowl.
Chill ..... until partially set.
Add ..... salt and mayonnaise, blending well.
Fold in ... remaining ingredients.
Pour ..... into 1-quart mold.
Chill ..... until firm.
Yields .... 6 servings/about 260 calories each.

Darlene Clevenger
Madison-Grant H. S., Fairmount, Indiana

CREAMY ORANGE-PINEAPPLE SALAD

1 8 1/2-oz. can crushed pineapple
1 3-oz. package orange Jell-O
1 3-oz. package cream cheese, softened
1 c. whipping cream, whipped
1 carrot, grated

Drain .... pineapple, reserving juice.
Add ..... enough water to reserved juice to
measure 1 cup liquid.
Bring .... liquid to a boil.
Add ..... to Jell-O and cream cheese in mix-
ing bowl.
Beat ..... until smooth.
Cool ..... stirring occasionally.
Fold in ... remaining ingredients.
Pour ..... into mold.
Chill ..... until firm.

Jo Etta Penn
Howe H. S., Howe, Texas

MIXED FRUIT SALAD

4 egg yolks, beaten
Juice of 6 lemons
1 10-oz. package miniature marshmallows
1 1/2 c. chopped nuts
1 bunch grapes
1 sm. can crushed pineapple
1 lg. can fruit cocktail, drained
6 bananas, sliced

1 c. coconut
1 c. whipped cream

Combine . egg yolks and lemon juice in large
saucepan.
Cook .... over low heat until thick, stirring
constantly.
Add ..... marshmallows, stirring until melted.
Add ..... 1 cup nuts and remaining ingredi-
ents except whipped cream, mixing
well.
Pour ..... into 2 bowls.
Chill ..... overnight.
Top ..... with whipped cream and remaining
nuts.

Hazel Rogers
Van Buren H. S., Van Buren, Arkansas

MANDARIN FRUIT SALAD

2 eggs, slightly beaten
1/4 c. frozen orange juice concentrate,
thawed
1/4 c. sugar
1 c. heavy cream, whipped
2 c. sweet cherries, drained
1 11-oz. can mandarin oranges, drained
2 c. green grapes
2 c. miniature marshmallows

Combine . first 3 ingredients in double boiler.
Cook .... until thick, stirring constantly.
Cool ..... to room temperature.
Fold ..... in whipped cream.
Combine . cream mixture with fruit and
marshmallows in large bowl, mixing
gently.
Chill ..... for 24 hours.

Linda F. Zwick
Norton H. S., Norton, Ohio

ORANGE CREAM JELL-O

1 3-oz. package orange Jell-O
1 3-oz. package lemon Jell-O
1 3/4 c. orange juice
1 No. 2 can crushed pineapple, drained
1 to 2 cans mandarin oranges, drained
1 1/2 c. small marshmallows
1 1/2 c. pineapple juice
1 c. sugar
1/3 c. flour
2 eggs, beaten

4 tbsp. butter
1 pkg. Dream Whip
Cheddar cheese, grated

Dissolve .. orange and lemon Jell-O in 2 cups boiling water in bowl.
Add ..... next 4 ingredients, mixing well.
Pour ..... into serving dish.
Chill ..... until firm.
Combine . pineapple juice, sugar, flour, eggs and butter in small saucepan, mixing well.
Cook .... over medium heat until thick, stirring constantly.
Prepare ... Dream Whip using package directions.
Fold ..... into cooled egg mixture.
Spread ... over Jell-O layer.
Sprinkle .. cheese over top.

Robyn H. Mower
American Fork Jr. H. S., American Fork, Utah

GOURMET BEEF SALAD VINAGRETA

1 1/2 lb. cooked roast beef, sliced 1/4-inch thick
2 tbsp. lemon juice
10 tbsp. oil
8 oz. fresh mushrooms, cut in half
1 7-oz. can artichoke hearts, drained, halved
2 to 3 tomatoes, cut in wedges
1/4 c. red wine
1/4 c. red wine vinegar
1/2 tsp. salt
1 pkg. Italian salad dressing mix
Bibb lettuce

Cut ...... beef into 1 x 3-inch strips.
Combine . lemon juice and 2 tablespoons oil in skillet.
Add ..... mushrooms, cooking until tender-crisp.
Combine . mushrooms, artichoke hearts, tomatoes and beef in large bowl.
Stir ...... next 3 ingredients into salad dressing mix in small bowl.
Add ..... remaining 1/2 cup oil, blending well.
Pour ..... over beef mixture.
Chill ..... covered, for 2 to 6 hours, stirring several times.
Line ..... serving bowl with lettuce leaves.
Arrange .. tomato wedges around edge of bowl.
Drain .... remaining salad.
Arrange .. in serving bowl.

Photograph for this recipe below.

CHICKEN SALAD

1 fryer chicken, cut up
Bay leaf
Parsley
1 can crushed pineapple, drained
1/2 c. celery, chopped
2 to 3 tbsp. mayonnaise

Boil ..... chicken pieces with bay leaf and parsley in water to cover in saucepan until tender.
Bone .... chicken and cut into bite-sized pieces.
Combine . chicken, pineapple, celery and mayonnaise in bowl, mixing well.
Serve .... on lettuce leaves and garnish with toasted slivered almonds.

Cheryl C. Evans
Westland H. S., Galloway, Ohio

GRANDMOTHER'S CHICKEN SALAD

6 c. cooked chopped chicken
2 c. chopped celery
12 hard-boiled eggs, chopped
3 c. chopped red Delicious apples
1 c. chopped sweet pickle
1/2 c. sweet pickle juice
1 1/2 c. chicken broth
3 c. Hellmann's mayonnaise
2 tbsp. sugar
Salt and pepper to taste

Combine . all chopped ingredients in large bowl.
Blend .... remaining ingredients in bowl.
Add ..... to chicken mixture, tossing until well mixed.
Serve .... on lettuce leaves.
Yield ..... 24 servings/about 375 calories each.

Jeanne B. Reed
Horn Lake Jr. H. S., Horn Lake, Mississippi

WOODEN BOWL SALAD

1/2 head lettuce, shredded
1 c. sliced water chestnuts
2 1/2 c. cooked, diced chicken

1 c. chopped celery
1/2 c. chopped green pepper
1/2 red onion, minced
1 pkg. frozen peas
1 pt. mayonnaise
3 tbsp. sugar
6 oz. Cheddar cheese, grated
8 slices crisp-cooked bacon, crumbled
3 hard-boiled eggs, sliced

Layer .... first 3 ingredients in wooden salad bowl.
Combine . next 4 ingredients in small bowl, mixing well.
Place .... evenly over chicken.
Spread ... mayonnaise over salad, sealing edges.
Sprinkle .. with sugar.
Chill ..... for at least 8 hours.
Top ..... with remaining ingredients.
Toss ..... just before serving.

Carla Voelkel
Texas City H. S., Texas City, Texas

CREAMY HAM AND NOODLE SALAD

2 c. rotini noodles
2 c. cooked ham, cubed
1 med. green pepper, diced
1   14-oz. can sweetened condensed milk
3/4 c. lime juice
1/4 c. oil
1/4 c. prepared mustard
2 tsp. onion salt
1 tbsp. celery seed

Cook .... noodles using package directions.
Combine . noodles with ham and green pepper in large bowl, tossing to mix.
Blend .... remaining ingredients in small bowl until smooth.
Pour ..... dressing over noodle mixture, mixing well.
Chill ..... for 3 hours or longer.
Yields .... 8 servings/about 410 calories each.

Anita Furrow
Jefferson County H. S., Tallahassee, Florida

Recipe on page 95.

TACO SALAD

1 lb. hamburger
1 8-oz. can tomato sauce
1 tsp. oregano
1/2 tsp. each salt, pepper
1 head lettuce, shredded
1 onion, chopped
12 oz. Colby cheese, grated
2 or 3 tomatoes, diced
1/4 c. taco sauce
1 bottle creamy Caesar salad dressing
1 lg. package Doritos, crushed

Brown . . . hamburger in skillet, stirring until crumbly.
Add . . . . . tomato sauce, oregano, salt and pepper.
Simmer . . covered, for 15 minutes.
Cook . . . . uncovered until thick.
Chill . . . . . in refrigerator until serving time.
Layer . . . . lettuce, onion, cheese, meat sauce, tomatoes, taco sauce, salad dressing and Doritos in large salad bowl.
Toss . . . . . to mix.

Mary Dean
Springboro Jr. H. S., Springboro, Ohio

CORNED BEEF AND CABBAGE MOLD

2 env. unflavored gelatin
1 tsp. salt
2 tbsp. lemon juice
1/4 tsp. Tabasco sauce
1 1/2 c. mayonnaise
2 tbsp. finely chopped onion
1/2 c. chopped sweet pickle
1 c. chopped celery
1 c. finely shredded cabbage
1 12-oz. can corned beef, finely chopped

Soften . . . gelatin in 1 cup cold water in saucepan.
Cook . . . . over low heat for 5 minutes or until dissolved, stirring constantly.
Stir . . . . . . in salt, lemon juice and Tabasco sauce.
Combine . with mayonnaise gradually in mixing bowl.

Recipes on pages 50 and 51.

Add . . . . . onion.
Chill . . . . until partially set, stirring occasionally.
Add . . . . . remaining ingredients, mixing well.
Pour . . . . . into 6-cup mold.
Chill . . . . until firm.
Garnish . . unmolded salad with salad greens and cherry tomatoes.

Photograph for this recipe on page 8.

SHRIMP SALAD

1 c. cold cooked rice
1 c. chopped cooked shrimp
3/4 tsp. salt
1 tbsp. lemon juice
1/4 c. slivered green pepper
1 tbsp. minced onion
2 tbsp. chopped stuffed olives
3/4 c. diced fresh cauliflower
Dash of pepper
1/3 c. mayonnaise

Combine . all ingredients in large bowl in order given.
Toss . . . . . gently until well mixed.
Serve . . . . in lettuce cups.
Yields . . . . 4 servings/about 235 calories each.

Patricia A. Boughner
New Trier East H. S., Winnetka, Illinois

SPAGHETTI CONFETTI

1 7-oz. package spaghetti
1 sm. head cabbage, chopped
1/2 c. carrots, grated
1/2 c. celery, chopped
1/2 c. green pepper, chopped
1/2 c. onion, chopped
1/2 pt. sour cream
1 c. mayonnaise
2 tsp. sugar
1 tsp. salt
1 tbsp. vinegar

Break . . . . spaghetti into 1-inch pieces.
Cook . . . . using package directions.
Rinse . . . . and drain well.
Combine . with remaining ingredients in bowl, mixing well.
Chill . . . . . covered, in refrigerator overnight.

Betty H. Knight
West Wilkes H. S., Millers Creek, North Carolina

FRESH BROCCOLI AND TOMATO SALAD

1 bunch fresh broccoli
1 carton cherry tomatoes, halved
6 slices crisp-cooked bacon, crumbled
1 bottle Green Goddess salad dressing
Garlic powder to taste
Juice of 1/2 lemon

Cut . . . . . . broccoli into bite-sized flowerettes.
Toss . . . . . broccoli, tomatoes and bacon in bowl.
Combine . remaining ingredients in small bowl, blending well.
Add . . . . . dressing just before serving.

Celeste Kelley
Enterprise H. S., Enterprise, Alabama

CAULIFLOWER SALAD

1 sm. head cauliflower, chopped
3 tbsp. chopped onion
1 lg. tomato, chopped
1/4 green pepper, chopped
Cheese, diced
Olives, chopped
1/2 c. sour cream
4 tsp. white vinegar
1/2 tbsp. sugar
Dash of salt

Combine . first 6 ingredients in bowl.
Blend . . . . remaining ingredients in small bowl.
Mix . . . . . dressing with vegetables.
Chill . . . . . in refrigerator overnight.

Marsha Kinsey
Marble Falls H. S., Marble Falls, Texas

CAULIFLOWER-AVOCADO SALAD

1 head cauliflower, separated into flowerettes
2 to 4 avocados, sliced
6 radishes, sliced
4 green onions, chopped
5 hard-boiled eggs, chopped
8 to 10 green olives, chopped
3/4 c. mayonnaise
1 pkg. Italian dressing (opt.)

Combine . first 6 ingredients in large bowl.
Blend . . . . mayonnaise and Italian dressing in small bowl.

Toss . . . . . vegetables with dressing until well-coated.
Chill . . . . . for several hours before serving.

Rita Hall
Flour Bluff H. S., Corpus Christi, Texas

MOLDED CUCUMBER SALAD

2 3-oz. packages lime gelatin
1 c. sour cream
1 med. cucumber, chopped
1 sm. onion, chopped

Combine . gelatin and 1 3/4 cups hot water in blender container.
Process . . . until gelatin is dissolved.
Add . . . . . remaining ingredients.
Process . . . until smooth.
Pour . . . . . into mold.
Chill . . . . . until firm.

Betty Lou Stomm
DeKalb H. S., Waterloo, Indiana

LAYERED SALAD

1 head lettuce, cut in bite-sized pieces
1 bell pepper, finely chopped
1 onion, finely chopped
1 sm. can Le Seur peas, drained
2 c. Hellman's mayonnaise
2 tbsp. sugar
1 c. Parmesan cheese

Layer . . . . first 4 ingredients in large bowl in order listed.
Spread . . . mayonnaise over vegetables.
Sprinkle . . with sugar.
Top . . . . . with cheese.
Chill . . . . . tightly covered, for 8 hours or longer.
Yields . . . . 10 servings/about 400 calories each.

Pam Byce
Greene County H. S., Greensboro, Georgia

SEVEN LAYER SALAD

1 10-oz. package frozen English peas, thawed
1 head lettuce, shredded

1/2 c. each chopped celery, bell pepper
1 pt. mayonnaise
2 tbsp. sugar
6 oz. Cheddar cheese, grated
1/4 c. Parmesan cheese
8 slices crisp-cooked bacon, crumbled

Drain .... peas on paper towel.
Place .... lettuce in large salad bowl.
Layer .... chopped vegetables and peas over lettuce.
Beat ..... mayonnaise until of spreading consistency.
Spread ... mayonnaise about 1/4 inch thick over peas.
Sprinkle .. sugar and cheeses over mayonnaise.
Top ..... with bacon.
Chill ..... tightly covered, for 8 hours.
Keeps .... up to 1 week.
Yields .... 8 servings/about 565 calories each.

Cindy J. Hall
C. F. Vigor H. S., Prichard, Alabama

VEGETABLE SALAD

1 head lettuce, torn into small pieces
1/4 c. chopped onions
1 c. water chestnuts, thinly sliced
1 c. chopped celery
1 pkg. frozen peas, thawed, drained
1 1/2 c. salad dressing
Parmesan cheese

Layer .... first 5 ingredients in order listed in large bowl.
Spread ... salad dressing over layers.
Sprinkle .. liberally with cheese.
Chill ..... covered, in refrigerator overnight.

Pat Wagoner
Salisbury H. S., Salisbury, North Carolina

THE SALAD

2 c. sliced carrots
1   10-oz. package frozen green peas
1 med. head iceberg lettuce, shredded
Salt and pepper
1 c. sliced celery
1/2 c. chopped Bermuda onion
2/3 c. sliced pimento-stuffed olives

1 lb. crisp-cooked bacon, crumbled
Blender Mayonnaise
1 tsp. sugar

Cook .... carrots in a small amount of boiling salted water until tender-crisp.
Drain .... and chill.
Cook .... peas using package directions.
Drain .... and chill.
Place .... lettuce in large glass salad bowl.
Season ... with salt and pepper.
Arrange .. carrots, celery, peas, onion, olives and bacon in layers over lettuce.
Spread ... 1 cup Blender Mayonnaise over top.
Sprinkle .. with sugar.
Garnish .. with parsley and additional olives.
Serve .. with remaining mayonnaise.

Blender Mayonnaise

1 1/2 c. oil
3 egg yolks
3 tbsp. wine vinegar
1 1/2 tsp. salt
3/4 tsp. dry mustard

Place .... 1/2 cup oil and remaining ingredients in blender container.
Process ... on High for 5 seconds.
Turn ..... speed to Low.
Add ..... remaining oil continuously in fine stream.
Blend .... until thoroughly combined.

Photograph for this recipe below.

CAROLINA POTATO SALAD

6 med. potatoes, cooked, diced
1 green pepper, chopped
1 sm. onion, chopped
1 lg. tomato, diced
2 stalks celery, chopped
3 sweet pickles, chopped
3 hard-boiled eggs
1/2 c. mayonnaise
2 tbsp. mustard (opt.)
Salt and pepper to taste

Combine . first 6 ingredients with 2 chopped hard-boiled eggs in large bowl, tossing to mix.
Add ..... mayonnaise, mustard and seasoning, mixing well.
Spoon ... into salad bowl lined with lettuce leaves.
Garnish .. with egg slices.
Yields .... 10 servings/about 175 calories each.

Myrtle Bailey
Holly Hill Jr. H. S., Holly Hill, Florida

COTTAGE CHEESE-POTATO SALAD

3 c. cooked, diced potatoes
1/2 c. sliced celery
1 tbsp. chopped green pepper
1 tbsp. chopped pimento
2 tbsp. minced onion
2 tbsp. chopped dill pickle
1 c. mayonnaise
1 tbsp. lemon juice
1 tsp. salt
1/8 tsp. pepper
1 tsp. dry mustard
1 c. cottage cheese

Combine . first 6 ingredients in bowl.
Chill ..... vegetables thoroughly.
Blend .... mayonnaise and lemon juice with seasonings in small bowl.
Combine . chilled vegetables, cottage cheese and dressing, tossing lightly.

Linda Owens
Mt. Vernon H. S., Mt. Vernon, Texas

ITALIAN POTATO SALAD

5 c. thinly sliced cooked potatoes
1 1/2 c. chopped celery
1 c. diced Provolone cheese
3/4 c. cubed hard Italian sausage
1/2 c. chopped green pepper
1/3 c. chopped onion
1/4 c. chopped peperoncini
1 1/2 c. sour cream
1/4 c. brine from peperoncini
1/2 tsp. oregano, crushed
1/2 tsp. salt
12 cherry tomatoes, cut in half

Toss ..... together first 7 ingredients in large bowl.
Blend .... sour cream, brine, oregano and salt in small bowl.
Add ..... to potato mixture, tossing to blend.
Fold ..... in half the tomatoes.
Chill ..... covered, for several hours.
Garnish .. with remaining tomatoes and parsley.

Photograph for this recipe on page 28.

LINDA'S MIXED VEGETABLE SALAD

2 pkg. frozen mixed vegetables, thawed
1/2 c. each finely chopped cauliflower, radishes, green onions, green pepper, carrots and cucumber
Salt to taste
1 lg. bottle Italian salad dressing
1/2 c. sugar
1/2 c. vinegar

Combine . all vegetables with salt in bowl.
Mix ..... remaining ingredients in small bowl, blending well.
Pour ..... over vegetables.
Chill ..... in refrigerator overnight.
Drain .... before serving.
Note ..... salad dressing may be reused.

Linda Downing
Hampshire H. S., Hampshire, Illinois

TOMATO ASPIC SALAD

2 c. tomato juice
1 slice onion
1 whole clove

Bay leaf
1/2 tsp. salt
2 tbsp. unflavored gelatin
2 tbsp. sugar
1/4 tsp. paprika
2 tbsp. mild vinegar

Combine . first 5 ingredients in saucepan.
Cook . . . . for 10 minutes and set aside.
Soften . . . gelatin in 1/4 cup cold water in small bowl for 5 minutes.
Add . . . . . softened gelatin, sugar, paprika and vinegar to tomato mixture.
Stir . . . . . . until gelatin dissolves and strain.
Rinse . . . . salad mold with cold water.
Pour . . . . . in tomato mixture.
Chill . . . . . until firm.
Garnish . . with mayonnaise, celery curls and carrot strips.

Lela Reed
Lyon Elementary, Lyon, Mississippi

FINGER-LICKING MAYONNAISE

1 tsp. prepared mustard
1/2 tsp. salt
1/8 tsp. paprika
1/4 tsp. sugar
1 egg
Salad oil
3 tbsp. white vinegar

Combine . first 5 ingredients in bowl, beating well.
Add . . . . . 2 cups oil gradually by drops, beating constantly.
Add . . . . . vinegar and additional oil alternately until mayonnaise holds shape.
Store . . . . covered, in refrigerator.

Mary Jo Lyle
Gatewood School, Eatonton, Georgia

FRUIT SALAD DRESSING

1 8-oz. can pineapple
1 egg, slightly beaten
1 tbsp. cornstarch
1/4 c. sugar
1/8 tsp. salt
1 c. whipped cream

Drain . . . . pineapple, reserving juice.
Add . . . . . enough water to reserved juice to measure 1 cup liquid.
Combine . egg, cornstarch, sugar and salt in 1 quart double boiler.
Add . . . . . pineapple juice, mixing well.
Cook . . . . over hot water until mixture thickens and set aside.
Fold . . . . . whipped cream into cooled custard.
Serve . . . . over Jell-O and fruit salad.

Marilyn L. Cobb
Foley H. S., Foley, Alabama

SOUR CREAM FRUIT SALAD DRESSING

3 tbsp. Miracle Whip
3 tbsp. sour cream
2 tbsp. sugar

Combine . all ingredients in small bowl, mixing well.
Pour . . . . . over fresh or canned fruit.

Jan Nell Reed
Rhodes Jr. H. S., Mesa, Arizona

HOT BACON DRESSING

4 strips bacon
2 tbsp. finely chopped onion
1 tbsp. cornstarch
1/4 c. vinegar
1 tbsp. sugar
1/4 tsp. salt
1/8 tsp. pepper

Cook . . . . bacon over medium heat until crisp.
Saute . . . . onion in bacon drippings in skillet for 1 to 2 minutes or until tender, stirring frequently.
Remove . . from heat and stir in cornstarch.
Add . . . . . 3/4 cup water and remaining ingredients gradually.
Bring . . . . to a boil over medium heat, stirring constantly, and boil for 1 minute.
Pour . . . . . over salad greens and vegetables.
Sprinkle . . with bacon.
Toss . . . . . lightly and serve immediately.

Photograph for this recipe on cover.

Vegetables and Side Dishes

No matter how they're prepared — steamed to creamed — vegetables make your meal more complete, and certainly more colorful. They're nutritious and one of today's best bargains at the grocery store.

Fresh is always best when serving vegetables plain. Lightly steamed, they add a delectable crunchiness to your meal. Save money, however, by buying canned or frozen vegetables when you plan to combine with sauces or in casseroles.

Here are a variety of flavorful vegetable recipes — as well as an excellent selection of side dishes of rice, eggs, cheese and more to complement your next meal!

TRICKS OF THE TRADE

- Freeze fresh herbs in small quantities and add, still frozen, to any dish before it's cooked.
- Green vegetables stay bright green if cooked uncovered.
- Rule of thumb for cooking vegetables: Vegetables grown *under ground;* cook covered. *Above ground* vegetables; cook uncovered.
- When cooking cauliflower, add a small amount of milk to water to keep it white.
- Don't throw away potato peels. Instead, add a small amount of oil and salt; spread on a pan and bake until crisp. A delicious snack!
- If you buy more mushrooms than you need, saute the extras; add 1 cup water. Cool; freeze in ice cube trays; repackage for later use.
- When you clean out your refrigerator, wash and chop celery, carrots, cabbage, lettuce, zucchini, etc. Go "Chinese" by sauteeing in butter with onion and garlic for a quick vegetable dish.
- For easy, inexpensive spaghetti, cook thinly sliced zucchini and stewed tomatoes just until tender. Tastes like a meat sauce!
- Remember, fresh vegetables stay fresh longer if stored in covered containers or plastic bags in the refrigerator.

CROCK•POT VERMONT BAKED BEANS

1 1/2 lb. yellow eye beans
1 med. onion, quartered
1/2 lb. salt pork
1/4 c. sugar
3/4 c. Grade B Vermont maple syrup
2 tsp. dry mustard
1/2 tsp. pepper
1 1/2 tbsp. salt

Soak . . . . . beans overnight in cold water in large saucepan.
Bring . . . . water to a boil.
Place . . . . onion in Crock·Pot.
Add . . . . . beans and salt pork.
Combine . remaining ingredients with 1 pint boiling water.
Pour . . . . . over beans, adding more water if necessary to cover.
Cook . . . . on Low for 7 to 9 hours.

Nancy Finck
Brattleboro Union H. S., Brattleboro, Vermont

LIMA BEAN CASSEROLE

1 lb. dry lima beans
3/4 c. packed brown sugar
2 tsp. salt
1 tbsp. dry mustard
1 tsp. dark syrup
Butter, melted
1/2 pt. sour cream

Soak . . . . . beans overnight in water to cover in large saucepan.
Drain . . . . beans and add fresh water to cover.
Cook . . . . until water is absorbed.
Combine . beans with next 4 ingredients and 1/2 cup butter in casserole, mixing well.
Stir . . . . . . in sour cream.
Drizzle . . . 1/3 cup butter over casserole.
Bake . . . . . at 300 degrees for 2 hours, stirring every half hour.

Ruth Beebe
Mauldin H. S., Mauldin, South Carolina

MICROWAVE CALICO BEAN POT

8 slices bacon
1 c. chopped onion
1 1-lb. can each green beans, kidney beans, butter beans and lima beans, drained
1 1-lb. can pork and beans
1/2 tsp. garlic salt
1/2 tsp. dry mustard

Place . . . . bacon in 3-quart microwave dish.
Microwave for 4 to 5 minutes or until crisp.
Remove . . bacon and add onion.
Saute . . . . onion in bacon drippings for 3 minutes.
Combine . remaining ingredients with onion, mixing lightly.
Microwave covered, at half power for 1/2 hour, stirring after 15 minutes.
Let stand . for 5 to 10 minutes before serving.
Crumble . . bacon over top.

Ruth Demins
Milwee Middle School, Longwood, Florida

SWEET AND SOUR BAKED BEANS

1 tbsp. dry mustard
1 tsp. garlic powder
1 c. cider vinegar
1 1/2 c. packed brown sugar
2 sm. cans butter beans
1 sm. can lima beans
1 lg. can oven-baked beans
2 lg. onions, sliced in rings
8 slices crisp-fried bacon, crumbled

Combine . first 4 ingredients with a small amount of bacon drippings in pan.
Simmer . . for 10 minutes.
Combine . beans, onions and sauce in casserole, mixing well.
Top . . . . . with bacon.
Bake . . . . . covered, at 350 degrees for 1 hour.

Leslie A. Nuttman
North Mason H. S., Belfair, Washington

BROCCOLI QUICHE

1 pkg. frozen chopped broccoli
1/3 c. imitation bacon bits
1 c. shredded Swiss cheese
2 tbsp. instant minced onion
2 c. milk
1 c. Bisquick
4 eggs
1/2 tsp. salt
1/8 tsp. pepper

Cook .... broccoli until almost tender, using package directions.

Place .... bacon chips, cheese, onion and broccoli in lightly greased deep-dish pie plate.

Beat ..... remaining ingredients in mixing bowl for 1 minute with electric beater or until smooth.

Pour ..... batter over broccoli.

Bake ..... at 400 degrees for about 40 minutes or until quiche is golden brown and tests done.

Ethelyn Oros
Keene H. S., Keene, New Hampshire

CHEEZY BROCCOLI

2 10-oz. packages frozen chopped broccoli
2 c. minute rice
2 cans cream of chicken soup
1 c. milk
1 16-oz. jar Cheez Whiz
1 tbsp. salt
1/2 tsp. pepper
1/2 c. chopped onion
1 c. chopped celery
1 can sliced water chestnuts, drained

Cook .... unopened broccoli in microwave for 4 to 5 minutes, turning over after 2 minutes.

Drain .... broccoli, separate stalks and set aside.

Combine . next 6 ingredients in large microwave dish.

Cook .... for 2 to 4 minutes or until cheese melts.

Add ..... 3/4 cup water, onion, celery, water chestnuts and broccoli, stirring thoroughly.

Spoon ... into 2 lightly greased 10 x 6 x 2-inch microwave dishes.

Cook .... 1 at a time, for 12 to 14 minutes, rotating after 5 minutes.

Let ...... stand for 5 minutes before serving.

Yields .... 12 servings/about 210 calories each.

Janet Mayer
LeRoy-Ostrander H. S., LeRoy, Minnesota

MARTHA'S BROCCOLI CASSEROLE

1 sm. jar sliced mushrooms
1 can sliced water chestnuts, drained

2 tbsp. butter
1 env. dry onion soup mix
2 pkg. frozen broccoli, cooked, drained
1/4 c. bread crumbs
1/2 c. grated cheese

Saute .... mushrooms and water chestnuts in butter and soup mix in skillet.

Combine . with broccoli in casserole.

Top ..... with bread crumbs and cheese.

Bake ..... at 325 degrees for 20 to 25 minutes or until bubbly.

Yields .... 6 servings/about 140 calories each.

Martha W. Rogers
G. C. Scarbourough Sr. H. S., Houston, Texas

GOLDEN PAVILION VEGETABLES

2 10-oz. packages frozen broccoli spears, thawed
2 tbsp. sesame seed
1/3 c. oil
1 head romaine, cut into bite-sized pieces
1 tsp. salt
1/2 tsp. monosodium glutamate (opt.)
2 Florida grapefruit, peeled, sectioned

Cut ...... broccoli spears in half lengthwise.

Brown ... sesame seed over medium heat in oil in large skillet.

Remove .. from skillet and set aside.

Add ..... broccoli.

Stir-fry ... until tender.

Add ..... next 3 ingredients.

Stir-fry ... for 2 minutes.

Remove .. from heat.

Add ..... sesame seed and grapefruit.

Yields .... 8 servings/about 140 calories each.

Photograph for this recipe below.

SALLY'S BROCCOLI CASSEROLE

1/2 c. chopped onion
6 tbsp. margarine
2 tbsp. flour
1 8-oz. jar process cheese
2 10-oz. packages chopped broccoli,
*   thawed, drained*
3 eggs, beaten
1/2 c. cracker crumbs
Butter

Saute .... onion in margarine in skillet until tender.
Stir ...... in flour and 1/2 cup water, blending until smooth.
Cook .... over low heat, stirring constantly, until thick.
Blend .... in cheese, stirring, until smooth.
Combine . cheese sauce, broccoli and eggs in 1 1/2-quart casserole, mixing well.
Top ..... with crumbs dotted with butter.
Bake ..... at 325 degrees for 1/2 hour.

Sally McDavid
Hoffman Estates H. S., Hoffman Estates, Illinois

DELICIOUS CARROT MARINADE

5 c. sliced cooked carrots, drained
1 bell pepper, sliced
1 onion, sliced
1 head fresh cauliflower, separated
1 can tomato soup
3/4 c. cider vinegar
1/2 c. oil
1 c. sugar
1 tsp. Worcestershire sauce
1 tsp. each salt, pepper

Place .... prepared vegetables in large bowl.
Combine . remaining ingredients in medium bowl, mixing well.
Pour ..... marinade over vegetables.
Chill ..... for 24 hours.
Yields .... 8 servings/about 283 calories each.

Claudia Aragon
Grant Middle School, Albuquerque, New Mexico

CARROT RING

3/4 c. shortening
1/4 c. packed brown sugar
1 egg
1/2 tsp. salt
1 tsp. baking powder
1 tsp. soda
1 1/4 c. sifted flour
1 c. grated carrots
1 tbsp. lemon juice

Cream ... shortening and sugar in bowl until fluffy.
Beat ..... in egg.
Combine . dry ingredients.
Add ..... to creamed mixture, blending well.
Stir ...... in remaining ingredients with 1 tablespoon water, mixing thoroughly.
Place .... in greased 1 1/2-quart ring mold.
Bake ..... at 350 degrees for 45 minutes.
Yields .... 6 servings/about 365 calories each.

Madonna Meeker
Ridgedale H. S., Morral, Ohio

CREOLE BLACK-EYED PEAS

2 1-lb. cans black-eyed peas
1 1-lb. can jalapeno black-eyed peas
1 lg. can tomatoes
1 c. chopped onion
1 c. chopped celery
1 1-lb. bag cut-up frozen okra (not breaded)

Combine . all ingredients in slow cooker.
Cook .... on High for 4 hours.
Yields .... 8 servings/about 150 calories each.

Donna Rychlik
Caldwell H. S., Caldwell, Texas

MARINATED VIDALIA ONIONS

1 c. sugar
1/2 c. white vinegar
4 lg. Vidalia onions, sliced
1/4 c. mayonnaise
Celery salt to taste

Combine . sugar, vinegar and 2 cups water in large bowl, stirring to dissolve sugar.
Separate .. onion slices into rings.
Marinate .. overnight.
Drain .... onions thoroughly.
Add ..... mayonnaise and celery salt, mixing well.

Emma Ruth Hester
Marietta H. S., Marietta, Georgia

MEXICAN CORN BAKE

1 8-oz. package cheese
1/4 c. margarine
1/4 c. evaporated milk
Garlic salt and red pepper to taste
2 cans whole kernel corn, drained
1 can chopped chiles, drained

Place .... cheese, margarine, evaporated milk, garlic salt and red pepper in small Dutch oven.
Cook .... over low heat until cheese melts, stirring until blended.
Add ..... corn and chiles, mixing well.
Bake ..... at 350 degrees for 20 minutes.

Ann Edwards
Duncanville H. S., Duncanville, Texas

MEXICAN ONION CASSEROLE

1 lg. onion, chopped
1 10 1/2-oz. can cream of chicken soup
1 can Ro-Tel chili sauce
1 med. bag Fritos
1/2 lb. American cheese, sliced

Combine . onion, soup, Ro-Tel and 2/3 cup water in bowl, mixing well.
Layer .... Fritos, soup mixture and cheese in greased 8-inch baking dish until all ingredients are used, ending with cheese.
Bake ..... at 375 degrees for 20 to 25 minutes.
Yields .... 4 servings/about 600 calories each.

Dorothy Moore
Central Jr. H. S., Sand Springs, Oklahoma

PEAS VINCENTA

1 No. 303 can peas, drained
1/2 c. pea liquid
1 1/2 tsp. seasoned chicken stock
1/4 tsp. ginger
1 tbsp. salad oil
1 5-oz. can water chestnuts, sliced
1 3-oz. can sliced mushrooms
1 1/2 tsp. cornstarch
1 tbsp. soy sauce

Combine . first 7 ingredients in saucepan.
Heat ..... covered, to boiling point.

Blend .... cornstarch and soy sauce in small bowl until smooth.
Stir ...... into peas gently.
Cook .... over low heat until thickened, stirring constantly.

Anglee Smith
Laurel County Sr. H. S., London, Kentucky

PIZZA CASSEROLE

2 c. cooked elbow macaroni
1/2 lb. Cheddar cheese, grated
1 pt. tomatoes, chopped
1 tsp. crushed oregano leaves
1/8 tsp. garlic powder
1 tsp. instant minced onions
1/4 lb. grated mozzarella cheese

Layer .... macaroni and Cheddar cheese alternately in 2-quart baking dish until all ingredients are used.
Combine . tomatoes and seasonings in bowl, mixing well.
Pour ..... tomato mixture over macaroni and cheese.
Bake ..... covered, at 400 degrees for 45 minutes.
Add ..... mozzarella cheese.
Bake ..... uncovered, for 15 minutes longer.
Yields .... 4 servings/about 430 calories each.

Dorothy S. Weirick
Cottonwood H. S., Salt Lake City, Utah

JIFFY POTATO-ONION PUFFS

2 c. instant mashed potatoes
1/3 c. pancake mix
1 tbsp. dry onion soup mix
1 tsp. finely snipped parsley

Prepare ... potatoes using package directions.
Add ..... remaining ingredients; mix well.
Drop .... by tablespoonfuls, several at a time, into deep fat at 365 degrees.
Fry ...... for about 1 to 1 1/2 minutes, until golden brown, turning to brown both sides.
Drain .... on paper towels.
Yields .... 18 puffs/about 25 calories each.

Pauline Shields
Webster Middle School, Oklahoma City, Oklahoma

POTATO CASSEROLE

2 lb. frozen hashed brown potatoes, thawed
1 8-oz. carton sour cream
1 8-oz. carton onion dip
1 can cream of chicken soup
10 oz. Cheddar cheese, grated
Salt and pepper to taste
6 tbsp. margarine, melted
3/4 c. butter, melted
2 c. crushed corn flakes

Mix . . . . . first 7 ingredients in large bowl, stirring well.
Pour . . . . . into greased casserole.
Mix . . . . . butter and corn flakes in bowl.
Press . . . . . onto top of potato mixture.
Bake . . . . . at 350 degrees for 1 1/2 hours.
Yields . . . . 10 servings/about 585 calories each.

Jeri O'Quinn
Jones County H. S., Gray, Georgia

POTATO CROQUETTES

4 c. hot mashed potatoes
2 egg yolks
Salt and pepper to taste
Cheddar cheese, softened
1 egg, beaten
Corn flakes, crushed

Combine . first 3 ingredients in bowl, mixing well.
Shape . . . . around small ball of cheese.
Dip . . . . . . in mixture of egg and 2 tablespoons water in bowl.
Roll . . . . . in corn flake crumbs.
Place . . . . in buttered casserole.
Bake . . . . . at 350 degrees until brown.

Eloise Guerrant
Robert Lee H. S., Robert Lee, Texas

POTATO QUICHE IDAHO

4 Idaho potatoes
6 eggs
2 tsp. salt
1/4 tsp. white pepper
1 tsp. ground nutmeg
1/4 lb. fresh mushrooms, sliced
1/3 c. chopped red pepper
2 tbsp. butter
1/4 lb. Jarlesberg cheese, diced

2 c. skim milk
1 tsp. pepper

Prick . . . . potatoes with fork.
Bake . . . . . at 425 degrees for 45 to 50 minutes or until tender.
Cut . . . . . . hot potatoes in half, scooping out pulp into bowl.
Mash . . . . potato pulp well.
Add . . . . . 1 beaten egg, 1 teaspoon salt, white pepper and 1 teaspoon nutmeg, mixing well.
Press . . . . . into deep 9-inch pie plate and prick with fork.
Bake . . . . . at 425 degrees for 12 minutes.
Remove . . from oven to cool slightly.
Reduce . . . temperature to 325 degrees.
Saute . . . . mushrooms and red pepper in butter in skillet until tender.
Arrange . . sauteed vegetables and cheese in pie shell.
Beat . . . . . 5 eggs with remaining ingredients in bowl.
Pour . . . . . over vegetables and cheese.
Bake . . . . . at 325 degrees for 30 minutes or until quiche tests done.
Cool . . . . . for 15 minutes before serving.
Yields . . . . 6 servings/about 430 calories each.

Photograph for this recipe on page 2.

SINFUL POTATOES

2 lb. frozen hashed brown potatoes, thawed
1/2 c. melted margarine
1 tsp. salt
1/4 tsp. pepper
1 can cream of mushroom soup
2 c. grated cheese
1/2 c. chopped onion
2 c. sour cream
Unseasoned bread crumbs

Combine . all ingredients except bread crumbs in large bowl, mixing well.
Spread . . . in 9 x 13-inch baking pan.
Top . . . . . with bread crumbs.
Bake . . . . . at 350 degrees for 1 hour.

Connie Hansen
Magee Jr. H. S., Tucson, Arizona

SUNDOWN BAKE

2 c. sliced mushrooms
1/3 c. chopped green pepper

4 Idaho potatoes, baked
Milk
4 tbsp. butter
1 egg
1 1/2 tsp. salt
6 slices crisp-cooked bacon, crumbled
2 tbsp. flour
1/4 tsp. pepper
1 c. shredded Cheddar cheese

Saute .... mushrooms and green pepper in 2 tablespoons bacon drippings in skillet until tender.
Cut ...... slice from top of each potato.
Scoop .... out pulp without breaking shells.
Mash .... potato with 3 tablespoons milk, 2 tablespoons butter, egg and 1 teaspoon salt, beating well.
Stir ...... in bacon and sauteed vegetables.
Spoon ... mixture into reserved shells.
Bake ..... at 350 degrees for 25 to 30 minutes.
Melt ..... remaining butter in saucepan.
Blend .... in flour.
Cook .... for 1 minute; remove from heat.
Stir ...... in 1 1/4 cups milk.
Cook .... over low heat until thick, stirring constantly.
Add ..... remaining 1/2 teaspoon salt, pepper and cheese.

Cook .... until cheese melts.
Serve .... warm over stuffed potatoes.
Yields .... 4 servings/about 490 calories each.

Photograph for this recipe below.

SPINACH PIE

1 med. onion, chopped
1 stick margarine
4 pkg. frozen chopped spinach, thawed, drained
Salt, pepper and garlic salt to taste
1 1/2 c. shredded Cheddar cheese
1 egg, beaten
1/2 lb. Swiss cheese, shredded

Saute .... onion in margarine in skillet.
Combine . onion with spinach and seasonings in bowl, mixing well.
Spoon ... half the mixture into buttered 9-inch pie plate.
Spread ... with Cheddar cheese.
Cover .... with remaining spinach mixture.
Spoon ... egg over layers.
Top ..... with Swiss cheese.
Bake ..... at 375 degrees for 40 minutes.
Yields .... 8 servings/about 370 calories each.

Denise Pollack
Plum Grove Jr. H. S., Rolling Meadows, Illinois

SQUASH-STUFFED TOMATOES

4 med. tomatoes
3/4 tsp. salt
2 zucchini, grated
1/3 c. chopped onion
1 c. grated Swiss cheese
1/4 tsp. each pepper, basil

Slice . . . . . stem end from each tomato.
Scoop . . . . out centers with spoon, reserving pulp.
Sprinkle . . with 1/2 teaspoon salt.
Invert . . . . on paper towel and let stand for 30 minutes.
Pat . . . . . . dry and place on baking sheet.
Combine . reserved tomato pulp, 1/4 teaspoon salt and remaining ingredients in bowl.
Spoon . . . into tomato shells.
Bake . . . . . at 350 degrees for 10 minutes. Do not overbake.
Yields . . . . 4 servings/about 85 calories each.

Photograph for this recipe on page 36.

SAVORY SQUASH

1 1/2 lb. yellow squash or zucchini, sliced
1/2 c. chopped onions
3 c. cooked rice
2 c. grated Cheddar cheese
1 tsp. seasoned pepper
1/2 tsp. salt
3 eggs, beaten
1/2 c. mayonnaise
1 c. soft bread crumbs
1/2 c. sliced almonds

Cook . . . . squash in a small amount of water in saucepan until tender.
Drain . . . . well.
Combine . with next 7 ingredients in large bowl, mixing well.
Turn . . . . . into shallow 2-quart buttered casserole.
Top . . . . . with crumbs and almonds.
Bake . . . . . at 350 degrees for 30 minutes.
Yields . . . . 6 servings/about 600 calories each.

Photograph for this recipe on page 42.

JOY'S SUMMER SQUASH CASSEROLE

2 lb. yellow summer squash, sliced
1/4 c. chopped onion

1 can cream of chicken soup
1 c. sour cream
1 c. shredded carrot
1 8-oz. package herb-seasoned stuffing mix
1/2 c. melted margarine

Cook . . . . squash and onion in a small amount of boiling salted water in saucepan for 5 minutes.
Drain . . . . squash well.
Combine . soup and sour cream in bowl, mixing well.
Fold . . . . . in carrots and squash, blending thoroughly.
Combine . stuffing mix and margarine in bowl until well mixed.
Spread . . . half of stuffing in bottom of 7 x 12-inch baking dish.
Spoon . . . in vegetable mixture.
Top . . . . . with remaining stuffing.
Bake . . . . . at 350 degrees for 25 to 30 minutes.
Yields . . . . 6 servings/about 445 calories each.

Joy L. Manson
Miami H. S., Miami, Arizona

STEAMED SUMMER VEGETABLES TWO WAYS

1/2 tsp. salt
3 med. potatoes, pared, sliced
1/2 lb. fresh green beans, cut in 1-in. pieces
1 lg. onion, sliced
2 zucchini, sliced
2 c. sliced yellow squash
Lemon Herb Butter
Zesty Marinade

Bring . . . . 1 1/2 cups water and salt to a boil in large skillet; reduce heat.
Place . . . . steamer in skillet.
Layer . . . . potatoes and green beans in steamer.
Simmer . . covered, for 5 minutes.
Add . . . . . remaining vegetables.
Simmer . . for 5 minutes or until tender-crisp.
Toss . . . . . half the vegetables with Lemon Herb Butter, serving hot.
Toss . . . . . remaining vegetables with Zesty Marinade.
Chill . . . . . covered, overnight.

Lemon Herb Butter

1/3 c. butter
1 tbsp. lemon juice
1/2 tsp. salt
Dash of pepper

Melt . . . . . butter in small saucepan.
Stir . . . . . . in remaining ingredients.
Toss . . . . . with steamed vegetables.

Zesty Marinade

1 /3 c. oil
1 tbsp. wine vinegar
2 tbsp. lemon juice
1 tsp. chopped fresh parsley
1/2 tsp. salt
1/2 tsp. dried leaf basil, crumbled

Combine . all ingredients in jar.
Shake . . . . covered, to blend well.
Toss . . . . . with steamed vegetables.
Chill . . . . . covered, overnight.

Photograph for this recipe on page 36.

FRESH STIR-FRY MELANGE

3 1/2 c. fresh green pepper strips
3 1/2 c. fresh red pepper strips
2 1/2 c. sliced mushrooms
1 c. sliced celery
2 tbsp. chopped fresh onion
1/2 clove of garlic, crushed
1/2 tsp. sugar
1/4 tsp. dried leaf oregano
3/4 tsp. salt
Dash of pepper
1/4 c. olive oil
1 tsp. wine vinegar
2 tomatoes, cut in wedges

Stir-fry . . . first 10 ingredients in hot oil in skillet over medium-high heat until peppers are tender-crisp.
Add . . . . . vinegar and tomatoes.
Cook . . . . until heated through.
Yields . . . . 6 servings/about 130 calories each.

Photograph for this recipe on page 36.

CHEESE-STUFFED EGGPLANT

1 med. eggplant
1/2 tsp. salt

4 tbsp. lemon juice
1 8-oz. can tomato sauce
1/4 tsp. crushed oregano leaves
1/2 c. chopped onion
1 tbsp. butter
1/2 lb. cooked ham, chopped
1/3 c. coarsely grated carrot
1/4 c. finely chopped celery
2 c. shredded Cheddar cheese

Cut . . . . . . eggplant in half lengthwise.
Scoop . . . . out pulp to within 1/2 inch of edge.
Bring . . . . 2 cups water, salt and 2 tablespoons lemon juice to a boil in 3-quart saucepan.
Place . . . . eggplant shells in boiling water; cover.
Parboil . . . for 5 minutes.
Drain . . . . and set aside.
Chop . . . . eggplant pulp.
Combine . pulp, tomato sauce, oregano and remaining 2 tablespoons lemon juice in 2-quart saucepan.
Heat . . . . . to boiling point; set aside.
Saute . . . . onion in butter in skillet until tender.
Remove . . from heat.
Stir . . . . . . in remaining ingredients.
Spoon . . . 2/3 of the tomato mixture into buttered 1 1/2-quart baking dish.
Arrange . . eggplant shells on top.
Spoon . . . ham mixture into shells.
Pour . . . . . remaining tomato sauce over top.
Bake . . . . . in preheated 375-degree oven for 25 to 30 minutes or until hot.
Yields . . . . 4 servings/about 540 calories each.

Photograph for this recipe below.

STUFFED MUSHROOMS

1 lb. fresh mushrooms
2 sm. green onions with tops, chopped
4 slices bread, cubed
1/4 tsp. garlic salt
1 tsp. lemon juice
1 egg

Remove .. mushroom stems and chop finely.
Saute .... chopped mushrooms and onions lightly in skillet in small amount of oil.
Add ..... bread cubes, garlic salt and lemon juice, tossing to mix.
Stir ...... in egg; simmer for 1 minute.
Stuff .... mushroom caps with mixture.
Arrange .. in oiled 5 x 12-inch baking dish.
Bake ..... at 350 degrees for 10 minutes, or microwave for 4 minutes.

Sandra C. Snipes
Bishop Moore H. S., Orlando, Florida

MOCK CHEESE SOUFFLE

12 slices white bread
12 slices American cheese
6 eggs
3 c. milk
1/2 tsp. paprika
1/4 tsp. mustard
1 tsp. salt

Remove .. crusts from bread.
Place .... 6 slices in bottom of baking dish.
Top ..... each slice with 2 slices cheese.
Place .... remaining bread on top.
Combine . remaining ingredients in blender container.
Process ... until well mixed.
Pour ..... over bread.
Place .... in refrigerator overnight.
Bake ..... at 350 degrees for 1 hour.

Ethel White
Sheepshead Bay H. S., Brooklyn, New York

QUICK QUICHE LORRAINE

1 can crescent dinner rolls
1 egg, beaten
1 c. evaporated milk
1/2 tsp. salt
1/2 tsp. Worcestershire sauce

1 c. shredded Swiss cheese
1 3 1/2-oz. can French-fried onions, crumbled
9 slices crisp-cooked bacon, crumbled

Separate .. roll dough into 8 triangles.
Place .... in 9-inch pie plate, pressing together to form crust.
Combine . next 5 ingredients in bowl, mixing well.
Sprinkle .. half the onions over crust.
Pour ..... egg mixture over onions.
Top ..... with bacon and remaining onions.
Bake ..... at 325 degrees for 25 to 30 minutes until quiche tests done.
Cool ..... for 5 minutes before serving.

Barbara E. Smoot
Wapahani H. S., Selma, Indiana

DAY-AHEAD EGGS

3 doz. eggs
1/2 c. milk
Butter
2 cans mushroom soup
1/2 lb. Cheddar cheese, grated
1/2 c. dry Sherry
1 lb. mushrooms, sliced

Mix ..... eggs and milk in large mixing bowl.
Cook .... in 1/2 cup butter in large skillet, stirring to scramble.
Combine . soup, cheese and Sherry in saucepan.
Cook .... until heated through.
Layer .... 1/3 of the egg mixture and 1/3 of the sauce in 3-quart casserole, repeating until all ingredients are used.
Cover .... and refrigerate for 1 day.
Saute .... mushrooms in butter in skillet.
Place .... over eggs.
Bake ..... covered, at 275 degrees for 50 minutes.

Murriel Riedesel
Wauconda H. S., Wauconda, Illinois

EGG CASSEROLE

3 tbsp. margarine
2 tbsp. flour
1/4 tsp. salt
1 c. milk

1 c. grated cheese
2 c. cracker crumbs
3 hard-cooked eggs, sliced

Melt . . . . . margarine in medium saucepan.
Add . . . . . flour and salt, stirring until smooth.
Add . . . . . milk and cheese.
Cook . . . . over medium heat until thick, stirring constantly.
Sprinkle . . 1 cup cracker crumbs over bottom of 8 x 8-inch casserole.
Place . . . . egg slices over crumbs.
Pour . . . . . cheese sauce over eggs.
Top . . . . . with remaining crumbs.
Yields . . . . 6 servings/about 390 calories each.

Ruth E. Montell
Russellville Middle School, Russellville, Kentucky

HOT EGG SALAD LOAF

1 4 x 16-in. loaf unsliced Italian bread
1 c. bread crumbs
2 tbsp. butter, melted
6 tbsp. mayonnaise
1 1/2 tbsp. prepared mustard
1 clove of garlic, minced
1 tsp. dried chives
1/4 c. chopped onion
1/2 c. chopped celery
1/2 c. chopped pimento-stuffed olives
6 hard-cooked eggs, coarsely chopped

Cut . . . . . . bread in half lengthwise.
Scoop . . . . out bread center to within 1/2-inch of crust.
Brush . . . . crust with butter.
Blend . . . . mayonnaise, mustard and garlic in bowl.
Add . . . . . remaining ingredients, mixing well.
Spoon . . . mixture into hollowed out crust.
Wrap . . . . each portion in foil.
Bake . . . . . at 425 degrees for 20 minutes or until heated through.

Photograph for this recipe on page 4.

CHEESE AND EGG PUFFS

Margarine
1/2 c. pancake mix
12 eggs
1/4 c. chopped green onions
1 1/2 c. shredded sharp Cheddar cheese

2 to 3 tbsp. chopped pimento
1/4 tsp. salt

Place . . . . 1/4 cup margarine and 1/2 cup water in medium saucepan.
Bring . . . . mixture to a boil.
Add . . . . . pancake mix, stirring until dough forms ball.
Remove . . from heat.
Add . . . . . 2 eggs, one at a time, beating well after each addition.
Spread . . . evenly in greased pie plate.
Bake . . . . . at 400 degrees for 15 to 18 minutes.
Mix . . . . . remaining ingredients in bowl.
Melt . . . . . 3 tablespoons margarine in large skillet.
Pour . . . . . in egg mixture.
Cook . . . . over low heat, stirring to scramble.
Spoon . . . eggs into center of puff and serve immediately.

Ruth Larson
Hickman H. S., Columbia, Missouri

CHEESE AND PEPPER ENCHILADAS

1 onion, chopped
10 banana peppers, chopped
6 to 8 tortillas
1 can cream of mushroom soup
1 lb. Cheddar cheese, shredded
1/2 soup can milk

Saute . . . . onion and peppers in small amount of margarine in skillet until tender.
Soften . . . tortillas over steam from vegetables.
Place . . . . 1 spoonful soup, 1 spoonful vegetables and 2 spoonfuls cheese in each tortilla.
Roll . . . . . tortillas to enclose filling.
Place . . . . seam side down in casserole.
Top . . . . . with remaining cheese and vegetables.
Add . . . . . milk to remaining soup, stirring to mix.
Pour . . . . . over enchiladas.
Bake . . . . . at 325 degrees for 15 to 20 minutes or until bubbly.
Yields . . . . 6 servings/about 465 calories each.

Durene French
Cameron H. S., Cameron, Oklahoma

FOOD PROCESSOR CHEESE SOUFFLE

6 eggs
1/2 c. heavy cream
1/4 c. grated Parmesan cheese
1/2 tsp. prepared mustard
1/2 tsp. salt
1/4 tsp. pepper
1/2 lb. sharp Cheddar cheese, shredded
11 oz. cream cheese, cubed

Attach ... steel blade to food processor.
Combine . eggs, cream, Parmesan cheese, mustard, salt and pepper in processor container.
Process ... mixture until smooth.
Add ..... Cheddar cheese and cream cheese while processor is running.
Process ... until cheeses are incorporated, then for 5 seconds longer.
Pour ..... into buttered souffle dish.
Bake ..... at 375 degrees for 45 to 50 minutes.

Ellen Jansson
J. B. Young H. S., Davenport, Iowa

GARY'S FAVORITE STUFFING

2 c. chopped celery
2 c. chopped onion
1 c. butter
1 lg. can oysters, chopped
5 c. dry bread cubes
1 1/2 c. cooked chopped giblets
1 3/4 tsp. salt
1 tsp. ground pepper
1/4 c. chopped parsley (opt.)
1/4 tsp. each sage, poultry seasoning
1 can cream of mushroom soup
1 can mushrooms, chopped

Saute .... celery and onion in 3/4 cup butter in large skillet until tender.
Drain .... oysters, reserving broth.
Combine . remaining 1/4 cup butter, oysters and next 7 ingredients in large bowl, tossing lightly.
Add ..... celery and onions, mixing lightly.
Mix ..... reserved oyster broth with soup in bowl.
Fold ..... into bread mixture, mixing thoroughly.

Add ..... mushrooms and enough water for desired moistness.
Pour ..... into baking pan.
Bake ..... at 325 degrees for 40 minutes.

Becky S. Groves
Humansville R-IV H. S., Humansville, Missouri

MANICOTTI

1/2 lb. mozzarella cheese, shredded
1/2 c. cottage cheese
2 eggs, slightly beaten
2 tbsp. Parmesan cheese
2 tbsp. soft butter
1/2 tsp. salt
1/2 tsp. pepper
8 manicotti shells
1 pkg. spaghetti sauce mix
1 c. tomato sauce

Combine . first 7 ingredients in bowl, mixing well.
Stuff .... uncooked manicotti shells with cheese mixture.
Place .... in baking dish.
Prepare ... spaghetti sauce using package directions with tomato sauce.
Pour ..... over manicotti.
Sprinkle .. with additional Parmesan cheese.
Bake ..... covered, at 350 degrees for 45 minutes.
Yields .... 4 servings/about 580 calories each.

Ellen Serfustini
Cyprus H. S., Magna, Utah

MICROWAVE RICE AND SPINACH DELUXE

2 tsp. butter
1 c. chopped onion
1 1/2 c. quick-cooking rice
1/2 tsp. salt
1 10-oz. package frozen chopped spinach
1 5-oz. jar sharp process cheese spread
1 10 3/4-oz. can cream of mushroom soup
1/8 tsp. nutmeg (opt.)

Melt ..... butter in 1 1/2-quart microwave casserole on High for 20 to 30 seconds.
Stir ...... in onion.
Cook .... for 3 to 4 minutes or until tender.

Add ..... rice, salt and 1 1/2 cups water, mixing well.
Microwave covered, on High for 2 to 3 minutes, bringing to a boil.
Let ...... stand until water is absorbed.
Place .... spinach in 1-quart microwave casserole.
Cook .... for 2 1/2 to 3 minutes.
Drain .... excess moisture.
Add ..... rice mixture and cheese spread.
Stir ...... until cheese spread melts.
Add ..... soup and nutmeg, mixing well.
Microwave for 7 to 9 minutes or to 150 degrees on microwave thermometer.
Yields .... 6 servings/about 298 calories each.

Glynda Hooper
Marlow H. S., Marlow, Oklahoma

BAKED RICE WITH MUSHROOMS

1 stick butter, melted
1 can onion soup
1 can beef broth
2 c. rice
1 tbsp. Worcestershire sauce
1 1/2 tsp. salt
1 can water chestnuts, sliced, drained
1 4-oz. can sliced mushrooms, drained

Place .... all ingredients in large baking dish; mix well.
Bake ..... covered, at 325 degrees for 1 hour and 20 minutes, stirring halfway through.

Janet S. Blackwood
Glen Oaks Jr. H. S., Baton Rouge, Louisiana

JEWEL RICE

1/2 c. chopped onion
2 tbsp. butter
1 c. rice·
1 chicken bouillon cube
1 tsp. salt
1/8 tsp. pepper
1/2 tsp. dried thyme
1 10-oz. package frozen peas, thawed, drained
1 1/2 c. Florida orange sections

Saute .... onion in butter in skillet until tender.

Add ..... rice, cooking until golden.
Stir ...... in next 4 ingredients and 2 cups water.
Simmer .. covered, for 15 minutes.
Add ..... peas.
Cook .... for 5 minutes longer or until rice is tender and water is absorbed.
Add ..... orange sections and heat through.
Yields .... 6 servings/about 220 calories each.

Photograph for this recipe on page 1.

RICE WITH CHILES

1 1/2 c. cooked rice
Salt and pepper to taste
2/3 can chopped green chiles
1 c. sour cream
1/4 lb. Monterey Jack cheese, sliced
Cheddar cheese, shredded (opt.)

Mix ..... rice with salt and pepper.
Layer .... rice, chiles, sour cream and Monterey Jack cheese in greased casserole until all ingredients are used, beginning and ending with rice.
Bake ..... at 350 degrees for 30 minutes.
Top ..... with Cheddar cheese.
Let ...... stand until cheese is melted before serving.

Deborah Jackson
Pine Tree H. S., Longview, Texas

RICE JARDIN

3/4 c. chopped onion
1 1/2 lb. zucchini, thinly sliced
3 tbsp. butter
1 1-lb. can whole kernel corn
1 1-lb. can tomatoes
3 c. cooked rice
1/4 tsp. each oregano, coriander
1 1/2 tsp. salt
1/4 tsp. pepper

Saute .... onion and zucchini in butter in skillet until tender.
Add ..... remaining ingredients, mixing well.
Simmer .. for 15 minutes, stirring occasionally.
Yields .... 8 servings/about 200 calories each.

Carolyn Preston
Sam Rayburn H. S., Pasadena, Texas

Meats

When your family asks "What's for dinner?" they usually mean, "What kind of meat?" Now, with your *All-Purpose Cookbook*, you can have a new and different dish for months!

Many all-time meat favorites are included in these pages but you'll find an excellent selection of new recipes you'll want to try too. Each is sure to please family and friends!

TRICKS OF THE TRADE

- Carve meat neatly and retain rich juices by allowing to stand 15 minutes after removing from the oven.
- Freeze extra broth and pan drippings in ice cube trays, then pop into plastic bags for storage. So easy and tasty to add to soups and gravies.
- To prevent spattering, sprinkle a small amount of salt into the frypan before adding fat.
- To prevent smoking while broiling, add one cup water to the bottom portion of the broiling pan to absorb smoke and grease.
- When browning meat for stew, place a few pieces at a time in the skillet since crowding steams the meat rather than browns it.

BEEF JERKY

1 tbsp. lemon pepper
1/2 c. soy sauce
1/2 tsp. garlic salt
2 lb. flank steak, cut in 1/4-in. strips

Combine . first 3 ingredients in bowl, mixing well.
Add . . . . . steak to marinate, stirring to coat all sides.
Place . . . . strips on cookie sheet.
Bake . . . . . at 200 degrees for 6 to 8 hours or until dried.

Sandra Souza
El Rancho Verde H. S., Hayward, California

BEEF STROGANOFF

1 lb. round steak, trimmed
1/4 c. butter
1 lb. fresh mushrooms, sliced
1 lg. onion, chopped
1 c. beef broth
2 1/2 tbsp. flour
1 c. sour cream
Salt and pepper to taste

Slice . . . . . steak into thin strips.
Brown . . . steak in butter in large skillet.
Remove . . from pan.
Saute . . . . mushrooms and onion in pan drippings in skillet.
Stir . . . . . . in steak and broth, heating to boiling point.
Combine . flour and sour cream in small bowl, blending well.
Add . . . . . sour cream mixture to steak, blending well; season with salt and pepper.
Cook . . . . over low heat until heated through, stirring occasionally.
Serve . . . . over buttered noodles.

Marie Caldorera
Independence H. S., Independence, Louisiana

CUBED STEAK PARMIGIANA

6 beef cubed steaks
3 tbsp. flour
1/2 tsp. salt
1/8 tsp. pepper
10 crackers, finely crushed
1/2 tsp. basil
Grated Parmesan cheese
1 egg, beaten
3 tbsp. oil
1   15-oz. can tomato sauce
1 tbsp. sugar
1 clove of garlic, crushed
1/2 tsp. ground oregano
1 oz. mozzarella cheese, sliced
Leaf oregano

Coat . . . . . steaks in flour seasoned with salt and pepper.
Combine . cracker crumbs, basil and 1/3 cup Parmesan cheese in small bowl.
Mix . . . . . egg with 2 tablespoons water in bowl.
Dip . . . . . . each steak into egg mixture.
Coat . . . . . each steak evenly with crumb mixture.
Heat . . . . . oil in 13 x 9-inch baking pan in 375-degree oven for 5 to 10 minutes.
Place . . . . steaks in baking pan.
Bake . . . . . uncovered for 25 to 30 minutes or until golden brown.
Pour . . . . . off drippings.
Combine . tomato sauce with sugar, garlic and ground oregano, pounding over steaks.
Sprinkle . . with 1/4 cup Parmesan cheese.
Bake . . . . . for 20 minutes longer.
Top . . . . . with mozzarella cheese and a sprinkle of leaf oregano.
Bake . . . . . for 3 to 5 minutes longer.
Yields . . . . 6 servings/about 405 calories each.

Cynthia Berend
Mt. Vernon H. S., Mt. Vernon, Texas

LUAU BEEF STRIPS

2 lb. round steak, 1/2 in. thick
1 tbsp. shortening
2 med. onions, thinly sliced
1   20-oz. can pineapple chunks
1/2 c. packed brown sugar
1 tsp. ginger
2 tbsp. cornstarch
1/3 c. soy sauce
2 tbsp. vinegar
1 can mushrooms
2 med. tomatoes, cut in wedges
1 med. avocado, sliced

Cut . . . . . . steak into 1/8 x 2-inch strips.
Brown . . . steak in shortening in skillet.
Add . . . . . onions and 1/2 cup water.
Simmer . . covered, for 30 minutes.
Drain . . . . pineapple, reserving juice.
Add . . . . . enough water to juice to measure 2/3 cup liquid.
Combine . with next 5 ingredients in saucepan.
Cook . . . . until thick, stirring constantly.
Add . . . . . sauce, pineapple and mushrooms to steak, mixing well.
Cook . . . . covered, for 5 minutes.
Fold . . . . . in tomatoes and avocado.
Cook . . . . until heated through.
Serve . . . . over rice.

Syd Burnett
Flour Bluff H. S., Corpus Christi, Texas

STEAK ROLL-UPS WITH MUSHROOMS

1 lb. round steak, pounded thin
Salt and pepper to taste
Dash of garlic salt
1 pkg. stuffing mix
1 can cream of mushroom soup

Cut . . . . . . steak into 6 pieces.
Sprinkle . . with seasonings.
Prepare . . . stuffing using package directions.
Spoon . . . 1 tablespoon on each piece of steak.
Roll . . . . . up, securing with toothpicks.
Brown . . . over medium heat in shortening in skillet for 2 minutes per side.
Remove . . rolls and pour off excess drippings.
Add . . . . . soup and 1 soup can water, stirring to mix well.
Return . . . steak rolls to skillet, spooning sauce over each.
Simmer . . over low heat for 1 hour, turning once.

Cindy Gedling
Sidney Phillips School, Mobile, Alabama

STIR-FRY BEEF WITH BROCCOLI

4 tbsp. oil
1 tbsp. cornstarch
1 tbsp. soy sauce
1 1/2 lb. round steak, thinly sliced
2 green onions, sliced
1 bunch fresh broccoli, chopped

Combine . 1 tablespoon oil, cornstarch and soy sauce in bowl.
Add . . . . . steak slices, mixing well.
Brown . . . onions in 2 tablespoons oil in skillet.
Add . . . . . steak, cooking until brown.
Add . . . . . remaining oil and broccoli.
Stir-fry . . . for 3 to 5 minutes.

Jo Burroughs
Trinity H. S., Trinity, North Carolina

ALL-AMERICAN POT ROAST

1/4 c. corn oil
1 4-lb. chuck roast
1 c. chopped onion
1 c. sliced celery
2 cloves of garlic, minced
3 c. beef bouillon
1/4 c. catsup
1 tsp. salt
1/2 tsp. dried thyme leaves
1/4 tsp. pepper
6 med. potatoes, peeled, quartered
4 carrots, peeled, cut in 2-in. pieces
1/2 lb. whole green beans
1/4 c. cornstarch

Heat . . . . . corn oil in 5-quart Dutch oven over medium heat.
Brown . . . chuck roast on all sides.
Add . . . . . next 8 ingredients.
Bring . . . . to a boil, covered.
Reduce . . . heat and simmer for 2 hours.
Add . . . . . potatoes and carrots.
Simmer . . covered, for 1/2 hour or until roast and vegetables are tender.
Add . . . . . green beans.
Simmer . . for 10 minutes longer until beans are tender-crisp.
Arrange . . meat and vegetables on platter.
Combine . cornstarch and 1/4 cup water, mixing until smooth.
Add . . . . . to liquid in Dutch oven.
Boil . . . . . for 1 minute, stirring constantly to thicken.
Serve . . . . gravy over roast and vegetables.

Photograph for this recipe on cover.

GRANDMA SMITH'S BARBECUE

1   3 to 4-lb. 7-bone roast
1 onion, minced
1 tbsp. butter
1 1/2 c. catsup
1/2 c. chili sauce
3 tbsp. vinegar
3 tbsp. brown sugar
1/2 tsp. dry mustard
1 tsp. chili powder
1 tsp. Worcestershire sauce

Wrap .... roast in foil.
Bake ..... at 325 degrees for 3 hours or until well done.
Cool ..... roast and cut meat from bones in strips.
Cook .... onion in butter in saucepan until transparent.
Add ..... remaining ingredients.
Simmer .. for 1 hour.
Add ..... beef to sauce.
Serve .... on buns.
Note ..... sauce will keep indefinitely in refrigerator.

Ann Porter
Carl Albert Sr. H. S., Midwest City, Oklahoma

FAVORITE POT ROAST

1   4-lb. beef chuck pot roast
1 env. dry onion soup mix
1 can cream of mushroom soup

Place .... roast on large sheet of aluminum foil in baking pan.
Sprinkle .. soup mix over roast.
Spread ... canned soup over all.
Seal ..... foil securely over roast.
Bake ..... at 300 degrees for 4 hours.
Yields .... 8 servings/about 640 calories each.

Judith Brown
Norwayne H. S., Creston, Ohio

POT ROAST WITH BEER

1   3 to 4-lb. pot roast
Flour
Salt and pepper
2 onions, sliced
8 carrots, sliced
1 stalk celery, diced
1/2 c. dark beer

1 sprig of parsley
1 bay leaf
1 can mushroom soup
1   4-oz. can button mushrooms

Rub ..... roast with seasoned flour.
Brown ... roast in shortening in skillet.
Cover .... roast with vegetables.
Add ..... beer, parsley and bay leaf.
Cook .... covered, over low heat for 3 hours or until tender.
Remove .. roast to serving plate.
Add ..... soup and mushrooms to drippings in skillet, heating through.
Serve .... over roast.

Mary Ann Prust
McClintock H. S., Tempe, Arizona

LONDON BROIL

1 lb. flank steak
2 med. onions, thinly sliced
1/4 tsp. salt
1 tbsp. butter
2 tbsp. oil
1 tsp. lemon juice
2 cloves of garlic, crushed
1/2 tsp. salt
1/4 tsp. pepper

Place .... steak on broiler rack.
Score .... both sides of steak in diamond pattern, 1/8 inch deep.
Saute .... onions with salt in butter in skillet until tender.
Set ...... aside, keeping warm.
Combine . remaining ingredients in bowl.
Brush .... steak with half the sauce.
Broil ..... 2 to 3 inches from heat source for 5 minutes.
Turn ..... steak and brush with remaining sauce.
Broil ..... for 5 minutes longer.
Slice ..... across the grain into thin slices.
Serve .... with onions.

Doris Stiles
Doss H. S., Louisville, Kentucky

MARINATED CHUCK STEAK

1   2 1/2 to 3-lb. chuck steak, 1 1/2 in. thick
1/4 c. oil
1/4 c. packed brown sugar
2 tbsp. dry mustard

2 tbsp. each Worcestershire sauce, horseradish
2 tsp. hot pepper sauce
Unseasoned meat tenderizer

Trim . . . . . chuck steak.
Combine . next 6 ingredients in 9 x 13-inch dish.
Sprinkle . . steak with meat tenderizer.
Add . . . . . to marinade, turning to coat.
Let . . . . . . stand for 20 minutes, turning once.
Broil . . . . . steak to desired degree of doneness, brushing with marinade.
Yields . . . . 6 servings/about 480 calories each.

Mrs. Pam Miller
Bradley Jr. H. S., Cleveland, Tennessee

PEPPER STEAK

1 green pepper, chopped
Margarine
1 steak, cut up
Mushrooms
2 med. cloves of garlic
Oregano to taste
1/2 c. catsup
1/8 c. Sherry
3 tomatoes, chopped
Salt and pepper to taste

Brown . . . green pepper in margarine in skillet.
Remove . . and set aside.
Brown . . . steak, mushrooms and garlic in pan drippings.
Add . . . . . oregano, catsup, Sherry and 1 tomato.

Steam . . . . covered, until meat is tender.
Add . . . . . remaining 2 tomatoes, green pepper, salt and pepper.
Cook . . . . until just heated.
Serve . . . . with rice.

Sharon Johnson
Upper Arlington H. S., Columbus, Ohio

GREEN PEPPER STEAK AND RICE

1 1/2 lb. sirloin steak, cut in 1/4-in. thick strips
1 tbsp. paprika
2 cloves of garlic, crushed
2 tbsp. butter
1 c. sliced green onions
2 green peppers, cut in strips
2 lg. fresh tomatoes, chopped
1 c. beef broth
2 tbsp. cornstarch
2 tbsp. soy sauce
3 c. hot cooked rice

Sprinkle . . steak with paprika.
Let . . . . . . stand for several minutes.
Brown . . . steak and garlic in butter in skillet.
Add . . . . . next four ingredients; cover.
Simmer . . for 15 minutes.
Blend . . . . cornstarch and soy sauce with 1/4 cup water in small bowl.
Stir . . . . . . into steak.
Cook . . . . until thick, stirring constantly.
Serve . . . . over rice.
Yields . . . . 6 servings/about 355 calories each.

Photograph for this recipe below.

ORIENTAL PEPPER STEAK

3 lb. round steak, cut into strips
3 tsp. Accent
1/2 c. oil
2 c. bouillon
1 tsp. sugar
1/2 tsp. ginger
2 tsp. soy sauce
3 lg. green peppers, cut into strips
2 med. onions, sliced
4 med. tomatoes, peeled, cut into wedges
4 tsp. cornstarch

Sprinkle .. steak with 2 teaspoons Accent.
Brown ... in oil in skillet.
Add ..... next 4 ingredients.
Bring .... to a boil and reduce heat.
Simmer .. for 15 minutes.
Add ..... vegetables and remaining 1 teaspoon Accent.
Cook .... for 5 minutes.
Combine . cornstarch with 4 teaspoons cold water, stirring to make smooth paste.
Add ..... paste to steak mixture.
Cook .... until mixture comes to a boil, stirring constantly.
Serve .... with rice or noodles.

Mary H. McMillin
Ripley H. S., Ripley, Mississippi

ALL-DAY BEEF STEW

2 lb. beef cubes
4 to 6 carrots, peeled, cut in fourths
4 to 6 potatoes, peeled, quartered
1 lg. onion, quartered
2 stalks celery, chopped
1 can golden mushroom soup
1 can cream of celery soup
1 can tomato soup
2 bay leaves
1 env. dry onion soup mix

Combine . all ingredients with 2 cups water in Dutch oven.
Bake ..... covered, at 275 degrees for 6 hours or longer.
Remove .. bay leaves before serving.

Debra Lang
Viewmont H. S., Bountiful, Utah

BEEF STEW WITH ONIONS

2 lb. lean beef, cubed
1/2 c. butter
18 sm. whole onions, peeled
1 No. 2 can tomatoes
1 tsp. pickling spices
1 tbsp. wine
Salt and pepper to taste

Saute .... beef in large skillet for 15 minutes.
Add ..... butter and cook for 5 minutes, browning on all sides.
Place .... beef in large saucepan.
Brown ... onions lightly in skillet.
Remove .. onions and reserve.
Add ..... tomatoes to skillet; cook for 5 minutes.
Pour ..... over beef in saucepan.
Add ..... last 4 ingredients with 3 cups hot water, mixing well.
Bring .... to a boil, cover and reduce heat.
Cook .... for 1 1/2 hours or until meat is tender.
Add ..... onions.
Cook .... for 1 hour longer.
Yields .... 5 servings/about 590 calories each.

Hazel C. Tassis
Imperial H. S., Imperial, California

FRENCH BEEF STEW

1 1/2 lb. beef stew meat, cubed
1 onion, chopped
1 8-oz. can mushrooms
4 beef-flavored bouillon cubes
4 tbsp. quick-cooking tapioca

Combine . all ingredients with 3 cups water in large baking pan, mixing well.
Bake ..... covered, at 350 degrees for 3 to 3 1/2 hours.
Serve .... over rice.

Carole Fisher
Martinsville H. S., Martinsville, Indiana

OVEN BEEF STEW

2 lb. stew beef, cubed
2 c. chopped potatoes
2 c. green beans
2 c. chopped carrots
2 c. peas
3/4 c. chopped onions

1 qt. tomato sauce
1 tbsp. tapioca
2 tbsp. brown sugar
1 bay leaf
Salt and pepper to taste
1/2 c. bread crumbs

Combine . all ingredients except bread crumbs in 4-quart baking pan, mixing well.
Top ..... with crumbs.
Bake ..... covered, at 250 degrees for 6 to 7 hours.

Nancy L. Bell
Mascenic Regional School
New Ipswich, New Hampshire

REUBEN CASSEROLE

1 8-oz. can sauerkraut, drained
1/2 tsp. caraway seed
1 sm. tomato, cut in thin wedges (opt.)
2 tbsp. Thousand Island salad dressing
1 3 or 4-oz. package thin-sliced corned beef, cut up
1/4 c. shredded Swiss cheese
1/4 c. soft rye bread crumbs
2 tsp. melted butter

Spread ... sauerkraut in baking dish.
Sprinkle .. with caraway seed.
Layer .... next 4 ingredients in order given over sauerkraut.
Toss ..... bread crumbs with butter.
Sprinkle .. over casserole.
Bake ..... at 375 degrees for 25 to 30 minutes or until heated through.
Yields .... 2 servings/about 350 calories each.

Paula Neth
St. Teresa's Academy, Kansas City, Missouri

AMERICAN CHOP SUEY

1 8-oz. package small macaroni
2 tsp. salt
1/2 c. chopped onion
1/2 c. chopped green pepper
3 stalks celery, finely sliced
2 tbsp. butter
1 lb. ground beef
2 tsp. chili powder
1 tsp. each garlic salt, pepper
1 1-lb. can tomatoes
1 8-oz. can tomato sauce
1 c. shredded Cheddar cheese

Cook .... macaroni in 3 cups boiling salted water in saucepan until tender.
Set ...... aside, covered, for 5 minutes; drain.
Saute .... onion, green pepper and celery in butter in skillet until golden; set aside.
Brown ... ground beef with seasonings in skillet, stirring until crumbly.
Pour ..... off drippings.
Add ..... sauteed vegetables, tomatoes and tomato sauce.
Simmer .. for 5 minutes.
Add ..... macaroni and 3/4 cup cheese, mixing well.
Pour ..... into greased 2-quart casserole.
Sprinkle .. with remaining cheese.
Bake ..... covered, at 375 degrees for 20 to 25 minutes.
Yields .... 6 servings/about 430 calories each.

Kaye Derryberry
Webster Middle School, Oklahoma City, Oklahoma

FAKE STEAK

1 lb. ground meat
1 egg, beaten
1/4 c. milk
1 c. bread crumbs
1 tsp. salt
1/2 lb. bacon
1 can tomato soup
1/2 c. packed brown sugar
1/4 c. vinegar
1 tbsp. Worcestershire sauce

Combine . first 5 ingredients in bowl, mixing well.
Shape .... into balls.
Wrap .... with bacon, securing with toothpicks.
Brown ... on all sides in skillet.
Pour ..... off drippings.
Combine . remaining ingredients with 1/2 cup water in bowl, blending well.
Pour ..... over meat.
Cook .... covered, over low heat until done or bake at 325 degrees for 30 to 45 minutes.
Yields .... 6 servings/about 415 calories each.

Sandra Tanner
Troy H. S., Troy, Texas

CABBAGE ROLLS

8 large cabbage leaves
1 lb. hamburger
1/2 c. cracker crumbs
Minced onions to taste
1/2 c. rice
1 green pepper, chopped
1 egg, beaten
Salt and pepper to taste
1 can tomato sauce
1 can tomatoes
2 tsp. sugar
1 tsp. each thyme, oregano
Garlic powder to taste

Boil . . . . . cabbage leaves in water to cover in saucepan until tender; drain and set aside.
Combine . next 7 ingredients in bowl with enough tomato sauce to moisten, mixing well.
Roll . . . . . hamburger mixture in cabbage leaves.
Place . . . . in baking dish.
Combine . remaining ingredients in saucepan.
Simmer . . for 5 minutes.
Pour . . . . . over cabbage rolls.
Bake . . . . . at 350 degrees for 1 hour.

Joyce A. Cole
Bell County H. S., Pineville, Kentucky

HAMBURGER PIE

1 pkg. refrigerator biscuits
1 lb. ground beef
2 tsp. minced onion
1 egg, slightly beaten
1/3 c. catsup
1/4 c. chopped green pepper
1/2 tsp. each chili powder, salt
Dash of pepper
3 slices cheese, halved diagonally

Press . . . . . biscuits into bottom of pie plate.
Bake . . . . . using package directions.
Brown . . . ground beef in skillet, stirring until crumbly.
Combine . remaining ingredients except cheese in bowl, mixing well.
Add . . . . . browned ground beef, stirring to mix.
Spoon . . . into baked shell.

Arrange . . cheese over top.
Bake . . . . . at 400 degrees for 5 minutes or until cheese melts.

Helen Webster
Newcomerstown H. S., Newcomerstown, Ohio

GOLDEN BEEF QUICHE

1 unbaked pie shell
1 tbsp. margarine, softened
3/4 lb. ground beef
1 med. onion, minced
1 11-oz. can Cheddar cheese soup
6 eggs
1/2 c. milk
1/2 tsp. thyme
1/8 tsp. pepper

Rub . . . . . pie shell with margarine.
Brown . . . ground beef and onion in medium skillet, stirring until crumbly.
Spoon . . . into pie shell.
Combine . remaining ingredients in large bowl, mixing well.
Pour . . . . . over ground beef.
Bake . . . . . at 375 degrees for 35 to 40 minutes or until quiche tests done.
Yields . . . . 6 servings/about 400 calories each.

D'Nelle Phillips
Texas H. S., Texarkana, Texas

HUNGRY MAN'S CASSEROLE

1 1/2 lb. ground beef
2 tsp. salt
2 tsp. sugar
1 16-oz. can tomatoes
1 8-oz. can tomato sauce
2 cloves of garlic, crushed
Pepper to taste
1 8-oz. package thin noodles, cooked
1 c. sour cream
3 oz. cream cheese, softened
3 green onions with tops, chopped
Grated cheese (opt.)

Brown . . . ground beef in skillet, stirring until crumbly.
Pour . . . . . off drippings.
Add . . . . . next 6 ingredients, mixing well.
Cook . . . . for 10 minutes.
Combine . remaining ingredients except grated cheese in bowl, mixing well.

Layer . . . . noodle mixture and ground beef mixture alternately in greased casserole until all ingredients are used.
Top . . . . . with cheese.
Bake . . . . . at 350 degrees for 30 to 35 minutes.

Roselen Bobo
Henderson H. S., Henderson, Texas

LAZY DAY CASSEROLE

2 sm. onions, chopped
1 1/2 c. diced celery
1 tbsp. oil
1 lb. ground chuck
1/2 c. rice
1 can cream of chicken soup
1 can cream of mushroom soup
1 can chow mein noodles

Saute . . . . onions and celery in oil in skillet.
Brown . . . ground chuck in skillet, stirring until crumbly.
Pour . . . . . off drippings.
Add . . . . . vegetables, rice and soups.
Pour . . . . . into 2-quart casserole.
Bake . . . . . covered, at 400 degrees for 35 minutes.
Sprinkle . . noodles over casserole.
Bake . . . . . uncovered, for 10 minutes.
Yields . . . . 6 servings/about 300 calories each.

Mrs. Wade H. Harris
Southwestern Randolph H. S.
Asheboro, North Carolina

MEAT LOAF SOUFFLE

1 1/2 lb. ground beef
1/2 c. dry bread crumbs
1/2 c. milk
1/2 c. chopped onion
4 eggs
Salt and pepper
4 oz. Cheddar cheese, shredded
2 tomatoes, sliced
1 c. sour cream
3/4 c. flour

Combine . first 4 ingredients with 1 egg, 1 1/2 teaspoons salt and 1/8 teaspoon pepper in bowl, mixing well.
Press . . . . . lightly into 9 x 9-inch baking dish.
Bake . . . . . at 350 degrees for 25 minutes.
Pour . . . . . off drippings.

Top . . . . . with cheese and tomato slices.
Separate . . remaining eggs.
Combine . egg yolks, sour cream, flour, 1/4 teaspoon salt and dash of pepper in bowl, beating until thick and creamy.
Beat . . . . . egg whites until stiff but not dry.
Fold . . . . . into sour cream mixture, blending well.
Spread . . . over tomato slices.
Bake . . . . . at 350 degrees for 30 to 40 minutes or until golden brown.
Let . . . . . . stand for 5 minutes before serving.
Yields . . . . 8 servings/about 390 calories each.

Mary F. Yost
Cairo-Durham H. S., Cairo, New York

MEAT LOAF SUPREME

2 eggs, beaten
3/4 c. soft bread crumbs
1/2 c. tomato juice
2 tbsp. snipped parsley
1/2 tsp. oregano
1/4 tsp. salt
1/4 tsp. pepper
1 clove of garlic, minced
1 1/2 lb. lean ground beef
8 oz. lean pork sausage
4 slices salami
1 1/2 c. shredded mozzarella cheese
3 slices mozzarella cheese, halved diagonally

Combine . first 10 ingredients in large bowl, mixing well.
Pat . . . . . . meat mixture into a 10 x 12-inch rectangle on waxed paper.
Arrange . . salami over meat, leaving small margin around edges.
Sprinkle . . with shredded cheese.
Roll . . . . . as for jelly roll from short end, sealing edges and ends.
Place . . . . seam side down in 9 x 13-inch baking pan.
Bake . . . . . at 350 degrees for 1 1/4 hours or until done.
Arrange . . cheese triangles over top.
Bake . . . . . for 5 minutes longer until cheese melts.
Yields . . . . 8 servings/about 370 calories each.

Shirley Wells
Douglas S. Freeman H. S., Richmond, Virginia

PICKLE MEAT LOAF MEAL

1/2 c. milk
1/4 c. sweet pickle liquid
2 eggs
4 slices white bread, quartered
1 med. onion, quartered
1 1/2 tsp. salt
1/4 tsp. pepper
2 lb. lean ground beef
5 tbsp. chopped parsley
2/3 c. finely chopped sweet gherkins
1 16-oz. can cut green beans, drained
1 16-oz. can waxed beans, drained
1 16-oz. can julienne beets, drained

Combine . first 7 ingredients in blender container.
Process . . . until smooth.
Add . . . . . to ground beef in large bowl, mixing until well blended.
Shape . . . . into 9 x 15-inch rectangle on waxed paper.
Sprinkle . . with parsley and pickles.
Roll . . . . . as for jelly roll from narrow end.
Place . . . . seam side down in large baking dish.
Bake . . . . . at 350 degrees for 1 hour.

Pour . . . . . off pan drippings and add vegetables.
Bake . . . . . covered for about 15 minutes longer or until vegetables are heated through.
Place . . . . meat loaf on serving plate; spoon vegetables around meat loaf.
Garnish . . with sour cream and pickle slices.
Yields . . . . 8 servings/about 380 calories each.

Photograph for this recipe above.

MOZZARELLA MEAT LOAF

1 1/2 lb. ground beef
1/2 c. dry bread crumbs
1 egg, slightly beaten
1 tsp. instant minced onion
3/4 tsp. salt
1/2 tsp. oregano
1 15-oz. can tomato sauce
1 1/2 c. shredded mozzarella cheese
1 4-oz. can mushrooms (opt.)

Combine . first 6 ingredients with 3/4 cup tomato sauce in bowl, mixing well.
Pat . . . . . . meat mixture into 9 x 13-inch rectangle on waxed paper.
Sprinkle . . with cheese and mushrooms.

Roll . . . . . as for jelly roll, sealing edge and ends.
Place . . . . seam side down in 8 x 12-inch baking pan.
Bake . . . . . at 375 degrees for 30 minutes.
Pour . . . . . off drippings.
Spoon . . . remaining tomato sauce over loaf.
Bake . . . . . for 30 minutes longer.
Yields . . . . 8 servings/about 255 calories each.

Jo Anne M. Stringer
Liberty H. S., Youngstown, Ohio

MEATBALL DINNER

1 lb. ground beef
2 tbsp. chopped onion
2 tbsp. chopped green pepper
1/2 c. yellow cornmeal
1 tsp. each salt, chili powder
1 1/2 tsp. dry mustard
1/2 c. milk
1 egg, beaten
6 carrots, halved
6 sm. onions
3 or 4 potatoes, peeled, quartered
1 can tomato soup

Combine . first 9 ingredients in bowl, mixing well.
Shape . . . . into small meatballs.
Place . . . . in baking dish.
Bake . . . . . at 400 degrees for 10 minutes.
Layer . . . . meatballs and vegetables in baking dish.
Pour . . . . . soup over top.
Bake . . . . . covered, at 350 degrees for 1 hour.
Yields . . . . 4 servings/about 525 calories each.

Carol S. Windus
Wheeling H. S., Wheeling, Illinois

MEATBALL STROGANOFF

1 lb. ground beef
1/2 c. finely chopped onion
1 egg
1 slice white bread, crumbled
1/2 tsp. salt
Pepper to taste
1 can cream of mushroom soup

1/2 c. sour cream
3 c. cooked wide noodles

Combine . first 6 ingredients in bowl, mixing well.
Shape . . . . into balls.
Brown . . . meatballs on all sides in skillet.
Pour . . . . . off drippings.
Add . . . . . soup and 1/3 cup water.
Simmer . . for 10 minutes, stirring occasionally.
Blend . . . . in sour cream and heat through.
Serve . . . . over noodles.

DeAnn B. Degelbeck
Tooele H. S., Tooele, Utah

PEPPER STEAK MEATBALLS

1 1/2 lb. ground beef
1/2 c. milk
3/4 c. seasoned bread crumbs
2 tbsp. parsley
1 tsp. each salt, pepper
1/4 c. margarine
1 can sliced mushrooms
2 onions, sliced
3 green peppers, cut in strips
3 tomatoes, quartered
1 tbsp. soy sauce
1 10-oz. can beef broth
1/4 c. Burgundy
3 tbsp. cornstarch

Combine . first 6 ingredients in bowl, mixing well.
Shape . . . . into 1-inch balls.
Brown . . . in margarine in skillet.
Add . . . . . vegetables and saute until tender.
Stir . . . . . . in next 3 ingredients with 1/3 cup water.
Simmer . . for 20 minutes.
Blend . . . . cornstarch with 1/4 cup cold water in small bowl until smooth.
Pour . . . . . cornstarch glaze over meatballs and vegetables.
Cook . . . . 2 to 3 minutes.
Serve . . . . over rice accompanied by curried fruit.
Yields . . . . 8 servings/about 370 calories each.

Darrelynn Barnett
Ore City H. S., Ore City, Texas

PLANTATION SUPPER

1 lb. ground beef
1/2 c. chopped onion
3/4 c. milk
1 can cream of mushroom soup
1 8-oz. package cream cheese, softened
1 1/2 c. whole kernel corn, drained
1/4 c. chopped pimento
8 oz. noodles, cooked
1 to 1 1/2 tsp. salt
Dash of pepper

Brown ... ground beef in skillet, stirring until crumbly.
Add ..... onion, cooking until tender.
Stir ...... in milk, soup and cream cheese until well blended.
Add ..... remaining ingredients, mixing well.
Cook .... until heated through.

Ann Morgan
Seabreeze Sr. H. S., Daytona Beach, Florida

LASAGNA

1 lb. ground beef
2 tbsp. chopped onions
1 qt. Ragu sauce with mushrooms
1 lb. cottage cheese
2 eggs, beaten
8 oz. mozzarella cheese, grated
1 pkg. lasagna noodles, cooked
1/2 c. Parmesan cheese

Brown ... ground beef and onions in skillet, stirring until crumbly.
Pour ..... off drippings.
Add ..... Ragu sauce, mixing well and simmering.
Combine . cottage cheese, eggs and mozzarella cheese in bowl, mixing until smooth.
Layer .... noodles, sauce and cheese mixture alternately in 9 x 13-inch baking dish until all ingredients are used.
Top ..... with Parmesan cheese.
Bake ..... covered, at 325 degrees for 50 minutes.
Uncover .. and bake for 10 minutes longer.

Rose Rinehardt
Trinity H. S., Trinity, North Carolina

EASY KETTLE LASAGNA

1 lb. ground beef
1 pkg. spaghetti sauce mix
2 c. cottage cheese
1 pkg. medium egg noodles
1 qt. whole tomatoes with juice
1 c. shredded mozzarella cheese

Brown ... ground beef in large skillet, stirring until crumbly.
Pour ..... off drippings.
Sprinkle .. half the spaghetti sauce mix over ground beef.
Spread ... cottage cheese on top.
Cover .... with noodles.
Sprinkle .. with remaining sauce mix.
Pour ..... tomatoes over all.
Simmer .. covered, over low heat for about 30 minutes or until noodles are tender.
Add ..... 3/4 to 1 cup water if necessary.
Sprinkle .. cheese on top.
Heat ..... until cheese melts.
Yields .... 6 servings/about 490 calories each.

Katy Jo Powers
Haysi H. S., Haysi, Virginia

ZUCCHINI-BEEF CASSEROLE

3 med. zucchini, sliced
1/2 onion, chopped
1 sm. green pepper, chopped
Salt and pepper to taste
1 c. cracker crumbs
1 can cream of chicken soup
Parmesan cheese
1/2 lb. ground beef

Arrange .. zucchini in greased 2-quart casserole.
Add ..... onion and green pepper.
Season ... with salt and pepper.
Cover .... with crumbs.
Pour ..... undiluted soup over all.
Sprinkle .. with cheese.
Bake ..... at 325 degrees for 45 minutes.
Brown ... ground beef in skillet, stirring until crumbly.
Season ... with salt and pepper.
Sprinkle .. over baked casserole.
Bake ..... for 25 minutes longer.
Yields .... 4 servings/about 390 calories each.

Merridy Leichty
Iowa Mennonite School, Kalona, Iowa

Recipe on page 76.

SAVORY LASAGNA

2 lb. ground beef
1 lb. sausage
1/4 c. onion flakes
1 18-oz. can tomato paste
1 tbsp. (heaping) each oregano, salt and
*   pepper*
1 tbsp. (heaping) parsley flakes
1 tbsp. basil
1/4 tsp. garlic powder
1 lb. lasagna noodles, cooked
2 lb. mozzarella
Grated Parmesan cheese

Brown ... ground beef and sausage in large skillet, stirring until crumbly.
Pour ..... off drippings.
Add ..... onion flakes, tomato paste and 2 tomato paste cans water, mixing well.
Add ..... seasonings and spices.
Simmer .. for 20 to 30 minutes.
Layer .... noodles, sauce and mozzarella cheese in two 9 x 14-inch pans. Top with Parmesan cheese.
Bake ..... at 350 degrees for 30 minutes.
Note ..... May be frozen before baking.

Barbara Pyke
Aubrey H. S., Aubrey, Texas

MANICOTTI

1 pkg. manicotti shells
2 lb. ground beef
1 onion, chopped
1 tsp. salt
2 tbsp. chopped parsley
1/2 tsp. each oregano, garlic salt
2 eggs, beaten
2 c. dry cottage cheese
1/2 c. Parmesan cheese
3/4 lb. mozzarella cheese, shredded
1 med. jar prepared spaghetti sauce

Cook .... manicotti shells using package directions.
Brown ... ground beef and onion in skillet, stirring until crumbly.
Pour ..... off drippings.
Stir ...... in seasonings, mixing well.

Recipe on page 78.

Combine . ground beef with next 3 ingredients and 1/3 of the mozzarella cheese, mixing well.
Stuff .... manicotti shells with mixture.
Arrange .. in baking dish.
Top ..... with any remaining ground beef mixture, spaghetti sauce and remaining cheese.
Bake ..... at 350 degrees for 30 minutes.

Nancy King
Hallsville H. S., Hallsville, Texas

MEAL-IN-ONE

4 slices bacon, chopped
1 1/2 lb. thin-sliced round steak, slivered
1 onion, chopped
1 16-oz. can tomatoes, cut up
1 beef bouillon cube
1 4-oz. can mushroom pieces, drained
2 tbsp. catsup
1/2 lb. spaghetti, cooked
Parmesan cheese

Brown ... bacon and round steak in skillet, stirring to brown all sides.
Add ..... next 5 ingredients, mixing well.
Simmer .. for 45 minutes or until meat is tender.
Stir ...... in spaghetti and heat through.
Serve .... sprinkled with Parmesan cheese.

Jane A. Solinsky
James B. Conant H. S., Hoffman Estates, Illinois

QUICK AND EASY CHILI

1 1/2 to 2 lb. ground beef
1/2 onion, chopped
2 pkg. French's Chili-O mix
1 tsp. sugar
2 No. 303 cans tomatoes
2 cans Mexican-style chili beans
Salt and pepper to taste

Brown ... ground beef and onion in skillet, stirring until crumbly.
Pour ..... off pan drippings.
Add ..... remaining ingredients with 2 cups water, mixing well.
Simmer .. for 1 hour, stirring frequently.

Becky Dubea
Bunkie H. S., Bunkie, Louisiana

MRS. J'S CHILI

1 lb. hamburger
1 lg. onion, chopped
2 cans light red kidney beans
3 c. tomato juice
1 tbsp. chili powder
1 tsp. cumin
2 cloves of garlic

Brown ... hamburger in skillet, stirring until crumbly.
Drain .... well and set aside.
Saute .... onion until soft.
Combine . all ingredients in skillet.
Simmer .. covered, for 2 hours.
Remove .. garlic before serving.

Betty Jackson
Sheridan H. S., Sheridan, Montana

CHILI MANANA

1 lb. ground beef
1 tsp. salt
1/2 tsp. pepper
1 tbsp. chili powder
1 8-oz. can evaporated milk
1 4-oz. can green chiles
1 10-oz. can chili
1 can cream of chicken soup
1/2 c. white cornmeal
1/2 c. milk
2 tbsp. oil
3 eggs
1 lb. Cheddar cheese, grated

Brown ... ground beef in skillet, stirring until crumbly.
Pour ..... off drippings.
Add ..... 1/2 teaspoon salt, pepper and chili powder.
Simmer .. for 5 to 10 minutes.
Add ..... next 4 ingredients.
Simmer .. for 20 minutes; set aside.
Combine . remaining ingredients except cheese in bowl, stirring well.
Spoon ... 2 tablespoons batter into hot 6-inch skillet, tilting to coat bottom.
Cook .... until slightly browned and turn.
Cook .... other side for several seconds.
Repeat ... until all batter is used, stirring batter frequently.

Layer .... tortillas, meat mixture and cheese in 3-quart casserole, ending with cheese.
Bake ..... covered, at 350 degrees for 20 minutes.
Bake ..... uncovered, until cheese starts to brown.
Note ..... May be made ahead, refrigerated and baked, covered, for 45 minutes and uncovered until cheese browns.

Linda Winget Kittelson
Holmes H. S., San Antonio, Texas

DORITO CASSEROLE

1 lb. hamburger
1 sm. can chopped green chili peppers
1 can enchilada sauce
1 can cream of mushroom soup
1 can cream of chicken soup
1 pkg. Doritos
1 pkg. Monterey Jack cheese, grated

Brown ... hamburger in skillet, stirring until crumbly.
Pour ..... off drippings.
Add ..... next 4 ingredients, mixing well.
Cook .... until bubbly.
Spread ... Doritos in baking dish.
Spoon ... soup mixture over Doritos.
Top ..... with cheese.
Bake ..... at 400 degrees until cheese melts.

Mary Lue Reed
Spiro H. S., Spiro, Oklahoma

CHEESE ENCHILADAS

1 lb. ground beef
1 tsp. salt
1/4 tsp. garlic
1 can cream of chicken soup
1 soup can of milk
1/2 lb. process cheese
1 pkg. onion soup mix
1 sm. can hot peppers, drained, chopped
1 sm. jar pimento, drained, chopped
20 tortillas
1/2 c. corn oil
1/2 lb. Cheddar cheese
1 c. chopped onions

Brown ... ground beef with salt and garlic in skillet, stirring until crumbly.

Combine . next three ingredients in saucepan.
Cook .... over low heat until cheese melts, stirring constantly.
Add ..... soup mix, peppers and pimento and set aside.
Soften ... tortillas, one at a time, in hot oil, draining on paper towel.
Add ..... Cheddar cheese and onions to cooled ground beef, mixing well.
Fill ...... tortillas with ground beef mixture.
Roll ..... to enclose filling.
Place .... in 9 x 13-inch casserole.
Pour ..... cheese sauce over enchiladas.
Bake ..... covered, at 350 degrees for 30 minutes.

Carol Tevebaugh
Hallsville H. S., Hallsville, Texas

BEEF ENCHILADAS

1 1/2 lb. ground beef
1/2 c. chopped onion
1 to 2 tbsp. chili powder
2 cans green chili salsa
Tortillas
1 can enchilada sauce
1/2 lb. grated cheese

Brown ... ground beef in skillet, stirring until crumbly; drain well.
Add ..... onion, chili powder, 1 can salsa and 1 cup water, mixing well.
Simmer .. until liquid is evaporated.
Warm .... tortillas.
Place .... spoonful of meat mixture in center of each tortilla; roll to enclose filling.
Place .... in baking dish.
Pour ..... remaining salsa and enchilada sauce over tortillas.
Top ..... with cheese.
Bake ..... at 350 degrees for 30 minutes or microwave for 7 minutes.

Donna E. Pernett
George Washington School, Miami, Arizona

ENCHILADA CASSEROLE

2 lb. ground beef
1 can cream of celery soup
1 can cream of mushroom soup
1 tsp. salt

Pepper and chili powder to taste
1 lg. bag Tostitos
2 lb. Cheddar cheese, shredded
1 can enchilada sauce

Brown ... ground beef in skillet, stirring until crumbly.
Pour ..... off drippings.
Stir ...... in soups and seasonings, mixing well.
Layer .... Tostitos, ground beef mixture and cheese alternately in large baking dish until all ingredients are used, ending with Tostitos.
Top ..... with enchilada sauce.
Bake ..... at 400 degrees for 15 minutes or until bubbly.

Ann Davis
Gentry H. S., Gentry, Arkansas

GREEN ENCHILADAS

1 lb. ground beef
1 tsp. salt
1/4 tsp. minced garlic
1 can cream of chicken soup
1/2 to 3/4 c. evaporated milk
1 lb. Velveeta cheese
1 pkg. green onion dip mix
1 sm. can green chiles
1 sm. jar pimento
1/2 lb. longhorn cheese, grated
1 c. chopped onion
18 tortillas
1/2 c. Wesson oil

Brown ... ground beef in skillet, stirring until crumbly.
Season ... and set aside to cool.
Combine . next 6 ingredients in double boiler, heating until Velveeta melts.
Mix ..... longhorn cheese and onion with ground beef.
Soften ... tortillas, one at a time, in hot oil in skillet.
Spoon ... 1 or 2 tablespoons of ground beef mixture on each tortilla and roll up.
Place .... in 8 x 10-inch baking dish.
Top ..... with cheese sauce.
Bake ..... covered, at 350 degrees for 30 minutes.

Diana McGregor
Como-Pickton ISD, Como, Texas

MEXICAN ENCHILADAS

Flour
1/2 c. cornmeal
1 1/4 c. milk
3 eggs
1 tbsp. melted butter
Salt
1 lb. ground beef
1/2 c. chopped onion
1/4 c. chopped green pepper
1 lg. can enchilada dip
1 sm. can taco sauce
2 c. grated cheese
1 tbsp. bacon drippings
1/2 tsp. each chili powder, pepper and
    garlic powder
1 can tomato sauce

Combine . 3/4 cup flour with next 4 ingredi-
            ents and a pinch of salt in small
            bowl, beating thoroughly.
Let . . . . . . stand for 1 hour.
Spoon . . . 2 tablespoons batter into hot 6-inch
            skillet tilting to coat bottom.
Cook . . . . until slightly brown, turn and cook
            for several seconds longer.
Brown . . . ground beef in skillet, stirring until
            crumbly.
Add . . . . . onion and green pepper, cooking
            until tender.
Pour . . . . . off drippings.
Add . . . . . enchilada dip and salt to taste, mix-
            ing well.
Dip . . . . . . each crepe in taco sauce.
Spread . . . with a small amount of ground beef
            mixture and 1 tablespoon cheese.
Roll . . . . . up and place in 9 x 13-inch baking
            dish.
Blend . . . . bacon drippings and 1 tablespoon
            flour in small saucepan until
            smooth. Do not brown.
Mix . . . . . in spices, 1/2 teaspoon salt and
            tomato sauce, heating through.
Pour . . . . . over crepes.
Top . . . . . with remaining cheese.
Bake . . . . . at 350 degrees for 20 minutes or
            until bubbly.

Pamela C. Towery
Caledonia School, Caledonia, Mississippi

MICROWAVE TACO CASSEROLE

1 lb. ground beef
1 15-oz. can tomato sauce
1 1 3/4-oz. envelope taco seasoning mix
1/4 c. pimento-stuffed olives, chopped (opt.)
1 6 1/2-oz. bag corn chips, crushed
1 16-oz. can refried beans
1/2 c. shredded Cheddar cheese

Place . . . . ground beef in 1 1/2-quart micro-
            wave casserole.
Microwave for 4 to 5 minutes or until beef
            loses its color, stirring after 2
            minutes.
Pour . . . . . off drippings.
Add . . . . . next 3 ingredients, mixing well.
Microwave for 3 minutes, bringing mixture to a
            boil.
Spread . . . corn chips in microwave pie plate.
Press . . . . . refried beans on top, forming a
            shell.
Fill . . . . . . with ground beef mixture.
Microwave for 3 minutes or until hot.
Top . . . . . with cheese.
Microwave for 1 minute.
Serve . . . . with taco sauce if desired.
Yields . . . . 6 servings/about 454 calories each.

Lillian M. Kwas
Warren Township H. S., Gurnee, Illinois

NAVAJO TACOS

2 c. flour
1 c. milk
1 tsp. baking powder
Salt
Oil
2 c. chopped onions
6 to 8 tsp. chili powder
2 lb. ground beef
1 15-oz. can tomato paste
2 16-oz. cans pinto beans

Combine . first 3 ingredients with 1/2 tea-
            spoon salt in bowl, mixing well.
Knead . . . on floured board until smooth.
Divide . . . into portions and roll out individual
            fry breads.
Fry . . . . . . in hot deep oil until brown.
Saute . . . . onions in 1/4 cup oil in skillet.
Add . . . . . 3 teaspoons salt and chili powder,
            cooking for 1 minute.

Add ..... ground beef and brown, stirring
until crumbly.
Stir ...... in tomato paste and beans, mixing
well.
Cook .... over low heat for 10 minutes, stirring occasionally.
Spoon ... into fry bread slit to form pockets.
Garnish .. with shredded lettuce, cheese, diced
tomatoes and green peppers.

Karen Ferre
American Fork Jr. H. S., American Fork, Utah

BEEF STEAK AND TORTILLA BAKE

1 1/2 lb. round steak, cut 3/4 in. thick
2 tbsp. shortening
1 1/2 tsp. salt
1/8 tsp. pepper
1 4-oz. can mushrooms
1 15-oz. can tomato sauce
1 10-oz. can mild enchilada sauce
1 c. finely chopped onion
1 clove of garlic, crushed
1 10-oz. package corn tortillas
1 c. shredded sharp Cheddar cheese

Slice ..... steak into 2 x 1/8-inch pieces.
Brown ... in shortening in skillet.
Pour ..... off pan drippings.
Season ... with salt and pepper.
Drain .... mushrooms, reserving liquid.
Add ..... enough water to reserved liquid to
measure 1 1/4 cups.
Add ..... to steak.
Cook .... tightly covered, over low heat for 1
hour.
Add ..... mushrooms, tomato sauce,
enchilada sauce, 1/2 cup onion and
garlic, mixing well.
Cook .... covered, for 20 minutes longer.
Dip ...... tortillas in hot sauce.
Place .... 2 teaspoons onion on one side and
roll up.
Arrange .. in 9 x 13-inch baking dish.
Stir ...... 3/4 cup cheese into remaining
sauce.
Spoon ... around rolled tortillas.
Sprinkle .. with remaining cheese.
Bake ..... tightly covered, at 350 degrees for
10 minutes or until heated through.

Photograph for this recipe below.

TACO STIR-FRY

1 lb. lean ground beef
1/4 c. chopped onion
1 tbsp. oil
1 c. whole kernel corn
1 1-lb. can tomatoes
2 tbsp. chili powder
1 tsp. sugar
1 tsp. oregano
1/4 tsp. salt
1/8 tsp. pepper
1 1/2 c. grated mild Cheddar cheese
1 9 1/2-oz. package corn chips
2 sm. heads Boston lettuce, shredded

Brown ... ground beef and onion in oil in large skillet, stirring until crumbly.
Pour ..... off drippings.
Stir ...... in corn, tomatoes and seasonings.
Bring .... to a boil.
Simmer .. covered, over low heat for 10 minutes.
Stir ...... in 1 cup cheese and corn chips.
Cook .... until cheese is partially melted.
Place .... lettuce on serving platter.
Spoon ... ground beef mixture over top.
Sprinkle .. with remaining 1/2 cup cheese.
Yields .... 6 servings/about 580 calories each.

Karen Anding Crook
Schaumburg H. S., Schaumburg, Illinois

PITA BREAD WITH MEDITERRANEAN MIX

1 lb. ground beef, cooked, drained
1 cucumber, peeled, seeded
1 med. onion, chopped
1/2 jar green olives, chopped
1/2 jar ripe olives, chopped
1 stalk celery, chopped
2 med. tomatoes, chopped
1/2 lb. Cheddar cheese, shredded
1/2 lb. Swiss cheese, shredded
1 clove of garlic, crushed
1 slice bread, cubed
2 slices hard salami, chopped
Pepper to taste
2 to 3 tbsp. olive oil
Pita bread

Combine . all ingredients except pita bread in large bowl, mixing to coat with oil.

Chill ..... in refrigerator for 2 to 3 hours.
Cut ...... pita bread into halves with scissors.
Pull ..... open to form pockets.
Fill ...... with chilled mixture.

Cathryn E. Springer
Northwest H. S., Canal Fulton, Ohio

FAR EAST POTATO TAFFEL

1 24-oz. package frozen Idaho Southern-Style hashed brown potatoes with butter sauce and onions
1 1/2 c. diced cooked lamb
2 tbsp. brown sugar
2 tbsp. lemon juice
1 tbsp. soy sauce
1 tsp. curry powder
1 1/2 tsp. cornstarch
3/4 tsp. Tabasco sauce
2 tbsp. diced pimento (opt.)

Brown ... potatoes in large skillet.
Stir ...... in lamb.
Blend .... next 6 ingredients with 1 cup water in small bowl.
Add ..... to potato mixture.
Cook .... over low heat, stirring constantly, until mixture boils and thickens.
Spoon ... into serving dish.
Sprinkle .. with pimento.
Serve .... with peanuts, coconut, raisins and chutney.
Yields .... 4 servings/about 455 calories each.

Photograph for this recipe on page 69.

MINTED GRAPEFRUIT LEG OF LAMB

1 onion, sliced
1 carrot, sliced
1 rib celery, sliced
1 7-lb. leg of lamb
1 tsp. salt
1/4 tsp. pepper
3 c. Florida grapefruit juice
1 tsp. dried mint

Arrange .. vegetables over bottom of roasting pan.
Rub ..... lamb with salt and pepper.
Place .... on top of vegetables.
Pour ..... grapefruit juice mixed with mint over lamb.

Bake . . . . . at 325 degrees for 2 hours, basting every 15 minutes with pan drippings.

Serve . . . . with strained pan drippings.

Photograph for this recipe on page 1.

CHOW MEIN

1/2 c. celery
1/2 c. green onions
2 tbsp. oil
2 c. cooked pork, cut into 2-inch slices
1 c. bean sprouts, drained
1 c. mushrooms
1 green pepper, chopped
1/2 c. thinly sliced tomato
1 c. consomme
1 tbsp. soy sauce
3 tbsp. Sherry
Salt and pepper to taste
Cornstarch (opt.)

Stir-fry . . . celery and onions in oil in large skillet for 3 minutes.

Add . . . . . next 4 ingredients.

Stir-fry . . . for 2 to 3 minutes.

Add . . . . . tomato and consomme.

Stir . . . . . . in remaining seasonings.

Thicken . . with cornstarch if desired.

Martha R. Phillips
Kennett H. S., Conway, New Hampshire

COUNTRY-BRAISED PORK CHOPS

4   3/4-in. thick pork chops, trimmed
1 tbsp. flour
1 sm. onion, chopped
2 tbsp. oil
1   10-oz. can cream of mushroom soup
1   3-oz. can sliced mushrooms
8 sm. new potatoes, peeled
4 med. carrots, thickly sliced
1 tsp. salt
1/2 tsp. rosemary
1/4 tsp. pepper

Coat . . . . . pork chops with flour.

Brown . . . onion in oil in skillet until tender.

Add . . . . . pork chops and brown on both sides.

Stir . . . . . in remaining ingredients.

Heat . . . . . to boiling point; reduce heat.

Simmer . . covered, for 1 hour or until pork chops are tender, stirring occasionally.

Yields . . . . 4 servings/about 573 calories each.

Katherine A. Winchester
Winter Park H. S., Winter Park, Florida

CRANBERRY PORK CHOPS

6 pork chops
1 can whole berry cranberry sauce
1 can cream of mushroom soup

Brown . . . pork chops in a small amount of shortening in Dutch oven.

Pour . . . . . cranberry sauce over chops.

Cover . . . . with soup.

Bake . . . . . covered, at 350 degrees for 45 minutes or until chops are tender.

Connie Y. Crouch
Palatka H. S., Palatka, Florida

PORK CHOP SUPPER

4 pork chops
2/3 c. long grain rice
4 tbsp. chopped onion
2 tsp. instant chicken bouillon
1/2 c. chopped apple

Brown . . . pork chops in a small amount of shortening in skillet.

Remove . . pork chops, setting aside.

Add . . . . . rice and onion.

Cook . . . . until golden brown, stirring constantly.

Add . . . . . 2 cups water and bouillon and bring to a boil.

Stir . . . . . . in apple.

Turn . . . . . into casserole, arranging pork chops on top.

Bake . . . . . covered, at 350 degrees for 30 minutes; uncover.

Bake . . . . . for 20 minutes longer or until pork chops are tender.

Yields . . . . 4 servings/about 440 calories each.

Sally G. Mace
Hendersonville H. S., Hendersonville, Tennessee

PORK CHOPS AND POTATO CASSEROLE

1 can cream of mushroom soup
1 carton sour cream
6 pork chops
Flour
Parsley flakes (opt.)
Salt and pepper to taste
5 c. 1/4-in. thick sliced potatoes

Combine . soup and sour cream in bowl, mixing well.
Coat . . . . . pork chops with seasoned flour.
Place . . . . potatoes in 9 x 13 x 2-inch buttered casserole.
Arrange . . pork chops on top.
Cover . . . . with sour cream mixture.
Bake . . . . . at 350 degrees for about 1 1/4 hours or until pork chops are tender.

Mrs. Carrie Ward
Baldwyn H. S., Baldwyn, Mississippi

BARBECUED SPARERIBS

4 lb. spareribs
2 tbsp. shortening
1 med. onion, finely chopped
2 tbsp. butter
2 tbsp. vinegar
4 tbsp. lemon juice
1 c. catsup
2 tbsp. brown sugar
1/8 tsp. cayenne pepper
1/2 tsp. mustard
2 tbsp. Worcestershire sauce
1/2 c. diced celery

Brown . . . ribs on both sides in shortening in Dutch oven.
Brown . . . onion in butter in skillet.
Add . . . . . remaining ingredients and 1 cup water to onion, heating until very hot.
Pour . . . . . over ribs.
Bake . . . . . at 375 degrees for 1 3/4 hours.

Stella Heath
John Marshall H. S., Oklahoma City, Oklahoma

LEMON-BARBECUED RIBS

3 or 4 lb. spareribs, cut into pieces
1/3 c. lemon juice
1/3 c. catsup
1 tsp. horseradish sauce
1 tsp. salt
Dash of Tabasco sauce
1 tbsp. Worcestershire sauce
1/2 c. orange juice
2 tsp. dry mustard
1/2 tsp. paprika
1/4 c. packed brown sugar
1 clove of garlic, crushed
2 lemons, sliced

Place . . . . ribs in large baking dish.
Brown . . . at 450 degrees for 45 to 50 minutes; drain.
Combine . remaining ingredients except lemon slices in bowl, mixing well.
Brush . . . . ribs with sauce.
Top . . . . . each piece with lemon slice.
Bake . . . . . at 350 degrees for 1 hour, basting frequently.
Yields . . . . 5 servings/about 850 calories each.

Sharon Kleven
San Gabriel H. S., San Gabriel, California

PORK RIBS WITH KRAUT

4 lb. pork ribs
1 lg. onion, chopped
1 green pepper, chopped
2 cans sauerkraut
1 tsp. pepper

Cook . . . . ribs in 3 cups water in large saucepan for 1 1/2 hours or until tender.
Add . . . . . remaining ingredients.
Cook . . . . for 15 minutes longer.
Yields . . . . 6 servings/about 700 calories each.

Gloria Whitted
Northwest Sr. H. S., Greensboro, North Carolina

WINTER PORK ROAST WITH FRESH VEGETABLES

2 lb. pork roast, boned, rolled
1 clove of garlic, mashed
1 lg. onion, sliced
4 med. turnips, peeled, quartered
3 carrots, cut in 1-in. chunks
2 c. shredded cabbage
1 tsp. each caraway seed, salt
1/4 tsp. pepper

1 bay leaf
1/2 c. dry white wine

Rub ..... roast with garlic.
Place .... in clay cooker.
Arrange .. vegetables over and around roast.
Sprinkle .. with seasonings.
Drizzle ... with wine.
Bake ..... covered, at 350 degrees for 2 hours or until tender.
Remove .. from oven and let stand for 15 minutes.
Yields .... 4 servings/about 575 calories each.

Photograph for this recipe on page 70.

BONELESS PORK LOIN ROTISSERIE-STYLE

1 3 to 6-lb. boneless pork loin roast
Barbecue sauce

Insert .... rotisserie rod through exact center of roast, using prongs to hold roast in place.
Insert .... meat thermometer so bulb is centered in roast but not in fat or on rod.
Cook .... at low temperature on rotisserie for 2 to 3 hours or to 170 degrees on meat thermometer.
Brush .... with barbecue sauce during last 30 minutes of cooking.

Photograph for this recipe on page 56.

HAM AND CHEESE QUICHE

3 c. cheese croutons
3 to 4 c. chopped ham
3 c. shredded Cheddar cheese
6 eggs
3 c. milk
1 1/2 tsp. each dry mustard, onion salt
1/2 tsp. pepper

Line ..... bottom of buttered 9 x 13-inch pan with croutons.
Sprinkle .. with ham and cheese.
Beat ..... eggs, milk and spices together in bowl.
Pour ..... over meat and cheese.
Refrigerate for several hours.
Bake ..... at 350 degrees for 35 minutes.

Mrs. Mary Ann McGovern
Truman H. S., Independence, Missouri

HAM SOUFFLE

Butter
8 slices white bread, crusts removed
2 c. ground ham
1 c. grated sharp Cheddar cheese
1 tbsp. prepared mustard
3 eggs, beaten
2 c. milk

Spread ... butter on both sides of bread.
Place .... in bottom of 9 x 13-inch baking dish to cover completely.
Combine . next 3 ingredients in bowl.
Spread ... over bread.
Mix ..... eggs and milk in bowl.
Pour ..... over ham mixture.
Chill ..... for several hours or overnight.
Bake ..... at 325 degrees for 1 1/4 hours.

Alice P. Schleg
Grayslake Community H.S., Grayslake, Illinois

UPSIDE-DOWN HAM LOAF

2 tbsp. butter
1/4 c. packed brown sugar
Whole cloves
1 20-oz. can pineapple chunks, drained
4 c. ground cooked ham
1 c. ground beef
1 c. fresh pork
1/2 c. pineapple juice
1/2 c. milk
1 c. dry bread crumbs
2 eggs, slightly beaten
1 tbsp. prepared mustard
1 tbsp. onion

Melt ..... butter in 9 1/2 x 5 1/4-inch loaf pan.
Sprinkle .. brown sugar over bottom.
Insert .... 1 clove in each pineapple chunk.
Place .... clove side down in butter mixture.
Combine . remaining ingredients in large bowl.
Shape .... into loaf.
Place .... on top of pineapple.
Set ...... inside large baking dish to catch drippings.
Bake ..... at 350 degrees for 1 1/2 hours.
Invert .... onto platter to serve.
Yields .... 6 servings/about 365 calories each.

Marlys Hauck-Fenner
Freeman H. S., Freeman, South Dakota

ITALIAN STEW

1 med. head cabbage, chopped
1/2 lb. hot sausage
1 lg. onion, quartered
1 lg. can whole tomatoes
1 med. can tomato sauce
2 potatoes, diced (opt.)

Boil ..... cabbage in water to cover in sauce-pan until tender.
Pour ..... off excess water.
Brown ... sausage in skillet, stirring until crumbly.
Add ..... sausage and remaining ingredients to cabbage, mixing well.
Simmer .. for 1 1/2 to 2 hours.

Sandi Taylor
Bearden Middle School, Knoxville, Tennessee

BREAKFAST SOUFFLE

1 1/2 lb. pork sausage
9 eggs, beaten
3 c. milk
1 1/2 tsp. dry mustard
1 tsp. salt
3 slices bread, cut into 1/4-in. cubes
1 1/2 c. shredded Cheddar cheese

Brown ... sausage over medium heat in skillet, stirring until crumbly.
Drain .... well on paper towels.
Combine . with remaining ingredients in large bowl, mixing well.
Pour ..... into greased 9 x 13-inch baking dish.
Chill ..... covered, in refrigerator overnight.
Bake ..... at 350 degrees for 1 hour.
Yields .... 8 servings/about 445 calories each.

Naomi Mayes
Warren East H. S., Bowling Green, Kentucky

SAUSAGE AND CHEESE BAKE

1 8-oz. can crescent rolls
1 8-oz. package brown and serve sausages
2 c. shredded cheese
4 eggs, slightly beaten
2 tbsp. chopped green pepper
1/2 tsp. salt
1/4 tsp. each pepper, oregano

Press ..... rolls into bottom and sides of 9 x 13-inch baking pan to form crust.

Arrange .. sausages over crust.
Sprinkle .. with cheese.
Combine . remaining ingredients in bowl, mixing well.
Pour ..... over cheese.
Bake ..... at 425 degrees for 20 to 25 minutes or until golden brown.
Yields .... 5 servings/about 450 calories each.

Beverly H. Kish
Seabreeze Jr. H. S., Daytona Beach, Florida

SAUSAGE-MUSHROOM SOUFFLE

8 slices white bread, crusts removed, cubed
3/4 lb. Cheddar cheese, cubed
1 1/2 lb. sausage, cooked, drained
4 eggs, beaten
Milk
1 tsp. salt
3/4 tsp. dry mustard
1 can cream of mushroom soup

Layer .... first 3 ingredients in order given in baking dish.
Combine . eggs with 2 1/2 cups milk and seasonings in bowl, mixing well.
Pour ..... over sausage.
Chill ..... in refrigerator overnight.
Combine . soup with 1/3 soup can milk in small bowl, blending until smooth.
Spread ... over top.
Bake ..... at 350 degrees for 1 hour.

Sharon Reddell
Churchill H. S., San Antonio, Texas

SAUSAGE-EGG BAKE

4 slices French bread, cubed
3/4 lb. country sausage, cooked
1 c. grated cheese
2 eggs, beaten
1/2 tsp. dry mustard
Milk
1/2 can mushroom soup

Spread ... bread cubes in buttered 7 x 11-inch baking dish.
Layer .... sausage and cheese over bread.
Combine . eggs and mustard with 1 generous cup milk in bowl, beating well.
Pour ..... over sausage and cheese.
Blend .... 1/4 cup milk with soup until smooth.

Pour . . . . . over all.
Bake . . . . . at 325 degrees for 30 to 35
minutes.
Yields . . . . 6 servings/about 350 calories each.

Shannon Wilson
Provo H. S., Provo, Utah

VEAL CORDON BLEU

8 veal cutlets
Salt and pepper to taste
4 slices Swiss cheese
4 thin slices ham
4 tbsp. flour
1 egg, beaten
1/2 c. fine dry bread crumbs
3 tbsp. butter
1 tbsp. oil

Pound . . . veal with mallet to flatten and work
in salt and pepper.
Place . . . . cheese and ham slice on each of
cutlets; do not overlap cheese and
ham.
Top . . . . . each cutlet with another and pound
edges to seal.
Roll . . . . . in flour, dip in egg and roll in
crumbs.
Saute . . . . in butter and oil until brown.
Place . . . . in baking dish.
Bake . . . . . at 375 degrees for 20 to 35
minutes.

Kristine Bown
American Fork H. S., American Fork, Utah

VEAL PICCATA

3/4 to 1 lb. veal
1 egg, beaten
Flour
Oil
8 oz. broth
1 tbsp. cornstarch
1/4 to 1/2 c. white wine
2 tsp. parsley
1/8 tsp. garlic powder
2 tbsp. lemon juice
Salt and pepper to taste

Dip . . . . . . veal into egg then into flour to
coat.
Brown . . . in oil in skillet; remove and keep
warm.

Add . . . . . broth to pan juices, stirring to
blend in meat particles.
Combine . cornstarch and wine and stir into
broth with remaining ingredients.
Cook . . . . until thickened, stirring constantly.
Pour . . . . . over veal and garnish with lemon
slices.

Kathleen O'Malley
North Arlington H. S., North Arlington, New Jersey

PEPPERONI BREAD

1 or 2 bell peppers, sliced
2 loaves frozen bread dough, thawed
1/2 lb. provolone cheese, sliced
1 pkg. sliced pepperoni
Parmesan cheese, grated

Saute . . . . bell peppers in oil in skillet until
tender.
Roll . . . . . out dough on floured surface into
12 x 24-inch rectangle.
Arrange . . provolone cheese, pepperoni and
bell peppers down center of dough,
overlapping slices.
Sprinkle . . Parmesan cheese and garlic salt over
top.
Fold . . . . . sides to enclose filling.
Seal . . . . . seam and ends well.
Brush . . . . top of loaf with oil.
Place . . . . on greased baking sheet.
Bake . . . . . at 350 degrees for 25 minutes or
until golden brown.
Slice . . . . . into serving portions.

Lois H. Webber
East Forsyth Sr. H. S., Kernersville, North Carolina

QUICK CHILI FRANKS

1 lb. lean ground beef
1 med. onion, chopped
Salt and pepper to taste
1 15-oz. can kidney beans
1 to 2 tsp. chili powder
1/2 lb. franks, browned
1 8-oz. can tomato sauce

Brown . . . ground beef with onion in skillet,
stirring until crumbly.
Stir . . . . . . in remaining ingredients.
Cook . . . . until heated through.
Yields . . . . 4 servings/about 530 calories each.

Shirley Leslie
J. D. Leftwich H. S., Magazine, Arkansas

Poultry and Seafood

Some of the most enjoyable dishes to prepare are poultry and seafood. Their versatility creates an unlimited variety of menus for the all-purpose menu planner

Succulent morsels from the sea can be seasoned simply with herbs and spices, or served in a rich creamy sauce garnished with almonds or lemon slices.

Lucky for budgets, there's no end to the recipe ideas for plump, nutritious poultry. Serve with all the trimmings for an elegant holiday dinner, or as super sandwiches for lunch. Either way, it's sure to please.

TRICKS OF THE TRADE

- Frozen chicken defrosts faster when immersed in a bowl of cold water.
- Next time, coat chicken with biscuit mix and a mixture of spices for a new taste treat.
- Freeze chicken livers in small plastic bags to accumulate enough for a meal, party snack or pate.
- The most economical turkey to buy is between 16 and 20 pounds.
- Buy chicken breasts with wings; remove and freeze. When you've accumulated enough, serve a dish using just the chicken wings. It's like having a free meal!
- Stretch shrimp servings by splitting shrimp lengthwise; cook and serve stir-fried with vegetables.
- Clams and oysters are simple to open: wash first with cold water; place in a plastic bag; freeze for 1 hour before opening.

ANN'S FINGER LICKIN' CHICKEN

4 lg. chicken breasts, boned
1 egg, beaten
1/3 to 1/2 lb. Ritz crackers, crushed
Margarine

Cut . . . . . . chicken breasts into serving size pieces.
Dip . . . . . . chicken in egg.
Roll . . . . . in cracker crumbs to cover.
Brown . . . on both sides in 1/4 pound margarine in skillet.
Reduce . . . heat to low and cook for 20 minutes longer, adding additional margarine if needed to prevent sticking.
Yields . . . . 6 servings/about 610 calories each.

Audrey Starkey
Keene H. S., Keene, New Hampshire

BEEF AND BACON-WRAPPED CHICKEN

1 sm. jar dried beef
6 chicken breasts, skinned
6 slices of bacon
1 can golden mushroom soup
1 pt. sour cream

Place . . . . 3 slices dried beef around each chicken breast.
Wrap . . . . with bacon slices.
Secure . . . with toothpicks.
Arrange . . chicken in 9 x 13-inch baking dish.
Mix . . . . . soup and sour cream together.
Spoon . . . over chicken, covering completely.
Bake . . . . . at 350 degrees for 1 hour.

Carol Stallard
Monroney Jr. H. S., Midwest City, Oklahoma

BREAST OF CHICKEN

4 whole chicken breasts, skinned, boned
1 14-oz. can hearts of palm, drained
Melted butter
Salt and pepper to taste.
1 can cream of mushroom soup
1 8 oz. package cream cheese, softened

Flatten . . . chicken breasts and wrap around hearts of palm stalks.
Place . . . . in baking dish.
Brush . . . . with butter, seasoning to taste.

Bake . . . . . at 400 degrees for 30 to 35 minutes, basting occasionally.
Combine . soup and cream cheese in saucepan.
Heat . . . . . over low heat until cheese melts and sauce is smooth, stirring often.
Serve . . . . with chicken.
Yields . . . . 4 servings/about 820 calories each.

Wanda Bain Gary
El Sereno Jr. H. S., Los Angeles, California

CHICKEN CORNELIA

4 chicken breasts, boned, skinned
2 c. sour cream
2 cans cream of chicken soup
1 1/2 env. dry onion soup mix
1 can Chinese noodles

Place . . . . chicken breasts in casserole in single layer.
Combine . next 3 ingredients in bowl, mixing well.
Pour . . . . . over chicken.
Bake . . . . . uncovered, at 400 degrees for 50 minutes.
Sprinkle . . noodles over chicken.
Bake . . . . . for 10 minutes longer.
Yields . . . . 4 servings/about 800 calories each.

Ruby Bundy
Laurel County H. S., London, Kentucky

CHICKEN DIVAN

2 10-oz. packages frozen broccoli spears
1/4 c. margarine
6 tbsp. flour
2 tsp. salt
Dash of pepper
2 c. chicken broth
1/2 c. half and half
3 cooked chicken breasts, halved
Grated Parmesan cheese

Cook . . . . broccoli using package directions; drain.
Melt . . . . . margarine in saucepan.
Blend . . . . in flour, salt and pepper.
Add . . . . . broth, blending well.
Cook . . . . until thick, stirring constantly.
Blend . . . . in half and half, stirring until smooth.
Place . . . . broccoli in single layer across 12 x 7 x 2-inch baking dish.
Arrange . . chicken over broccoli.

Stir . . . . . . 1/4 cup Parmesan cheese into sauce.
Pour . . . . . over chicken.
Top . . . . . with additional cheese.
Bake . . . . . at 350 degrees for 20 minutes or until heated through.
Broil . . . . . for 5 minutes or until sauce is golden.
Yields . . . . 6 servings/about 360 calories each.

Brenda Eskew
Bowling Green R-1 H. S., Bowling Green, Missouri

CHICKEN POTPIE

4 to 6 chicken breasts
1 sm. onion, diced
1 can cream of mushroom soup
1 chicken bouillon cube
Salt and pepper to taste
3 or 4 potatoes, peeled, cubed
2 or 3 carrots, peeled, diced
1 can green peas
Cornstarch (opt.)
1   10-count can refrigerator biscuits

Place . . . . chicken breasts in large saucepan.
Add . . . . . next 5 ingredients and 2 soup cans water.
Bring . . . . to a boil.
Reduce . . . heat and simmer for 45 minutes.
Remove . . chicken and chop meat into bite-sized pieces.
Add . . . . . vegetables to stock.
Cook . . . . for 15 minutes.
Return . . . chopped chicken to stock.
Thicken . . with cornstarch if necessary.
Spoon . . . into 9 x 13-inch baking dish.
Slice . . . . . each biscuit in half and arrange over chicken mixture.
Bake . . . . . at 400 degrees for 10 to 15 minutes until biscuits are brown.

Marilyn Andrus
Pearland H. S., Pearland, Texas

CHICKEN IMPERIAL

8 oz. fresh mushrooms, sliced
1/4 c. chopped onions
2 tbsp. butter
2 lg. whole chicken breasts, halved
2 tbsp. flour
1/4 c. white wine

1 c. whipping cream
1 tsp. salt
Dash of pepper

Saute . . . . mushrooms and onions in butter in skillet until tender.
Arrange . . chicken in baking dish.
Blend . . . . flour and wine in small bowl to make smooth paste.
Add . . . . . cream, salt and pepper, mixing well.
Stir . . . . . . into vegetables and spoon over chicken.
Bake . . . . . covered, at 350 degrees for 45 minutes.
Serve . . . . over rice.

Barbara King
Kaufman H. S., Kaufman, Texas

ORIENTAL CHICKEN

4 lg. chicken breasts, boned, skinned
Salt and pepper to taste
1/4 c. cornstarch
Oil for deep frying
1 bunch celery, sliced
1 can bean sprouts, drained
1 can bamboo shoots, drained
1 can water chestnuts, drained
1 sm. onion, chopped
3 green onions, chopped
1/2 lb. fresh mushrooms
Pimento, chopped
1/4 c. soy sauce
1 can chicken broth

Pound . . . chicken breasts between waxed paper to 1/4-inch thickness.
Sprinkle . . with salt and pepper.
Cut . . . . . . into 1/2 x 1-inch strips.
Roll . . . . . in cornstarch.
Fry . . . . . . in hot deep oil until crisp and brown; drain.
Stir-fry . . . vegetables until tender-crisp and colors intensify.
Combine . 1/3 cup water with soy sauce and broth in bowl.
Stir . . . . . . into vegetables.
Add . . . . . chicken.
Cook . . . . until sauce thickens, stirring constantly.
Serve . . . . over white rice.

Stephanie Alvarez
McCollum H. S., San Antonio, Texas

PRUNE-CHICKEN SAUTE

1 clove of garlic
2 tbsp. butter
2 tbsp. olive oil
1 3-lb. broiler-fryer, cut up
Salt and pepper to taste
1/2 onion, thinly sliced
1/4 c. chopped celery
1/4 tsp. crushed tarragon
1/2 c. California prunes
1 c. dry white wine

Saute .... garlic in butter and oil in skillet until golden.
Remove .. garlic and discard.
Season ... chicken with salt and pepper.
Brown ... chicken in oil.
Sprinkle .. remaining ingredients except wine over chicken.
Pour ..... wine over all.
Cook .... covered, for 45 minutes to 1 hour.

Photograph for this recipe on page 82.

CHICKEN-IN-A-GARDEN

1 1/2 c. diced cooked chicken
1 can cream of chicken soup
1 can Veg-All, drained
1 can French-fried onions
1 baked 9-in. pie shell

Combine . chicken, soup, Veg-All and half the onions in bowl, mixing well.
Pour ..... into pie shell.
Bake ..... at 350 degrees for 30 minutes.
Sprinkle .. remaining onions over pie.
Bake ..... until onions are toasted.
Yields .... 6 servings/about 315 calories each.

Martha Tyra
Anderson Jr. H. S., Booneville, Mississippi

CHICKEN PIE

1 onion, chopped
2 stalks celery, chopped
3 tbsp. butter
Flour
1 1/2 tsp. salt
Pepper to taste
2 c. milk

1 c. chicken broth
1 can mushroom soup
1 sm. can pimentos (opt.)
1 chicken, cooked, boned
3 tbsp. oil
3 tsp. baking powder
3 c. grated sharp cheese

Saute .... onion and celery in butter in skillet until tender.
Blend .... in 4 tablespoons flour, 1/2 teaspoon salt and pepper.
Stir ...... in 1 1/2 cups milk and chicken broth.
Cook .... until smooth and thick, stirring constantly.
Add ..... soup and pimentos, blending well.
Place .... with chicken in large baking dish.
Combine . 1 1/2 cups flour, 1 teaspoon salt, 1/2 cup milk and remaining ingredients except cheese in bowl, mixing well.
Roll ..... out on floured surface to 8 x 12-inch rectangle.
Spread ... cheese over dough.
Roll ..... as for jelly roll and slice.
Place .... slices over casserole.
Bake ..... at 375 degrees until biscuits are brown.

Doris S. Johnson
Atlanta H. S., Atlanta, Texas

CRUNCHY CHICKEN CRESCENTS

2 tbsp. margarine, softened
2 3-oz. packages cream cheese with chives, softened
1 1/2 c. cubed cooked chicken
1 8-count pkg. crescent dinner rolls, separated
3/4 c. melted margarine
1 c. seasoned stuffing mix

Cream ... softened margarine and cream cheese together in bowl.
Add ..... chicken, mixing well.
Spoon ... 1/4 cup chicken mixture onto each roll.
Wrap .... dough to enclose filling, sealing well.
Dip ...... each roll into melted margarine.
Coat ..... with stuffing mix.

Place . . . . on baking sheet.
Bake . . . . . at 375 degrees for 20 minutes.

Judy McClenny
Highland Springs H. S., Highland Springs, Virginia

CHICKEN CASSEROLE ANGOSTURA

1   3 to 4-lb. chicken, cut up
Salt and pepper to taste
Flour
4 tbsp. butter
4 carrots, diced
2 sm. turnips, diced
2 onions, diced
3 med. potatoes, diced
6 med. tomatoes, peeled, sliced
1 tsp. sugar
2 chicken bouillon cubes
1 tbsp. Angostura aromatic bitters

Season . . . chicken with salt and pepper.
Coat . . . . . chicken with flour.
Brown . . . chicken in butter in skillet.
Remove . . chicken from skillet.
Brown . . . carrots, turnips, onions and potatoes in pan drippings.
Add . . . . . tomatoes, 1/2 teaspoon salt, 1/4 teaspoon pepper and sugar, stirring to blend.
Remove . . vegetables.
Dissolve . . bouillon cubes in 2 cups boiling water.
Blend . . . . 2 tablespoons flour into pan drippings.
Add . . . . . bouillon and bitters gradually.
Cook . . . . until slightly thickened, stirring constantly.
Arrange . . vegetables in bottom of deep casserole.
Pour . . . . . half the gravy over vegetables.
Arrange . . chicken pieces over vegetables.
Pour . . . . . remaining gravy over top.
Bake . . . . . covered, at 350 degrees for 45 minutes.

Photograph for this recipe below.

CHICKEN PILAF

3/4 c. coarsely chopped celery
1 med. onion, chopped
2 tbsp. butter
1/4 c. chopped red sweet pepper
2 c. cooked rice
1 1/2 c. chicken, chopped
Salt and pepper to taste

Saute . . . . celery and onion in butter in skillet until tender.
Add . . . . . remaining ingredients.
Simmer . . for 10 minutes, stirring constantly.
Yields . . . . 4 servings/about 290 calories each.

Mrs. Dorothy W. Reese
C. L. Harper H. S., Atlanta, Georgia

QUICK CHICKEN AND DRESSING

1 stick margarine, melted
1 pkg. corn bread stuffing mix
1   3-lb. fryer, cooked, boned, chopped
2 cans cream of chicken soup
2 soup cans chicken broth

Combine . margarine and stuffing mix in bowl, tossing to mix well.
Spread . . . in 9 x 13-inch greased baking dish, reserving 3/4 cup.
Arrange . . chicken over dressing.
Pour . . . . . soup and broth over chicken.
Top . . . . . with reserved stuffing mix.
Bake . . . . . at 350 degrees for 30 minutes.

Helen Joiner
Campbell H. S., Fairburn, Georgia

MARY JO'S CHICKEN CASSEROLE

1 pkg. wild rice mix
3 c. chopped cooked chicken
1 can cream of celery soup
1   4-oz. jar diced pimento
1 onion, chopped
2 c. French-style green beans, drained
1 c. mayonnaise
1 can water chestnuts
Salt and pepper to taste

Cook . . . . wild rice mix using package directions.
Add . . . . . remaining ingredients, mixing well.
Pour . . . . . into buttered 3-quart casserole.

Bake . . . . . at 350 degrees for 30 minutes.
Yields . . . . 6 servings/about 565 calories each.

Mary Jo Campbell
Liberty H. S., Liberty, Mississippi

STIR-FRY CHICKEN AND BROCCOLI

1/3 c. soy sauce
2 tbsp. brown sugar
3 tbsp. Sherry
1 clove of garlic, crushed
1 tsp. ginger
1 tsp. cornstarch
1 1/2 lb. chicken, cut in bite-sized pieces
3 tbsp. oil
1 bunch broccoli, cut in flowerets
1 lg. onion, cut in wedges

Combine . first 6 ingredients with 1/4 cup water in bowl, mixing well.
Marinate . . chicken in sauce for 10 minutes or longer.
Drain . . . . chicken, reserving marinade.
Heat . . . . . oil in skillet.
Add . . . . . chicken, in small amounts to prevent overcrowding.
Stir-fry . . . over high heat until brown.
Remove . . from skillet and set aside.
Add . . . . . broccoli and onion to hot skillet.
Stir-fry . . . for 1 minute.
Add . . . . . 1/4 cup water; cover and steam for 3 minutes or until broccoli is tender-crisp.
Return . . . chicken to skillet, adding marinade.
Heat . . . . . through, stirring constantly.
Serve . . . . over rice.
Yields . . . . 4 servings/about 330 calories each.

Jane D. Cooper
Lamar County Comprehensive H. S.,
Barnesville, Georgia

CHICKEN ENCHILADAS

1 doz. tortillas
1/2 c. cooking oil
1 c. chopped, cooked chicken
3/4 c. chopped onion
2 c. shredded Monterey Jack cheese
4 to 6 jalapeno peppers, seeded, cut into strips
1/4 c. margarine
1/4 c. flour

2 c. chicken broth
1 c. sour cream

Soften ... tortillas, one at a time, in hot oil in skillet for 15 seconds on each side.
Combine . chicken, onion and 1 cup cheese in bowl.
Spoon ... 3 tablespoons chicken mixture onto each tortilla.
Roll ..... to enclose filling.
Place .... seam side down in baking dish.
Saute .... peppers in margarine in saucepan.
Add ..... flour, stirring until smooth.
Add ..... broth gradually.
Cook .... over low heat until thick and bubbly, stirring constantly.
Stir ...... in sour cream until heated through.
Pour ..... sauce over enchiladas.
Bake ..... at 425 degrees for 20 minutes.
Sprinkle .. with remaining 1 cup cheese.
Bake ..... for 5 minutes longer.

Billie J. Garner
Keller H. S., Keller, Texas

CHICKEN OLE

3 to 4 lb. chicken, cooked, cubed
1 can cream of mushroom soup
1 can cream of chicken soup
1 soup can chicken broth
1 lg. onion, chopped
1 med. can chili salsa
1 sm. can chopped green chiles
1 pkg. flour tortillas
1/2 lb. Cheddar cheese, shredded

Combine . first 7 ingredients in large bowl, mixing well.
Cut ...... tortillas into 1 1/2-inch strips.
Layer .... chicken mixture, tortilla strips and cheese in buttered 9 x 13-inch baking dish, repeating until all ingredients are used ending with cheese.
Chill ..... covered, in refrigerator overnight.
Bake ..... at 325 degrees for 1 hour.
Yields .... 6 servings/about 600 calories each.

Marian B. Dobbins
Catalina H. S., Tucson, Arizona

RO-TEL CHICKEN

1 can cream of mushroom soup
1 can cream of chicken soup
1/2 can Ro-Tel tomatoes with green chiles
1 c. chicken broth
1 med. onion, finely chopped
1 lg. bag cheese-flavored corn chips, crushed
1 boiled chicken, cut in bite-sized pieces
1/2 to 1 c. grated cheese

Combine . first 5 ingredients in saucepan.
Heat ..... to boiling point; set aside.
Spread ... half the corn chips in greased 8 x 12-inch baking dish.
Layer .... half the chicken and soup mixture over chips.
Repeat ... layers of corn chips, chicken and soup.
Bake ..... at 350 degrees for 25 to 35 minutes.
Sprinkle .. cheese on top.
Bake ..... for 5 minutes longer.

Renee A. Jenkins
Glenmore Academy, Memphis, Tennessee

ALMOND CHICKEN BAKED IN CREAM

1 tsp. each celery salt, paprika and salt
1/2 tsp. each curry powder, crushed oregano and pepper
7 tbsp. melted butter
3 1/2 lb. chicken pieces
Flour
3/4 c. sliced almonds
1 1/2 c. half and half
1/2 c. sour cream
3 tbsp. fine dry bread crumbs

Blend .... seasonings with 6 tablespoons butter in bowl.
Coat ..... chicken pieces with flour.
Dip ...... chicken in seasoned butter.
Arrange .. in single layer in large baking dish.
Sprinkle .. with almonds.
Pour ..... half and half around chicken pieces.
Bake ..... covered, at 350 degrees for 45 minutes.
Spoon ... 1/2 cup pan drippings into sour cream, mixing well.
Pour ..... evenly over chicken.
Sprinkle .. with crumbs mixed with remaining tablespoon butter.
Bake ..... uncovered, for 15 minutes longer.

Evelyn L. McMurtray
Rincon H. S., Tucson, Arizona

CHEESY CHICKEN

1 clove of garlic
1/2 c. corn oil
1 c. fine dry bread crumbs
1/2 c. finely grated sharp Cheddar cheese
1/4 c. Parmesan cheese
1 tsp. Accent
1 tsp. salt
1/8 tsp. pepper
1 fryer, cut up

Combine . garlic and corn oil, letting stand for 20 minutes before removing garlic.
Mix . . . . . next 6 ingredients in bowl.
Dip . . . . . . chicken pieces in garlic oil, then in crumb mixture.
Place . . . . in large shallow baking pan 1 inch apart.
Pour . . . . . remaining oil over chicken pieces.
Bake . . . . . at 350 degrees for 45 minutes or until fork-tender, basting occasionally.
Yields . . . . 6 servings/about 755 calories each.

Kathy Fulmer
Cale H. S., Cale, Arkansas
Terry Rakes
Elmwood Jr. H. S., Rogers, Arkansas

CHICKEN-POTATO STEW

1   3 1/2 to 4-lb. broiler-fryer
2 chicken bouillon cubes
4 Idaho potatoes, well scrubbed
1 1/2 c. chopped onion
2 tsp. crushed tarragon
4 carrots, sliced
1   10-oz. bag fresh spinach, washed, trimmed
1 1/2 c. skim milk
2 tsp. salt
1/4 tsp. hot pepper sauce

Place . . . . chicken in large kettle.
Fill . . . . . . half full with water; add bouillon cubes, potatoes, onion and tarragon.
Bring . . . . to a boil, covered; reduce heat.
Simmer . . for 30 minutes or until potatoes are tender.
Remove . . potatoes; add carrots.
Peel . . . . . and mash potatoes; set aside.
Cook . . . . chicken and carrots for 20 to 30 minutes longer or until tender.

Remove . . chicken from kettle; debone.
Add . . . . . mashed potatoes, chicken and remaining ingredients to kettle.
Heat . . . . . through. Do not overcook spinach.
Yields . . . . 6 servings/about 434 calories each.

Photograph for this recipe on page 2.

TURKEY PIE

2 c. herb-seasoned stuffing mix
1/2 c. melted butter
1 can cream of celery soup
1/2 c. milk
1 1/2 c. cooked turkey chunks
3/4 c. cooked peas
1 tbsp. dried minced onion
1/8 tsp. pepper

Combine . 1 1/4 cups stuffing mix with 1/4 cup butter in bowl, mixing well.
Press . . . . . into bottom and side of 9-inch pie plate.
Blend . . . . soup and milk in saucepan over low heat until smooth, stirring constantly.
Add . . . . . turkey, peas, onion and pepper, mixing well.
Spoon . . . into stuffing shell.
Roll . . . . . 3/4 cup stuffing into fine crumbs.
Combine . with 1/4 cup butter, mixing well.
Spoon . . . around rim of pie plate in border.
Bake . . . . . at 425 degrees for 10 minutes or until browned and bubbly.
Yields . . . . 6 servings/about 335 calories each.

Arlene Maisel
Highland Park H. S., Highland Park, New Jersey

TURKEY-RICE BAKE

1 c. long grain rice
3 tbsp. margarine
1 can onion soup
1/2 c. chopped green pepper
1 tbsp. chopped pimento
1/2 c. diced celery
1 c. diced cooked turkey
1 can sliced mushrooms, drained
4 slices process cheese, halved diagonally

Brown . . . rice in margarine in skillet, stirring constantly.
Place . . . . in casserole.

Add ..... next 6 ingredients and 1 1/3 cups water, mixing well.
Bake ..... covered, at 350 degrees for 20 to 25 minutes or until rice is cooked.
Arrange .. cheese slices in pinwheel on casserole.
Bake ..... uncovered, until cheese melts.
Yields .... 6 servings/about 290 calories each.

Gloria Gauthier
F. J. Brennan H. S., Windsor, Ontario, Canada

TURKEY CUTLET PACIFICA

1 egg, slightly beaten
1/2 c. milk
6 thick slices cooked turkey
Flour
Dry bread crumbs
1/4 c. butter
Salt and pepper to taste
1 1-lb. can diced tomatoes in puree
1/2 tsp. oregano
1/2 tsp. sugar
6 slices mozzarella cheese
2 California avocados, peeled, sliced

Mix ..... egg and milk together in small bowl.
Dip ...... turkey in flour, then egg mixture.
Roll ..... in bread crumbs, coating well.
Brown ... in butter in skillet.
Season ... to taste.
Place .... in baking dish.
Mix ..... tomatoes with oregano and sugar.
Spoon ... over turkey.
Top ..... with cheese.
Broil ..... until bubbly.
Garnish .. with avocado slices.
Yields .... 6 servings/about 550 calories each.

Photograph for this recipe on this page.

WHITE CLAM SAUCE

1 med. onion, chopped
2 cloves of garlic, minced
1/2 c. butter
1/2 c. oil
1/4 c. parsley
1/2 lb. mushrooms, sliced
Juice of 1 lemon
1/2 c. white wine

2 10-oz. cans baby clams with broth
1 lb. thin spaghetti, cooked
Parmesan cheese

Saute .... onion and garlic in butter and oil in skillet.
Add ..... parsley and mushrooms.
Cook .... until vegetables are tender.
Add ..... lemon juice and wine.
Stir ...... clams into sauce.
Pour ..... sauce over hot spaghetti.
Sprinkle .. with Parmesan cheese.

Sue L. Fry
Atlantic H. S., Delray Beach, Florida

COD FILLET SUPREME

1 pkg. frozen cod fillets
1 6 1/2-oz. can crab meat
1 can cream of mushroom soup
1/2 c. shredded Swiss cheese
Almonds

Place .... cod fillets in buttered casserole.
Sprinkle .. crab meat on top.
Pour ..... soup over crab meat.
Sprinkle .. Swiss cheese over top.
Garnish .. with almonds.
Bake ..... covered, at 350 degrees for 1 1/2 hours.
Yields .... 4 servings/about 375 calories each.

Julia A. Arnett
Madison County Technical Center, Huntsville, Alabama

ALTURAS CASSEROLE

3 Idaho potatoes, cut in half crosswise
1 lb. fillet of sole
1 tbsp. lemon juice
1 tsp. salt
1 med. onion, sliced
1 med. red pepper, sliced
1 med. green pepper, sliced
1/2 tsp. white pepper
1 lg. tomato, sliced
2 tsp. butter

Cook .... potatoes in 1-inch boiling salted water in covered saucepan for 20 to 25 minutes or until tender but not crumbly.
Drain .... and peel; cut into 1/8-inch slices.
Arrange .. sole in single layer in shallow baking dish.
Sprinkle .. with lemon juice and 1/2 teaspoon salt.
Let ...... stand for 30 minutes.
Place .... layer of potatoes in shallow 2-quart casserole.
Layer .... half the onion and red and green pepper slices over potatoes.
Arrange .. sole in single layer over vegetables; sprinkle with salt and pepper.
Layer .... onion, pepper slices, tomato and potatoes in order listed.
Dot ..... with butter.
Bake ..... at 250 degrees for 30 minutes.
Yields .... 4 servings/about 345 calories each.

Photograph for this recipe on page 2.

COD AU GRATIN

3 tbsp. margarine
6 tbsp. flour
1/2 tsp. salt
1/8 tsp. pepper
2 c. milk
4 c. cooked cod, flaked
1 c. grated cheese

Melt ..... margarine in skillet.
Add ..... flour, salt and pepper, stirring until smooth.
Add ..... milk gradually.
Cook .... until thick, stirring constantly.
Arrange .. fish in casserole.

Cover .... with sauce.
Top ..... with cheese.
Bake ..... at 350 degrees for 30 minutes.

Mrs. Pauline Quinton
Morris Academy, Mount Pearl, Newfoundland, Canada

PARTY SALMON CREPES

1 c. pancake mix
3 1/2 c. milk
Butter, melted
1 egg, slightly beaten
1/4 c. minced onion
1/2 c. chopped celery
1/4 c. all-purpose flour
1/2 tsp. salt
2/3 c. grated Parmesan cheese
2 c. salmon
1 8-oz. can peas

Combine . pancake mix with 1 1/4 cups milk, 1 tablespoon butter and egg in bowl.
Stir ...... lightly until just mixed.
Pour ..... 1/3 cup batter onto hot, lightly buttered griddle.
Bake ..... until set.
Turn ..... to brown other side.
Saute .... onion and celery in 1/4 cup butter in skillet until tender.
Blend .... in flour and salt to make smooth paste.

Add ..... 2 1/4 cups milk gradually, stirring constantly.
Cook .... until thick, stirring constantly.
Remove .. from heat.
Add ..... cheese, stirring until melted.
Set ...... aside 1 1/3 cups sauce.
Add ..... salmon and peas to sauce in pan, heating and stirring until hot and blended.
Spread ... pancakes with salmon mixture and roll up.
Place .... in 9 x 11-inch baking dish.
Bake ..... at 350 degrees for 15 to 20 minutes.
Reheat ... reserved sauce to pour over crepes.

Photograph for this recipe on opposite page.

MICROWAVE SALMON DUMPLINGS

1 7 1/2-oz. package refrigerator biscuits
1 7 3/4-oz. can salmon
1 can Cheddar cheese soup
1 c. milk
2 tbsp. flour
2 tbsp. chopped green pepper
1 tbsp. parsley

Arrange .. biscuits over bottom of 1 1/2-quart microwave casserole.
Combine . remaining ingredients in bowl, blending well.
Spoon ... over biscuits.
Microwave on High for 12 minutes, spooning sauce over biscuits after 6 minutes.
Yields .... 4 servings/about 340 calories each.

Marilyn L. Burrows
Putnam City North H. S., Oklahoma City, Oklahoma

CRAB MEAT IMPERIAL

1 tbsp. chopped green pepper
1 tbsp. chopped pimento
3 tbsp. butter
3 tbsp. flour
1/2 tsp. salt
Dash each of pepper, paprika
1 c. milk
1 egg yolk, beaten
1/4 tsp. dry mustard
1 tbsp. capers, drained

1/2 to 1 tsp. Worcestershire sauce
2 6-oz. packages frozen king crab, thawed

Saute .... green pepper and pimento in butter in saucepan until tender.
Add ..... next 4 ingredients, stirring until smooth.
Add ..... milk gradually.
Cook .... until thick, stirring constantly.
Stir ...... a small amount of hot mixture into egg yolk.
Stir ...... egg yolk into hot mixture.
Add ..... mustard, capers and Worcestershire sauce, blending well.
Fold in ... crab meat.
Pour ..... into casserole.
Bake ..... at 350 degrees for 30 minutes.
Yields .... 3 servings/about 290 calories each.

Lucille H. Wiggins
I. C. Norcom H. S., Portsmouth, Virginia

HOT CRAB MEAT ROSE

1 lb. crab meat
1/4 c. rose wine
1/2 c. sour cream
1/2 tsp. dry mustard
1/2 tsp. salt
Dash of cayenne pepper
Pinch of thyme
1 c. sliced celery
2 hard-cooked eggs, chopped
1/2 c. slivered almonds
1/4 c. grated Parmesan cheese
1/4 c. melted butter.

Marinate .. crab meat in wine in bowl for 30 minutes.
Combine . sour cream, mustard, salt, cayenne and thyme in bowl, blending well.
Toss ..... crab meat and wine with sour cream mixture.
Stir ...... in celery and eggs.
Pour ..... into buttered casserole.
Combine . almonds, cheese and butter, sprinkling over top.
Bake ..... at 325 degrees for 25 minutes.
Brown ... under broiler if necessary.
Yields .... 4 servings/about 470 calories each.

Gerald A. Hils
Keene H. S.-Cheshire Vocational Center
Keene, New Hampshire

OYSTER BAKE CASSEROLE

36 Ritz crackers, crushed
1 17-oz. can creamed corn
2 8-oz. cans oysters, drained
1 10 1/2-oz. can cream of mushroom soup
1/4 c. milk
1 c. cubed mild Cheddar cheese
1/2 c. butter
1 c. flour
Dash of pepper

Sprinkle .. half the cracker crumbs over bot-
            tom of 8-inch casserole.
Spread ... corn over crackers.
Arrange .. oysters over corn.
Combine . soup, milk and cheese in bowl.
Spoon ... over oysters.
Cut ...... butter into flour in bowl until
            crumbly.
Add ..... remaining cracker crumbs and pep-
            per, mixing well.
Sprinkle .. over casserole.
Bake ..... at 450 degrees for 10 minutes.
Reduce ... heat and bake at 350 degrees for 30
            minutes.
Note ..... ham, shrimp or tuna may be substi-
            tuted for oysters.

Marilyn Ziegler
Bloomington H. S. South, Bloomington, Indiana

HOUSTON SHRIMP CREOLE

2 med. onions, chopped
1 green pepper, chopped
1/2 c. chopped celery
4 tbsp. bacon drippings
3 tbsp. tomato paste
4 c. canned tomatoes
3 tbsp. Worcestershire sauce
1 sm. bay leaf, crumbled
1 tbsp. minced celery leaves
2 tbsp. minced fresh parsley
1/2 tsp. Tabasco sauce
4 c. medium shrimp, cooked, shelled
Salt to taste

Saute .... first 3 ingredients in bacon drip-
            pings until onions are golden.
Add ..... tomato paste, tomatoes, seasonings
            and herbs.
Simmer .. for about 40 minutes until
            thickened.

Add ..... shrimp and salt.
Simmer .. for 15 minutes.
Serve .... with cooked rice.
Yields .... 6 servings/about 170 calories each.

Judith C. Tyler
Ross S. Sterling H. S., Baytown, Texas

SHRIMP CASSEROLE HARPIN

2 lb. shrimp
1 tbsp. lemon juice
3 tbsp. oil
1/4 c. chopped green pepper
1/2 c. chopped onion
2 tbsp. butter
1 c. heavy cream
1 tsp. salt
1/4 tsp. pepper
1/8 tsp. mace
Dash of cayenne pepper
1 can tomato soup
1/2 c. Sherry
1 1/2 c. cooked rice
1/4 c. slivered almonds

Mix ..... first 3 ingredients in buttered
            casserole.
Saute .... pepper and onion in butter in
            skillet.
Add ..... with remaining ingredients except
            almonds to shrimp mixture.
Stir ...... carefully.
Top ..... with almonds.
Bake ..... at 350 degrees for 1 hour.

Eunice Roberts
Walters Jr. H. S., Fremont, California

COMPANY TUNA BAKE

1 c. elbow macaroni
1 3-oz. package cream cheese, softened
1 can cream of mushroom soup
1 can tuna, drained, flaked
1 tbsp. chopped pimento
1 tbsp. chopped onion
1 tsp. prepared mustard
1/3 c. milk
1/2 c. bread crumbs
2 tbsp. butter, melted

Cook .... macaroni using package directions.
Beat ..... cream cheese and soup in bowl
            until smooth.

Add . . . . . next 5 ingredients and macaroni, mixing well.
Pour . . . . . into 1 1/2-quart casserole.
Combine . bread crumbs and butter in bowl.
Sprinkle . . over tuna mixture.
Bake . . . . . at 375 degrees for 20 minutes.
Yields . . . . 4 servings/about 435 calories each.

Margaret Brown
Woodward Jr. H. S., Wilkesboro, North Carolina

SPECIAL OCCASION TUNA CASSEROLE

2 c. stuffing mix
1 13-oz. can tuna
1 can cream of mushroom soup
2 c. finely chopped celery
1/2 c. Miracle Whip
1 c. sour cream
1 tbsp. lemon juice
8 oz. sliced water chestnuts
1 c. sliced mushrooms
1/2 c. each onion, green pepper
1 tsp. each salt, pepper and garlic powder
1 c. grated Cheddar cheese

Combine . 1 1/2 cups stuffing mix and remaining ingredients except cheese in 9 x 13-inch baking pan.
Top . . . . . with cheese.
Bake . . . . . at 350 degrees for 30 minutes.
Sprinkle . . remaining 1/2 cup stuffing mix on top.
Bake . . . . . for 10 minutes longer.
Yields . . . . 6 servings/about 635 calories each.

Linda J. Dobbins
Indian River H. S., Chesapeake, Virginia

TUNA JACKSTRAWS

1 7 1/2-oz. can tuna, drained
1 can mushroom soup
2/3 c. evaporated milk
1 lg. can shoestring potatoes
1/2 c. peas (opt.)
2 tbsp. pimento (opt.)

Combine . all ingredients in bowl, mixing well.
Spoon . . . into casserole.
Bake . . . . . at 350 degrees for 30 minutes.

Cloyann Fent
Perry H. S., Perry, Oklahoma

TUNA-STUFFED BAKED POTATOES

8 potatoes, baked
2 tbsp. butter
2 7-oz. cans tuna
1 tbsp. grated onion
1 tbsp. parsley
1 10 3/4-oz. can Cheddar cheese soup
1/4 tsp. paprika
2 drops of Tabasco sauce
1/4 tsp. salt
4 slices American cheese, cut into halves

Cut . . . . . . potatoes in half and scoop out meat.
Combine . potatoes with remaining ingredients except cheese in bowl, mixing well.
Spoon . . . into potato shells.
Top . . . . . each potato with cheese slice.
Bake . . . . . at 350 degrees for 15 minutes or until cheese melts.

Debbie Bacher
Moore H. S., Moore, Oklahoma

TUNA VEGETABLE PILAF

2 tbsp. butter
1/2 c. chopped scallions
2 c. brown rice
3 1/2 c. clear vegetable broth
1 tsp. salt
1/2 tsp. Tabasco sauce
1/2 c. hulled sunflower seeds
1/2 c. diced pared carrot
1 med. zucchini, halved lengthwise, sliced 1/2 in. thick
1 10-oz. package frozen broccoli spears, thawed, cut into 1-in. pieces
3 7-oz. cans tuna in oil

Melt . . . . . butter in 3-quart Dutch oven.
Add . . . . . scallions and rice.
Cook . . . . until rice is golden brown, stirring frequently.
Stir . . . . . . in broth.
Bring . . . . to a boil.
Bake . . . . . covered, at 375 degrees for 45 minutes.
Stir . . . . . . in remaining ingredients except tuna.
Bake . . . . . for 20 to 25 minutes longer.
Stir . . . . . . in tuna before serving.
Yields . . . . 6 servings/about 575 calories each.

Photograph for this recipe on page 35.

Breads

Even the simplest meals become a special occasion when steaming homemade bread is served. Piping hot biscuits for breakfast ... coffee cakes for a special group of visiting friends ... loaves of bread with a flavor no grocery could ever match ... and holiday breads for a gourmet gift.

Bread-making is a unique joy. And the all-purpose homemaker who masters it holds a very special place of honor with family and friends.

TRICKS OF THE TRADE

- If you like crusty biscuits, leave space between each one on the baking sheet; for softer biscuits, place closer together.
- To make biscuits that split open easily; roll dough to ¼ inch thickness; fold dough in half; then cut biscuit rounds.
- Bread has risen enough if indentation remains when your finger presses into the dough.
- Be sure to check the package date for freshness before using yeast. If in doubt, dissolve yeast in water according to the recipe. Add a pinch of sugar; set aside to become frothy.
- Unused egg wash can be frozen until needed.
- Bread freezes well up to three months.
- To slice freshly baked bread, cut with a hot knife.

BAKING POWDER BISCUITS

2 c. sifted flour
2 tsp. baking powder
1 tsp. salt
1/3 c. shortening
3/4 c. milk

Sift . . . . . . dry ingredients together into bowl.
Cut . . . . . . in shortening until crumbly.
Add . . . . . milk, stirring until just mixed.
Knead . . . lightly, on floured surface, 6 to 8 times.
Pat . . . . . . out to 1/2-inch thickness.
Cut . . . . . . with floured cutter, placing 1/2-inch apart on baking sheet.
Bake . . . . . at 450 degrees for 10 to 15 minutes or until golden brown.
Yields . . . . 10 biscuits.

Carolyne E. Ray
West Jr. H. S., Kansas City, Kansas

MEXICAN CORN BREAD

1 to 1 1/2 pkg. Mexican corn bread mix
1 chopped jalapeno pepper
1 tsp. jalapeno pepper juice
1 med. can cream-style corn
1 to 2 lb. ground beef
1 tbsp. chopped onion
Salt and pepper to taste
1 c. grated American cheese

Prepare . . . corn bread mix using package directions.
Add . . . . . next 3 ingredients, mixing well.
Brown . . . ground beef, onion, salt and pepper in skillet, stirring until crumbly.
Drain . . . . pan drippings.
Spread . . . half the corn bread batter in 2-quart casserole.
Spoon . . . ground beef over top.
Sprinkle . . with cheese.
Cover . . . . with remaining batter.
Bake . . . . . at 400 degrees for 45 minutes.
Yields . . . . 5 servings/about 715 calories each.

· Gwendolyn S. Doyle
Slidell Sr. H. S., Slidell, Louisiana

SUPER SPECIAL SPOON BREAD

2 c. yellow cornmeal, sifted twice
1 tbsp. salt
4 tbsp. melted shortening
1 1/2 c. milk
2 tbsp. sugar (opt.)
3 egg yolks, beaten
3 egg whites, stiffly beaten

Mix . . . . . cornmeal with 1 cup boiling water in bowl, stirring until smooth.
Add . . . . . 1 cup boiling water, salt, shortening, milk, sugar and egg yolks, mixing well.
Fold . . . . . in egg whites.
Pour . . . . . into greased 2-quart baking dish.
Bake . . . . . at 350 degrees for 45 minutes.
Top . . . . . with butter.
Let . . . . . . stand for 15 minutes before serving.
Yields . . . . 6 servings/about 340 calories each.

Mary Delores Williams Keyes
Marshall Walker H. S., Richmond, Virginia

BAKED APPLE DOUGHNUTS

1 1/2 c. flour
1 3/4 tsp. baking powder
1/2 tsp. each salt, nutmeg
Sugar
1/3 c. shortening
1 egg, beaten
1/4 c. milk
1/2 c. grated unpeeled apple
1 tsp. cinnamon
1/2 c. melted butter

Sift . . . . . . first 4 ingredients and 1/2 cup sugar together into bowl.
Cut . . . . . . in shortening until crumbly.
Stir . . . . . . in egg, milk and apple, mixing well.
Fill . . . . . . greased muffin cups 2/3 full.
Bake . . . . . at 350 degrees for 20 minutes.
Mix . . . . . 1/3 cup sugar and cinnamon in small bowl.
Remove . . doughnuts from pan and roll in butter, then in sugar mixture.

M. Van Dan
Alden-Hebron H. S., Hebron, Illinois

CHOCOLATE DOUGHNUTS

2 tbsp. shortening, melted
1 1/2 sq. unsweetened chocolate, melted
1 1/4 c. sugar
3/4 c. buttermilk
1 tsp. vanilla extract
2 tsp. baking powder

1 tsp. soda
1 tsp. salt
2 eggs
3 c. flour

Combine . all ingredients except 1 1/2 cups flour in bowl, beating until smooth with mixer at low speed.
Increase .. speed and beat for 1 minute longer.
Stir . . . . . . in remaining flour to make soft dough.
Chill . . . . . for 1 hour.
Roll . . . . . . out 1/2 inch thick on well-floured surface.
Cut . . . . . . with floured doughnut cutter.
Deep . . . . fry at 370 degrees.

Diane Gibbs
New Bloomfield R-III, New Bloomfield, Missouri

RAGGLETS

2 tbsp. butter
1 c. sifted flour
4 eggs
Oil for deep frying
Cinnamon (opt.)
Sugar (opt.)

Bring . . . . butter and 1 cup water to a boil in saucepan.
Remove .. from heat and add flour.
Beat . . . . . until smooth.
Add . . . . . eggs, 1 at a time, beating well after each addition.
Drop . . . . by teaspoonfuls into deep fat at 375 degrees.
Fry . . . . . . until golden brown on both sides.
Drain . . . . on paper towel and roll in cinnamon and sugar mixture.

Mrs. Pat Gant
Dell Rapids St. Mary's H. S.
Dell Rapids, South Dakota

COWBOY COFFEE CAKE

1 1/4 c. sifted flour
1 c. packed brown sugar
1/4 tsp. salt
1/3 c. shortening
1 tsp. baking powder
1/4 tsp. each soda, cinnamon and nutmeg

1/2 c. sour milk
1 egg, beaten

Combine . first 4 ingredients in bowl, stirring until crumbly.
Reserve .. 1/4 cup.
Add . . . . . baking powder, soda and spices to remaining crumbs, mixing well.
Add . . . . . milk and egg, mixing well.
Pour . . . . . into greased and floured 8 x 8-inch pan.
Top . . . . . with reserved crumbs.
Bake . . . . . at 375 degrees for 15 to 20 minutes.

Lucinda B. Helton
Conway Jr. H. S., Orlando, Florida

MORAVIAN SUGAR CAKE

1 pkg. hot roll mix
Butter, melted
1/3 c. sugar
1/3 c. instant nonfat dry milk
2 eggs
1/3 c. instant mashed potato flakes
2/3 c. packed brown sugar
1 tsp. cinnamon

Dissolve .. yeast from hot roll mix in 3/4 cup very warm water in large bowl.
Stir . . . . . . half the flour from mix, 1/3 cup butter, sugar, milk, eggs and potato flakes into yeast mixture.
Beat . . . . . for 2 minutes at medium speed of electric mixer.
Add . . . . . remaining flour, mixing well.
Cover . . . . and let rise in warm place for about 45 minutes or until doubled in bulk.
Stir . . . . . . dough down.
Spread . . . in greased 9 x 13-inch pan.
Cover . . . . and let rise for about 45 minutes or until doubled in bulk.
Press . . . . . dough with floured finger tip to make pockets.
Combine . brown sugar and cinnamon in bowl.
Sprinkle .. over dough.
Drizzle . . . with 1/2 cup butter.
Bake . . . . . at 375 degrees for 15 to 20 minutes.

Helen M. Godwin
Northwest Sr. H. S., Greensboro, North Carolina

BASIC MIX COFFEE CAKE

4 1/2 c. sifted flour
2 tbsp. baking powder
1 1/2 tsp. salt
1 c. shortening
1/4 c. sugar
1 egg, well beaten
2/3 c. milk
1/4 c. melted butter
1/2 c. packed brown sugar
1 c. Special K
1/2 tsp. cinnamon

Sift . . . . . . first 3 ingredients into large bowl.
Cut . . . . . . in shortening until crumbly.
Measure . . 2 cups of mixture for this recipe, reserving remainder for future use by storing in covered container.
Combine . with sugar, mixing well.
Beat . . . . . egg with milk in small bowl.
Add . . . . . to flour mixture, stirring until just mixed.
Spread . . . in 8 x 8-inch greased pan.
Combine . remaining ingredients in small bowl, mixing well.
Sprinkle . . over batter.
Bake . . . . . at 400 degrees for 25 minutes.

Betsy-Anne Sheffield
Bloomfield Jr. H. S., Halifax, Nova Scotia, Canada

QUICK COFFEE CAKE

1/2 c. butter
1/2 c. shortening
1/2 tsp. salt
Sugar
3 eggs
3 c. flour
4 tsp. baking powder
1 lg. can evaporated milk
1 tsp. vanilla extract
Cinnamon
Chopped walnuts

Cream . . . first 3 ingredients and 2 cups sugar together in bowl.
Add . . . . . eggs, 1 at a time, beating well after each addition.
Sift . . . . . . flour and baking powder together.
Add . . . . . to creamed mixture alternately with milk, beating constantly.
Stir . . . . . . in vanilla.

Pour . . . . . half the batter into 8 x 12-inch baking pan.
Sprinkle . . with sugar and cinnamon.
Cover . . . . with remaining batter.
Sprinkle . . with sugar, cinnamon and nuts.
Bake . . . . . at 350 degrees for 40 to 50 minutes.

Pamela J. Ramsey
Wintersville H. S., Wintersville, Ohio

WHITE SOUR CREAM COFFEE CAKE

1/2 c. shortening
1 c. sugar
2 eggs, slightly beaten
1/2 pt. sour cream
2 c. sifted flour
1 tsp. baking powder
1 tsp. soda
1/4 tsp. salt
1 tsp. vanilla extract
1 c. chopped nuts
1 tsp. cinnamon

Cream . . . shortening and 3/4 cup sugar together in bowl.
Combine . eggs and sour cream.
Add . . . . . to creamed mixture.
Sift . . . . . . next 4 ingredients together.
Add . . . . . to creamed mixture, blending well.
Stir . . . . . . in vanilla, beating well.
Pour . . . . . half the batter into buttered tube pan.
Combine . remaining 1/4 cup sugar, nuts and cinnamon.
Sprinkle . . over batter.
Cover . . . . with remaining batter.
Bake . . . . . at 350 degrees for 40 to 45 minutes.

Polly Webster
Mattanawcook Academy, Lincoln, Maine

PINEAPPLE-BUTTERCRUMB COFFEE CAKE

3/4 c. butter, softened
1 c. sugar
1/8 tsp. almond extract
1/2 tsp. vanilla extract
1 egg
2 1/2 c. sifted flour
2 1/2 tsp. baking powder
1 tsp. salt

1/2 c. milk
1 1-lb 4 1/2-oz. can pineapple tidbits,
   drained
1/4 tsp. cinnamon

Blend . . . . 1/2 cup butter, 1/2 cup sugar and flavorings in bowl until light.
Beat . . . . . in egg.
Sift . . . . . . 2 cups flour, baking powder and salt together.
Add . . . . . alternately with milk to sugar mixture, beating well after each addition.
Reserve . . 1/2 cup pineapple for topping.
Stir . . . . . . remaining pineapple into batter.
Spoon . . . into greased and floured 1 1/2-quart mold.
Arrange . . reserved pineapple over top.
Combine . 1/4 cup butter, 1/2 cup sugar, 1/2 cup flour and cinnamon in small bowl, mixing until crumbly.
Sprinkle . . crumbs over pineapple and batter.
Bake . . . . . at 350 degrees for 45 to 50 minutes or until cake tests done.

Photograph for this recipe above.

FRENCH BREAD MONTEREY

1 long loaf French bread
Butter, softened
1 c. mayonnaise
1/2 c. grated Parmesan cheese

1/2 c. grated onion
1/2 tsp. Worcestershire sauce

Cut . . . . . . bread in half lengthwise.
Spread . . . surfaces with butter.
Bake . . . . . bread in 350-degree oven until heated through.
Mix . . . . . next 4 ingredients together in bowl.
Spread . . . cheese mixture on hot bread.
Dust . . . . . with paprika.
Bake . . . . . until delicately browned.
Cut . . . . . . crosswise and serve.

Sharon Richter
Lebanon Sr. H. S., Lebanon, Missouri

FUNNY EGGS

1 stick butter
1/4 c. packed brown sugar
1 can refrigerator biscuits
1 1-lb. can apricots, drained
1/2 c. apricot liquid
Paprika

Melt . . . . . butter in round layer pan.
Sprinkle . . with brown sugar.
Dip . . . . . . biscuits in butter mixture to coat both sides and arrange in pan.
Make . . . . apricot-sized indentation in each biscuit and fill with apricot.
Pour . . . . . apricot liquid over top.
Sprinkle . . with paprika.
Bake . . . . . at 400 degrees for 15 minutes.

Deborah Casados
Mexia H. S., Mexia, Texas

HERB STICKS

4 hot dog buns, split
1/2 c. butter, melted
1/4 tsp. each dried savory, paprika
1/2 tsp. each celery seed, thyme
Cayenne pepper to taste
1 clove of garlic, minced

Cut . . . . . . bun halves into 4 long strips each.
Combine . remaining ingredients in bowl, letting stand for several hours.
Brush . . . . butter mixture on all sides of bread.
Place . . . . on cookie sheet.
Bake . . . . . at 275 degrees for 45 to 60 minutes or until lightly browned.
Store . . . . in airtight container.

Lynn MacIntyre
Maine Twp. H. S. West, Des Plaines, Illinois

FRENCH POUFS

1/3 c. shortening
1 c. sugar
1 egg
1 1/2 c. sifted flour
1 1/2 tsp. baking powder
1/2 tsp. salt
1/4 tsp. nutmeg
1/2 c. milk
1 tsp. cinnamon

Combine . shortening, 1/2 cup sugar and egg in bowl, mixing well.
Sift . . . . . . next 4 ingredients together.
Add . . . . . to creamed mixture alternately with milk, beating well after each addition.
Fill . . . . . . greased muffin cups 2/3 full.
Bake . . . . . at 350 degrees for 20 to 25 minutes.
Dip . . . . . . immediately in melted butter and then in mixture of 1/2 cup sugar and cinnamon.

Phyllis Dunlap
Dysart-Geneseo School, Dysart, Iowa

QUICK HERB ROLLS

1/2 c. butter, softened
1 1/2 tsp. parsley flakes
1/2 tsp. dillweed
1 tbsp. onion flakes
2 cans refrigerator biscuits
2 tbsp. Parmesan cheese

Spread . . . .butter over bottom of 9-inch pie pan.
Combine . next 3 ingredients and sprinkle over butter.
Cut . . . . . . biscuits into halves, placing in pie pan.
Sprinkle . . Parmesan cheese on top.
Bake . . . . .at 425 degrees for 12 to 15 minutes.

Andrea Gay Mitchell
Morrison H. S., Morrison, Oklahoma

BABY FOOD QUICK BREAD

1 c. sugar
1/3 c. shortening
1 egg, beaten
1 jar Jr. baby food of desired flavor
1/2 c. milk
1 1/2 c. flour
1 tsp. soda
1/2 tsp. salt
Chopped nuts (opt.)

Cream . . . first 4 ingredients in bowl.
Add . . . . . remaining ingredients, mixing well.
Pour . . . . . into greased and floured loaf pan.
Bake . . . . . at 350 degrees for 1 hour or until loaf tests done.

Mary Broadway
Midway H. S., Waco, Texas

BANANA BREAD

1 stick margarine, softened
1 c. sugar
2 eggs, beaten
3 lg. bananas, mashed
2 c. flour
1 tsp. soda
1 tsp. vanilla extract
Pinch of salt
1 c. broken pecans

Cream . . . margarine and sugar together in bowl.
Add . . . . . eggs and bananas, mixing well.
Sift . . . . . . flour and soda together into batter, blending thoroughly.
Stir . . . . . . in remaining ingredients.
Pour . . . . . into loaf pan.
Bake . . . . . at 350 degrees for 50 minutes.

Lynn Wagner
Newton H. S., Newton, Mississippi

BEER BREAD

3 c. self-rising flour
3 tbsp. sugar
Dash of salt
1 can warm beer
2 tbsp. melted butter

Combine . first 3 ingredients in bowl.
Add . . . . . beer, stirring until just mixed.
Pour . . . . . into greased loaf pan.
Drizzle . . . butter over batter.
Bake . . . . . at 350 degrees for 1 hour.

Edwynna Nolan
Bloomington H. S. South, Bloomington, Indiana

Recipe on page 112.

CHEESECAKE BREAD RING

1 pkg. hot roll mix
3/4 c. sugar
3 eggs
1/2 c. sour cream
6 tbsp. butter, melted
1 8-oz. package cream cheese, softened
1 tsp. vanilla extract

Dissolve .. yeast from roll mix in 1/4 cup warm water.
Combine . roll mix and 1/4 cup sugar in bowl.
Add ..... yeast, 1 egg, sour cream and butter, mixing well.
Place .... in greased bowl, turning to grease surface.
Chill ..... covered, for 2 to 3 hours.
Roll ..... into 18-inch circle on floured surface.
Fit ...... into 6 cup ring mold, allowing dough to cover center hole and hang over edge.
Beat ..... cream cheese, 1/2 cup sugar and vanilla together in bowl.
Add ..... 2 eggs, one at a time, beating well after each.
Pour ..... into mold.
Slash .... an X across center of mold.
Fold ..... dough from sides and center to enclose filling, sealing edges.
Let ...... rise until doubled in bulk.
Bake ..... at 350 degrees for 35 to 40 minutes or until cake tests done.
Cool ..... for 10 minutes before turning onto rack.
Sprinkle .. with confectioners' sugar.

Margaret Ann Larson
Paul Revere Middle School, Houston, Texas

POPPY SEED BREAD

1 1/2 tsp. salt
1 1/2 tsp. poppy seed
3 c. flour
1 1/2 tsp. baking powder
2 1/2 c. sugar
3 eggs
1 1/2 c. oil

Recipe on page 156.

1 1/2 tsp. butter flavoring
1 1/2 tsp. vanilla extract
2 tsp. almond extract
Milk
1 c. confectioners' sugar

Combine . first 5 ingredients in bowl, mixing well.
Add ..... next 4 ingredients with 1 1/2 teaspoons almond extract and 1 1/2 cups milk, beating well.
Pour ..... into 4 greased and floured 4 x 8-inch pans.
Bake ..... at 350 degrees for 40 minutes.
Blend .... confectioners' sugar with 2 tablespoons milk and 1/2 teaspoon almond extract.
Drizzle ... over loaves.

Lana Couch
Cassville H. S., Cassville, Missouri

PUMPKIN BREAD

1 1/2 c. melted butter
3 c. sugar
5 eggs
2 c. mashed pumpkin
3 1/2 c. flour
1 1/2 tsp. salt
1 tsp. each soda, cinnamon and nutmeg
1 tsp. vanilla extract
Chopped nuts (opt.)
4 c. confectioners' sugar
2 tsp. orange juice
1 tsp. grated orange rind

Cream ... 1 cup butter and sugar together in bowl.
Beat ..... in 4 eggs and pumpkin.
Sift ...... next 5 dry ingredients into batter, mixing well.
Add ..... 3/4 cup water, vanilla and nuts, mixing well.
Pour ..... into 2 large loaf pans.
Bake ..... at 350 degrees for 1 hour.
Combine . confectioners' sugar with remaining 1/2 cup butter, egg and orange juice and rind in bowl, mixing well.
Spread ... over warm loaf.

Karen Robinson
Alta H. S., Sandy, Utah

CHEESE-ONION BREAD

1 c. chopped onion
4 tbsp. butter, melted
2 eggs, slightly beaten
1 c. milk
2 1/2 c. Bisquick
1 c. grated Cheddar cheese
1 tbsp. poppy seed

Saute . . . . onion in 2 tablespoons butter until tender.
Combine . eggs, milk, Bisquick and 2/3 cup cheese in bowl, mixing well.
Add . . . . . onions, stirring to blend.
Pour . . . . . into greased 5 x 9-inch loaf pan.
Mix . . . . . remaining 2 tablespoons butter, 1/3 cup cheese and poppy seed.
Sprinkle . . topping over batter.
Bake . . . . . at 400 degrees for 20 to 25 minutes or until loaf tests done.

Carolyn Cotton
Bristow H. S., Bristow, Oklahoma

CHEDDAR-APPLE BREAD

1/2 c. sugar
1/2 c. shortening
1 egg
1 No. 2 can apple pie filling
2 1/2 c. sifted flour
1 tsp. each salt, soda and baking powder
1 c. shredded Cheddar cheese
1/2 c. chopped pecans

Cream . . . sugar and shortening together in bowl.
Add . . . . . egg, mixing well.
Beat . . . . . in pie filling.
Sift . . . . . . dry ingredients together.
Add . . . . . dry ingredients, cheese and pecans to batter.
Bake . . . . . at 350 degrees for 1 1/2 hours.

Photograph for this recipe on page 96.

LEMON LOAF

1/2 c. butter, softened
1 1/2 c. sugar
2 eggs
1 1/2 c. flour
1 tsp. baking powder
1/4 tsp. salt

1/2 c. milk
Grated rind and juice of 1 lemon

Cream . . . butter and 1 cup sugar together in bowl.
Add . . . . . eggs, beating well.
Sift . . . . . . dry ingredients together.
Add . . . . . to creamed mixture alternately with milk, beating well after each addition.
Stir . . . . . . in rind.
Pour . . . . . into 5 x 9-inch loaf pan.
Bake . . . . . at 350 degrees for 45 minutes.
Mix . . . . . lemon juice with remaining 1/2 cup sugar.
Spoon . . . over hot bread.
Cool . . . . . in pan.

Pat Leeser
Montgomery County R-11 H. S.
Montgomery City, Missouri

STRAWBERRY BREAD

3 c. (heaping) flour
1/2 tsp. soda
1 tbsp. cinnamon
1 tsp. salt
1 1/4 c. sugar
4 eggs, beaten
1 1/4 c. oil
1   10-oz. package frozen sliced strawberries, thawed
1 1/4 c. chopped nuts (opt.)

Combine . dry ingredients in bowl, mixing well.
Add . . . . . remaining ingredients, beating well.
Pour . . . . . into 2 greased and floured loaf pans.
Bake . . . . . at 375 degrees for 45 minutes to 1 hour.

Sharon Swallow
Payson H. S., Payson, Utah

LEMON TEA BREAD

1/2 c. milk
2 eggs
1/3 c. margarine, melted
1 1/2 tsp. grated lemon peel
1 1/4 c. sugar
1 1/4 c. flour

1 tsp. baking powder
1 tsp. salt
1/2 c. chopped nuts
3 tbsp. lemon juice

Combine . first 4 ingredients with 1 cup sugar in bowl, mixing well.
Add ..... dry ingredients, beating until smooth.
Stir ...... in nuts.
Pour ..... into greased loaf pan.
Bake ..... at 350 degrees for 45 to 50 minutes or until loaf tests done.
Combine . lemon juice with 1/4 cup sugar in bowl, blending well.
Drizzle ... over hot loaf.
Let ...... cool for 10 minutes before removing from pan.

Martha Momary
Jackson Jr. H. S., Orlando, Florida

SWEET POTATO BREAD

2 c. self-rising flour
1 c. sugar
1/4 c. oil
2 eggs
1 c. cooked, mashed sweet potatoes
1/2 tsp. allspice
1/2 c. milk
1 c. chopped pecans

Combine . all ingredients except pecans in large mixer bowl.
Beat ..... at low speed for 30 seconds and medium speed for 2 minutes.
Stir ...... in pecans.
Pour ..... into greased loaf pan.
Bake ..... at 350 degrees for 50 to 60 minutes or until loaf tests done.
Cool ..... for 10 minutes before removing from pan.

Mrs. Eloise Scott
Mooreville H. S., Mooreville, Mississippi

SPICY HARVEST FRUITS BREAD

1 1/2 c. whole wheat flour
1 tsp. baking powder
1/2 tsp. each soda, nutmeg
1/4 tsp. salt
1/2 to 2 tsp. cinnamon

4 egg whites
1 c. sugar
1/3 c. honey
1/2 c. corn oil
1 carrot, shredded
1 yam, shredded
1 c. chopped raisins

Sift ...... first 6 ingredients together.
Beat ..... next 4 ingredients together in bowl.
Add ..... 1 to 2 tablespoons hot water, mixing well.
Stir ...... in shredded vegetables.
Add ..... dry ingredients and raisins, mixing well.
Pour ..... into greased and floured 2-pound coffee can.
Place .... inside Crock-Pot.
Cover .... can with damp paper towel.
Cook .... partially covered, on high for 3 1/2 to 4 hours.

Nancy J. Evans-Freed
Reynoldsburg Jr. H. S., Whitehall, Ohio

GARDEN ZUCCHINI BREAD

1 c. sugar
1/2 c. oil
2 eggs
1 tsp. lemon peel, grated
1/2 tsp. orange extract
1 1/2 c. flour
2 tsp. baking powder
1/2 tsp. soda
1/2 tsp. salt
1/8 tsp. each nutmeg, ginger
1 c. unpeeled grated zucchini
1/2 c. chopped nuts

Beat ..... first 5 ingredients together in bowl.
Sift ...... dry ingredients together.
Add ..... alternately with zucchini to sugar mixture, beating well after each addition.
Stir ...... in nuts.
Pour ..... into greased loaf pan.
Bake ..... at 375 degrees for 55 to 60 minutes.
Cool ..... for 15 minutes before removing from pan.

Mrs. Adeline Brill
Jefferson Jr. H. S., Jamestown, New York

WHOLE WHEAT-ZUCCHINI BREAD

3 eggs
1 c. oil
1 c. packed brown sugar
2 c. grated zucchini
1 tsp. vanilla extract
2 c. whole wheat flour
1 c. all-purpose flour
1 tsp. soda
1 tsp. salt
1/4 tsp. baking powder
1 tbsp. cinnamon
1 c. chopped nuts

Beat . . . . . eggs in bowl until frothy.
Add . . . . . next 4 ingredients, mixing well.
Sift . . . . . . dry ingredients together.
Add . . . . . to egg mixture, beating well.
Stir . . . . . . in nuts.
Pour . . . . . into 2 greased 4 x 8-inch pans.
Bake . . . . . at 325 degrees for 1 hour or until loaves test done.
Remove . . from pans and cool on rack.

Vi Raddatz
Port Townsend H. S., Port Townsend, Washington

MAYONNAISE ROLLS

1 c. self-rising flour
3 tbsp. mayonnaise
1/2 c. milk
1/2 tsp. sugar

Combine . all ingredients in bowl until just mixed.
Spoon . . . into greased muffin cups.
Bake . . . . . at 425 degrees until golden brown.
Yields . . . . 6 muffins/about 135 calories each.

Margie Petro
Cannon County H. S., Woodbury, Tennessee

APPLE MUFFINS

3/4 c. milk
1 egg, beaten
1/4 c. oil
2 c. flour
1/2 c. sugar
1 tbsp. baking powder
1/2 tsp. salt
1 tsp. cinnamon
1 c. finely chopped apples
1/4 c. raisins

Combine . milk and egg in small bowl.
Stir . . . . . . in oil.
Combine . dry ingredients in bowl.
Add . . . . . apples and raisins, tossing to coat.
Stir . . . . . . in liquid ingredients until just mixed.
Fill . . . . . . muffin cups 2/3 full.
Bake . . . . . at 400 degrees for 20 to 25 minutes or until golden brown.

Jean Johnson
Conway Jr. H. S., Orlando, Florida

BASIC SWEET MUFFINS

1 egg, beaten
1/2 c. milk
1/4 c. oil
1 1/2 c. flour
1/2 c. sugar
2 tsp. baking powder

Combine . first 3 ingredients in bowl, mixing well.
Mix . . . . . dry ingredients together.
Add . . . . . to liquid mixture, stirring until just mixed.
Fill . . . . . . muffin cups 2/3 full.
Bake . . . . . for 20 minutes.
Yields . . . . 1 dozen/about 175 calories each.

Marcy Poulton
Millcreek Jr. H. S., Bountiful, Utah

BLUEBERRY MUFFINS

1 3/4 c. self-rising flour
3/4 c. sugar
1 egg, beaten
3/4 c. milk
1/3 c. oil
1/2 tsp. vanilla extract (opt.)
3/4 c. blueberries

Combine . first 6 ingredients in bowl, mixing to blend.
Fold . . . . . in blueberries.
Spoon . . . into greased and floured muffin cups.
Bake . . . . . at 400 degrees for 25 minutes.
Yields . . . . 1 dozen/about 210 calories each.

Marcia F. Swanson
Henry County Sr. H. S., McDonough, Georgia

BREAKFAST BRAN MUFFINS

2 c. milk
2 c. whole bran cereal
2 eggs
1/2 c. oil
1/2 c. honey
2 1/2 c. whole wheat flour
4 tsp. baking powder
1/2 tsp. soda
1 tsp. salt

Combine . milk and bran in bowl.
Let . . . . . . stand for 1 minute.
Add . . . . . eggs, oil and honey, beating well.
Stir . . . . . . remaining ingredients together.
Add . . . . . to liquid ingredients, stirring until just mixed.
Spoon . . . into greased muffin cups, filling 2/3 full.
Bake . . . . . at 400 degrees for 20 to 25 minutes.
Yields . . . . 1 dozen/about 250 calories each.

Jo Ann Glass
Meade County Middle School, Brandenburg, Kentucky

SIX-WEEK MUFFINS

3 c. sugar
2 1/2 c. flour
2 1/2 c. whole wheat flour
1   15-oz. box Raisin Bran cereal
5 tsp. soda
2 tsp. salt
4 eggs, beaten
1 qt. buttermilk
1 c. melted margarine

Combine . first 6 ingredients in large bowl.
Add . . . . . eggs, buttermilk and margarine, mixing well.
Fill . . . . . . lined muffin cups 2/3 full.
Bake . . . . . at 400 degrees for 15 to 20 minutes.
Note . . . . . May be refrigerated, covered, for up to six weeks.

Nicolette Gabrysiak
Warren Township H. S., Gurnee, Illinois

NEVER-FAIL POPOVERS

1 egg
1/2 c. milk
1/2 c. flour
Dash of salt

Combine . all ingredients in bowl, mixing well.
Spoon . . . into well-greased muffin cups.
Place . . . . in cold oven set to 425 degrees.
Bake . . . . . for 30 minutes.
Yields . . . . 1/2 dozen/about 65 calories each.

Penelope J. Byrd
Elk Grove H. S., Elk Grove Village, Illinois

GRANDPA'S HOT CAKES

2 c. buttermilk
2 eggs, separated
1 tbsp. melted margarine
1 1/2 c. flour
1 tsp. soda
1/2 tsp. salt
1 tbsp. sugar

Blend . . . . buttermilk, egg yolks and margarine in bowl.
Sift . . . . . . dry ingredients except sugar slowly into milk mixture, mixing well.
Beat . . . . . egg whites, adding sugar slowly, until stiff.
Fold . . . . . gently into batter.
Spoon . . . by tablespoonfuls onto hot griddle, turning when bubbles appear.

Katie Johnston
Mohave School, Scottsdale, Arizona

SWEDISH PANCAKES

2 c. rolled oats
2 1/8 c. buttermilk
1/2 c. flour
2 tbsp. sugar
1 tsp. baking powder
1 tsp. soda
2 eggs, lightly beaten
1/4 c. butter, melted

Combine . oats and buttermilk in bowl.
Refrigerate covered, overnight.
Sift . . . . . . dry ingredients together.
Stir . . . . . . into oatmeal mixture.
Add . . . . . remaining ingredients, mixing well.
Bake . . . . . on hot griddle using 2 tablespoons batter per pancake.
Yields . . . . 24 pancakes/about 70 calories each.

Mrs. Margaret Sloan
Devon H. S., Devon, Alberta, Canada

JAPANESE PANCAKE

1/4 c. margarine
2 eggs
1/2 c. flour
1/2 c. milk

Melt . . . . . margarine in pie plate.
Combine . remaining ingredients in bowl, mixing well.
Bake . . . . . at 400 degrees for 12 minutes.
Serve . . . . with confectioners' sugar, syrup or jelly.

Rose McCullough
Forrest H. S., Chapel Hill, Tennessee

HAWAIIAN TOAST WITH CUSTARD SAUCE

2 eggs
1/2 c. milk
1 tbsp. honey
1/2 tsp. salt
1/4 tsp. vanilla extract
1 tbsp. butter, softened
6 slices bread
3/4 c. finely crushed corn flakes
6 pineapple slices, drained
2 oranges, peeled, sliced
Custard Sauce

Combine . first 5 ingredients in bowl, beating slightly.
Spread . . . butter over 10 x 15 x 1-inch baking dish.
Dip . . . . . . bread in egg mixture; drain.
Coat . . . . . with crumbs.
Place . . . . in buttered dish.
Bake . . . . . at 400 degrees for 5 minutes; turn.
Bake . . . . . for 5 to 7 minutes or until crisp.
Top . . . . . each slice of toast with pineapple and orange slices and 1/2 cup Custard Sauce.

Custard Sauce

1/3 c. honey
2 tbsp. flour
1/2 tsp. salt
2 c. milk
3 eggs
1 tsp. grated orange rind

Combine . first 3 ingredients in bowl, blending well.

Stir . . . . . . in milk, mixing well.
Cook . . . . over low heat until smooth and thick, stirring constantly.
Beat . . . . . eggs and orange rind in small bowl.
Stir . . . . . . a small amount of hot mixture into eggs.
Add . . . . . eggs to hot mixture, stirring constantly.
Cook . . . . over low heat until thickened, stirring constantly.

Photograph for this recipe above.

BANANA WAFFLES

1 3/4 c. sifted flour
2 tsp. baking powder
1/2 tsp. salt
1 tbsp. sugar
3 eggs, separated
2 to 4 tbsp. oil
1 1/2 c. milk
2 med. bananas, mashed

Sift . . . . . . first 4 ingredients into bowl and make a well in center.
Combine . egg yolks with remaining ingredients in bowl, beating well.
Beat . . . . . egg whites until stiff but not dry.
Pour . . . . . banana mixture into dry ingredients, stirring until just mixed.
Fold . . . . . in egg whites until barely blended.

Bake . . . . . in waffle iron using appliance directions.

Yields . . . . 4 waffles/about 390 calories each.

Lyle Ann Miller
Bear River H. S., Tremonton, Utah

CHOCOLATE WAFFLES

1 c. flour
3/4 c. sugar
1/2 c. cocoa
1/2 tsp. baking powder
1/2 tsp. soda
1/4 tsp. salt
2 eggs
1 c. buttermilk
1/4 c. butter, melted
1 tsp. vanilla extract

Combine . first 6 ingredients in bowl.

Add . . . . . eggs and buttermilk, mixing until just blended.

Add . . . . . butter gradually, beating constantly.

Stir . . . . . . in vanilla.

Bake . . . . . in waffle iron using appliance directions.

Kathy Callahan
East H. S., Cheyenne, Wyoming

A BREAKFAST SANDWICH

1 pkg. yeast
2 1/2 c. sifted flour
1 tbsp. sugar
1/2 tsp. salt
3 tbsp. shortening
1/2 c. lukewarm buttermilk
Butter, melted
1 lb. sausage, sliced

Dissolve . . yeast in 1/4 cup lukewarm water.

Sift . . . . . . dry ingredients together into bowl.

Cut . . . . . . in shortening until crumbly.

Stir . . . . . . in buttermilk and yeast.

Knead . . . lightly on floured board.

Roll . . . . . out 1/4 inch thick and cut with 2-inch biscuit cutter.

Brush · · · · with butter and place, 2 biscuits stacked, on baking sheet.

Let . . . . . . rise until doubled in bulk.

Bake . . . . . at 425 degrees for 10 to 12 minutes.

Fry . . . . . . sausage.

Place . . . . sausage between biscuit halves.

Store . . . . covered, in refrigerator or freezer.

Reheat . . . in microwave or oven.

Betty J. Canter
Western Brown Sr. H. S., Mt. Orah, Ohio

ANGEL BISCUITS

6 c. biscuit mix
1/4 c. sugar
1 pkg. dry yeast
1/3 c. shortening
1 1/4 to 2 c. milk
Margarine, melted

Combine . first 3 ingredients in bowl.

Cut . . . . . . in shortening until crumbly.

Add . . . . . milk, stirring to make soft dough.

Roll . . . . . out on lightly floured surface to 1/2-inch thickness.

Cut . . . . . . with biscuit cutter, placing on baking sheet.

Brush . . . . with margarine.

Bake . . . . . at 425 degrees for 10 to 12 minutes or until golden brown.

Joni Sturm
Muenster Public School, Muenster, Texas

GLADY'S ANGEL BISCUITS

3 c. flour
1 tsp. salt
4 1/2 tsp. baking powder
2 tbsp. sugar
1/2 tsp. lemon peel (opt.)
1/2 c. shortening
1 env. dry yeast
1 c. milk

Sift . . . . . . first 5 ingredients into bowl.

Cut . . . . . . in shortening until crumbly.

Soften . . . yeast in 3 tablespoons warm water.

Combine . yeast and milk and add to flour mixture.

Knead . . . on floured surface until smooth.

Roll . . . . . out 5/8 inch thick; cut with biscuit cutter.

Let . . . . . . rise, on baking sheet, for 20 minutes.

Bake . . . . . at 450 degrees for 10 minutes or until golden.

Brush . . . . tops with melted butter.

Mary Ellen Benedict
Palatka H. S., Palatka, Florida

ENGLISH MUFFINS

1 1/4 c. milk, scalded
3/4 tsp. salt
1 pkg. yeast
4 c. sifted all-purpose flour
3 tbsp. melted shortening

Combine . milk and salt in large bowl; cool to lukewarm.
Dissolve .. yeast in 1/4 cup warm water.
Add ..... to cooled milk.
Add ..... half the flour, beating well.
Stir ...... in shortening, mixing well.
Add ..... remaining flour to make soft dough.
Place .... in greased bowl and brush top of dough with a small amount of water.
Let ...... rise, covered, in warm place until doubled in bulk.
Knead ... gently on lightly floured surface.
Roll ..... out 1/2 inch thick and cut into 3 to 4-inch rounds.
Place .... on board sprinkled with cornmeal.
Let ...... rise, covered, for 45 minutes or until light.
Bake ..... over low heat on slightly greased, moderately hot griddle for about 10 minutes on each side.
Yields .... 12 muffins/about 180 calories each.

Marie Heltzel
Union County H. S., Lake Butler, Florida

ENGLISH MUFFIN BREAD

4 1/4 c. flour
1 c. wheat bran cereal
2 pkg. Fleischmann's Active Dry Yeast
1 tbsp. sugar
2 tsp. salt
1/4 tsp. soda
2 c. milk
Cornmeal

Combine . 2 1/2 cups flour and next 5 ingredients in large bowl.
Heat ..... milk and 1/2 cup water in saucepan to 130 degrees.
Add ..... to dry ingredients, beating well.
Stir ...... in enough remaining flour to make stiff batter.

Sprinkle .. 2 greased 8 x 4 x 2-inch microwave loaf pans with cornmeal.
Spoon ... in batter and sprinkle with additional cornmeal.
Let ...... rise, covered, in warm place for 45 minutes.
Microwave each loaf separately on High for 6 1/2 minutes.
Let ...... rest for 5 minutes.
Slice ..... and toast to serve.

Photograph for this recipe on page 103.

PIZZA

2 1/2 to 3 c. flour
1 1/2 tsp. sugar
3 tsp. salt
1 pkg. dry yeast
2 tbsp. oil
1 8-oz. can tomato sauce
1/2 tsp. each oregano, pepper
1 tbsp. minced onion
1/2 c. Parmesan cheese
1/2 lb. mozzarella cheese

Combine . 1 cup flour, with sugar, 2 teaspoons salt and yeast in bowl, mixing well.
Add ..... oil and 1 cup hot water gradually, beating well.
Beat ..... for 1 minute.
Stir ...... in enough remaining flour to make soft dough.
Knead ... on floured surface until smooth and elastic.
Let ...... rise, covered, for 45 minutes.
Punch .... down and divide into halves.
Prepare ... 2 pizza pans by greasing lightly and sprinkling with cornmeal.
Press ..... dough into pans.
Combine . remaining ingredients except cheeses in bowl, mixing well.
Spread ... over crusts evenly.
Top ..... with cheeses.
Bake ..... at 425 degrees for 20 to 25 minutes.

Ann S. Casper
Viewmont H. S., Bountiful, Utah

POTATO DOUGHNUTS

1/2 c. shortening
2 c. milk, scalded

1 1/2 pkg. yeast
3 eggs, beaten
1 c. sugar
1 1/2 tsp. salt
1 c. freshly mashed potatoes
1/2 tsp. cinnamon
1/2 tsp. lemon extract
8 c. flour
Oil for deep frying
3/4 c. sifted confectioners' sugar
1/2 tsp. vanilla extract

Add ..... shortening to milk, stirring until melted; set aside to cool.
Dissolve .. yeast in 1/4 cup warm water.
Beat ..... eggs in bowl until frothy.
Beat ..... in sugar and salt gradually.
Stir ...... in next 3 ingredients, milk mixture and yeast, mixing well.
Add ..... flour, 1 cup at a time, to make soft dough.
Knead ... on lightly floured surface until smooth and elastic.
Place .... in greased bowl, turning to grease surface.
Let ...... rise, covered, until doubled in bulk.
Roll ..... out 1/2 inch thick; cut with floured doughnut cutter and place on greased cookie sheet.
Let ...... rise, covered with moist cloth, until doubled in bulk.
Deep .... fry at 350 degrees.
Combine . remaining ingredients with 3 to 4 teaspoons water in small bowl, blending until smooth.
Drizzle ... over doughnuts.

Rita Stacks
Independence H. S., Independence, Missouri

ALICE'S RICH BATTER BREAD

1 pkg. yeast
1/8 tsp. ginger
3 tbsp. sugar
1 13-oz. can evaporated milk
2 tbsp. oil
1 tsp. salt
4 to 4 1/2 c. flour

Dissolve .. yeast in 1/2 cup warm water in bowl.

Blend .... in ginger and 1 tablespoon sugar.
Let ...... stand for 15 minutes.
Stir ...... in milk, oil, salt and remaining 2 tablespoons sugar.
Beat ..... in 3 cups flour, 1 cup at a time, with electric mixer at low speed.
Stir ...... in enough remaining flour to make heavy, sticky dough.
Place .... in greased 2-pound coffee can.
Let ...... rise, covered, until doubled in bulk or until above top of can.
Bake ..... at 350 degrees for 60 minutes.
Brush .... with butter.
Cool ..... 5 to 10 minutes on rack before removing bread.

Patricia Sperry
Kecoughtan H. S., Hampton, Virginia

BULGAR-HONEY BREAD

1 c. dry bulgar wheat
1/2 c. honey
2 tbsp. oil
1 tbsp. salt
2 pkg. dry yeast
7 1/2 to 8 c. flour

Combine . first 4 ingredients and 3 cups boiling water in large bowl; cool to lukewarm.
Dissolve .. yeast in 1/2 cup warm water.
Add ..... to cooled bulgar mixture, mixing well.
Add ..... flour by thirds, beating well after each addition.
Knead ... on lightly floured surface for 5 minutes or until smooth and elastic.
Place .... in greased bowl, turning to grease surface.
Let ...... rise, covered, in warm place for 2 hours or until doubled in bulk.
Punch .... dough down and shape into 2 loaves.
Place .... in greased 9 x 5-inch loaf pan.
Let ...... rise, covered, for 1 hour or until doubled in bulk.
Bake ..... at 350 degrees for 45 to 50 minutes.
Brush .... with butter.

Virginia E. Grafe
Bertrand Community School, Bertrand, Nebraska

BEST WHEAT BREAD

2 tbsp. yeast
8 c. flour
4 c. whole wheat flour
2 tbsp. salt
2/3 c. oil
2/3 c. honey

Dissolve .. yeast in 1/2 cup warm water.
Combine . 5 cups hot water, 4 cups flour, whole wheat flour and salt in large mixer bowl, mixing until smooth.
Add ..... yeast, remaining 4 cups flour, oil and honey.
Mix ..... for 10 minutes, adding enough flour to make soft dough.
Place .... on oiled surface.
Shape .... into 4 loaves.
Place .... in greased loaf pans.
Let ...... rise 1 to 2 inches above pan.
Heat ..... oven to 400 degrees; reduce heat.
Bake ..... at 350 degrees for 30 minutes.

Carol Winter
Millcreek Jr. H. S., Bountiful, Utah

BOHEMIAN NUT SLICES

1 pkg. dry yeast
Sugar
2 c. flour
1/2 tsp. salt
3/4 c. butter
2 eggs, separated
1 tsp. vanilla extract
1/2 c. chopped nuts

Sprinkle .. yeast over 1/4 cup warm water.
Add ..... 1 teaspoon sugar and let stand until dissolved.
Sift ...... flour and salt together in bowl.
Cut ...... in butter until crumbly.
Combine . egg yolks and yeast.
Stir ...... into flour mixture.
Mix ..... until dough forms smooth ball.
Beat ..... egg whites in bowl until soft peaks form.
Beat ..... in 1/2 cup sugar gradually until stiff and glossy.
Fold ..... in vanilla and nuts.
Divide ... dough in half.
Roll ..... out each half on lightly floured surface to 9 x 13 inches.

Spread ... each rectangle with half the egg white mixture.
Roll ..... as for jelly roll.
Place .... on greased baking sheet.
Make .... 1/2-inch deep slit down center of each roll.
Bake ..... at 375 degrees for 22 minutes.
Sprinkle .. with confectioners' sugar while warm.
Slice ..... diagonally.

Ethel M. Spahn
Bell Jr. H. S., San Diego, California

ST. TIMOTHY'S BREAD

1 pkg. dry yeast
2 c. milk
1/2 c. oil
1/2 c. honey
2 tsp. salt
1/4 c. wheat germ
2 1/2 c. whole wheat flour
4 c. all-purpose flour

Dissolve .. yeast in 1/4 cup warm water, letting stand for 5 minutes.
Add ..... next 5 ingredients, mixing well.
Stir ...... in flours gradually until blended.
Let ...... stand, covered, in cool place for 8 to 14 hours. Do not refrigerate.
Sprinkle .. top with flour and stir dough down.
Knead ... on floured surface for 5 to 10 minutes or until smooth and elastic.
Shape .... into 2 loaves and place in greased loaf pans.
Let ...... rise for 1 to 2 hours or until doubled in bulk.
Bake ..... at 350 degrees for 30 to 40 minutes.

Karen J. Barker
Monterey H. S., Monterey, California

COFFEE CAN BREAD

1 1/4 c. whole wheat flour
1 pkg. dry yeast
1/2 c. oil
1/2 c. sugar
1/2 c. milk
1 tsp. salt
2 eggs
2 c. all-purpose flour

Combine . whole wheat flour and yeast in saucepan.

Add . . . . . 1/2 cup water and next 4 ingredients.

Warm . . . . slightly over low heat, mixing well.

Beat . . . . . in eggs.

Add . . . . . all-purpose flour, mixing well. Batter will be lumpy.

Grease . . . 2 one-pound coffee cans, placing half of batter in each.

Let rise . . . covered with plastic lids in warm place to 1 inch from top of can.

Bake . . . . . uncovered at 375 degrees for 35 to 40 minutes.

Jeannette H. Mercer
Dublin H. S., Dublin, Georgia

POTATO-CHEESE LOAF

1 1/4 c. milk
1 1/4 c. shredded Cheddar cheese
1 tsp. salt
1 tbsp. sugar
1 tbsp. butter
1/2 c. Idaho instant mashed potato flakes
1 pkg. dry yeast
1 egg
2 1/2 to 3 c. flour

Combine . milk, cheese, salt, sugar and butter in saucepan.

Heat . . . . . until cheese is melted, stirring frequently.

Stir . . . . . . in potato flakes.

Cool . . . . . to lukewarm.

Dissolve . . yeast in 1/4 cup warm water in large bowl.

Beat . . . . . in cheese mixture and egg until smooth.

Add . . . . . enough flour to make soft, sticky dough.

Turn . . . . . onto floured surface.

Knead . . . until smooth and elastic, adding flour as necessary to keep dough from sticking to board.

Shape . . . into ball; place in greased bowl, turning to grease surface.

Let . . . . . . rise, covered, in warm place until doubled in bulk.

Punch . . . . dough down; turn onto floured surface.

Knead . . . for a few minutes.

Shape . . . . into loaf.

Place . . . . in greased 9 x 15-inch loaf pan.

Let . . . . . . rise, covered, until doubled in bulk.

Bake . . . . . at 375 degrees for 35 to 40 minutes or until brown.

Photograph for this recipe below.

HIGH PROTEIN BREAD

1 pkg. yeast
2 tbsp. honey
6 c. unbleached flour
1/2 c. soy flour
3/4 c. dry skim milk powder
3 tbsp. wheat germ
2 tsp. salt
2 tbsp. melted butter

Dissolve .. yeast and honey in 3 cups luke-warm water in large bowl.
Let stand . for 5 minutes.
Sift ...... next 3 ingredients together in bowl.
Stir ...... in wheat germ.
Add ..... salt and half the dry ingredients to yeast, beating well until elastic.
Add ..... butter and enough remaining flour to make soft dough.
Knead ... on floured surface until smooth and elastic.
Place .... in greased plastic bag.
Chill ..... overnight.
Punch .... dough down and shape into 2 large or 3 small loaves.
Place .... in greased loaf pans.
Let ...... rise until doubled in bulk.
Bake ..... at 350 degrees for 50 to 60 min-utes, covering with foil if bread browns too quickly.

Jan Fairbanks
Mission San Jose H. S., Fremont, California

SOURDOUGH YOGURT BREAD

2 tbsp. yeast
2 tbsp. sugar
1 1/2 tsp. salt
1 tbsp. shortening
1 1/2 c. plain yogurt
5 to 7 c. flour

Dissolve .. yeast and sugar in 1/2 cup warm water in large bowl.
Mix ..... next 3 ingredients in bowl.
Add ..... to yeast mixture.
Add ..... enough flour gradually to make stiff dough.
Knead ... on lightly floured surface until smooth and elastic.
Place .... dough in greased bowl, turning to grease surface.

Let ...... rise, covered, in warm place until doubled in bulk.
Punch .... dough down and shape into loaves.
Place .... in greased loaf pans, greasing tops of loaves.
Let ...... rise until doubled in bulk.
Bake ..... at 375 degrees for 30 to 40 minutes.
Brush .... tops with butter.

Becky Low
Nevada Girls Training Center, Caliente, Nevada

WHEAT GERM-YOGURT BREAD

3 1/2 c. whole wheat flour
3/4 c. skim milk powder
5 tbsp. salt
2 pkg. dry yeast
1 c. plain yogurt
1/4 c. each honey, molasses
2 tbsp. oil
3 1/2 to 4 c. flour
1 c. each wheat germ, bran
1 egg, beaten

Combine . first 4 ingredients in large bowl, mixing well.
Heat ..... 2 3/4 cups water, yogurt, honey and molasses in saucepan to 115 degrees on thermometer.
Add ..... to dry ingredients, beating well.
Add ..... oil and 2 cups flour, beating well.
Stir ...... in wheat germ and bran.
Add ..... enough remaining flour to make soft dough.
Knead ... on floured surface for 4 to 5 min-utes or until smooth and elastic.
Place .... in greased bowl, turning to grease surface.
Let ...... rise, covered, in warm place until doubled in bulk.
Punch .... dough down.
Divide ... into 12 equal parts.
Shape .... dough into 12-inch ropes.
Braid .... 3 ropes together to make 4 loaves.
Place .... in greased pans.
Let ...... rise, covered, until doubled in bulk.
Brush .... with egg and sprinkle with wheat germ.
Bake ..... at 350 degrees for 25 to 35 minutes.

Elsie Klassen
Georges P. Vanier School, Donnelly, Alberta, Canada

BUTTERHORNS

1 pkg. dry yeast
1/2 c. milk, scalded
1/3 c. sugar
1/2 c. butter
3/4 tsp. salt
1 egg
4 c. sifted flour

Dissolve .. yeast in 1/2 cup warm water.
Combine . next 4 ingredients in bowl; cool to lukewarm.
Add ..... yeast, egg and half the flour, beating well.
Add ..... enough remaining flour to make soft dough.
Knead ... lightly on floured surface.
Place .... in greased bowl, turning to grease surface.
Let ...... rise, covered, in warm place for 1 hour or until doubled in bulk.
Divide ... into halves.
Roll ..... each portion on floured surface to 12-inch circle.
Cut ...... into 12 wedges and roll up from wide end.
Place .... on greased baking sheets.
Let ...... rise for 30 minutes or until doubled in bulk.
Bake ..... at 400 degrees for 15 minutes.

Fleda Lambert
Duncanville H. S., Duncanville, Texas

CINNAMON ROLLS

2 c. milk, scalded, cooled
1 c. sugar
1 c. flour
2 pkg. yeast
3/4 c. margarine, melted
2 eggs, beaten
4 1/2 c. flour
2 tsp. (scant) salt
Raisins
Butter, softened
Cinnamon
Sugar
Chopped nuts (opt.)

Combine . first 4 ingredients in bowl, mixing well.

Let ...... rise for 1 hour.
Add ..... next 5 ingredients, mixing well.
Let ...... rise, covered, in warm place until doubled in bulk.
Knead ... on floured surface until smooth and elastic.
Roll ..... out on floured surface.
Spread ... with butter.
Sprinkle .. with mixture of cinnamon, sugar and nuts.
Roll ..... as for jelly roll and cut into slices.
Place .... in greased baking pan.
Let ...... rise until doubled in bulk.
Bake ..... at 375 degrees for 10 minutes or until golden brown.
Frost .... while warm.

Ann Iverson
Skyline H. S., Salt Lake City, Utah

COTTAGE CHEESE ROLLS

3 pkg. dry yeast
4 c. sifted flour
6 tbsp. sugar
1 tsp. salt
3/4 c. shortening
12 oz. cottage cheese, mashed
2 eggs, beaten
6 tbsp. butter, melted
1 1/2 c. packed brown sugar
1 c. ground nuts
1 tsp. vanilla extract

Dissolve .. yeast in 1/4 cup warm water.
Sift ...... flour, sugar and 1/2 teaspoon salt together in bowl.
Cut ...... in shortening until crumbly.
Add ..... yeast, cottage cheese and eggs, mixing well.
Roll ..... out on floured surface to 1/4-inch thickness.
Combine . 1/2 teaspoon salt and remaining ingredients in small bowl.
Spread ... over dough.
Roll ..... as for jelly roll and slice.
Place .... in greased baking pan.
Let ...... rise for 2 1/2 hours.
Bake ..... at 400 degrees for 15 to 20 minutes.

Natalie Iverson
Lake Preston H. S., Lake Preston, South Dakota

DOUBLE-QUICK BATTER ROLLS

1 pkg. dry yeast
2 tbsp. sugar
1 tsp. salt
2 1/4 c. sifted flour
1 egg
2 tbsp. soft shortening

Dissolve .. yeast in 1 cup warm water in bowl.
Stir . . . . . . in sugar, salt and half the flour.
Add . . . . . egg and shortening, mixing well.
Beat . . . . . in remaining flour until smooth.
Let . . . . . . rise, covered, for about 30 minutes or until doubled in bulk.
Stir . . . . . . dough down.
Fill . . . . . . greased muffin cups 1/2 full.
Let . . . . . . rise for 20 to 30 minutes or until batter reaches tops of cups.
Bake . . . . . at 375 degrees for 15 to 20 minutes.

Deborah Frizzell
Fordsville Jr. H. S., Fordsville, Kentucky

HOMEMADE YEAST ROLLS

2 c. milk
1/2 c. sugar
1/2 c. shortening
1 to 2 pkg. yeast
4 to 6 c. flour
1 tbsp. salt
1/2 tsp. soda
1/2 tsp. baking powder
Melted margarine

Combine . milk, sugar and shortening in saucepan.
Warm . . . . over low heat until shortening melts; set aside to cool.
Dissolve .. yeast in 1/4 cup warm water in large bowl.
Add . . . . . milk and 2 to 3 cups flour, beating to consistency of cake batter.
Let . . . . . . rise, covered, in warm place for 1 hour or until doubled in bulk.
Stir . . . . . . down and add salt, soda and baking powder, mixing well.
Beat . . . . . in enough additional flour to make stiff dough.
Knead . . . on floured surface.
Shape . . . . into rolls; place in greased pans and brush with margarine.

Let . . . . . . rise until doubled in bulk or refrigerate overnight.
Bake . . . . . at 400 degrees until golden brown.

Camille M. Yates
Lee Academy, Clarksdale, Mississippi

HOT ROLLS

1 c. shortening
3/4 c. sugar
2 pkg. yeast
2 eggs, well beaten
6 c. flour
2 tsp. salt

Cream . . . first 2 ingredients together in bowl.
Add . . . . . 1 cup boiling water and cool.
Dissolve .. yeast in 1 cup warm water.
Add . . . . . to sugar mixture.
Add . . . . . eggs, mixing well.
Sift . . . . . . 3 cups flour and salt together.
Stir . . . . . . into egg mixture, blending well.
Chill . . . . . covered with wet cloth, until ready to use.
Add . . . . . remaining flour and shape as desired.
Place . . . . on buttered baking sheet.
Let . . . . . . rise for 2 hours.
Bake . . . . . at 350 degrees for 20 minutes.

Joyce Mann
Harmony Grove School, Camden, Arkansas

KAREN'S REFRIGERATOR ROLLS

1 pkg. yeast
1/4 c. shortening
1/2 c. sugar
1 tsp. salt
1 egg, beaten
6 c. flour

Dissolve .. yeast in 1/2 cup warm water.
Stir . . . . . . shortening and sugar with 1 1/2 cups boiling water in large bowl; cool to lukewarm.
Add . . . . . salt, yeast, egg and 2 cups flour, mixing well.
Stir . . . . . . in remaining flour to make soft dough.
Place . . . . dough in oiled tightly covered bowl.
Chill . . . . . in refrigerator for 2 hours.
Shape . . . . into rolls, placing in greased pan.
Let . . . . . . rise until doubled in bulk.

Bake . . . . . at 400 to 425 degrees for 30 minutes.

Note . . . . . dough will keep in refrigerator for 1 week.

Yields . . . . 24 rolls/about 160 calories each.

Karen L. Berrier
Pasadena H. S., Pasadena, Texas

ONE-HOUR ROLLS

2 pkg. dry yeast
1 1/2 c. lukewarm buttermilk
1/4 c. sugar
1/2 c. melted shortening
1 tsp. salt
4 1/2 c. sifted flour
1/2 tsp. soda

Dissolve . . yeast in 1/4 cup warm water.

Combine . buttermilk, sugar, shortening and salt in bowl.

Stir . . . . . . in yeast, mixing well.

Sift . . . . . . in flour and soda, mixing well.

Let . . . . . . stand for 10 minutes.

Shape . . . . into rolls.

Let . . . . . . rise for 30 minutes.

Bake . . . . . at 400 degrees for 15 to 20 minutes until brown.

Sharon Wilson
Mexia H. S., Mexia, Texas
Ann L. Champion
Jackson H. S., Jackson, Georgia

OVERNIGHT REFRIGERATOR ROLLS

2 pkg. yeast
8 to 8 1/2 c. flour
3/4 c. oil
3/4 c. sugar
2 1/2 tsp. salt
2 eggs, well beaten

Soften . . . yeast in 2 1/2 cups warm water in mixer bowl.

Add . . . . . 4 cups flour and remaining ingredients.

Beat . . . . . for 1 minute or until smooth.

Stir . . . . . . in remaining flour.

Chill . . . . . covered, overnight.

Punch . . . . dough down.

Shape . . . . into rolls and place in greased 9 x 9 x 2-inch baking pan.

Let . . . . . . rise, covered, for 1 1/2 hours or until doubled in bulk.

Bake . . . . . at 400 degrees for 10 to 12 minutes.

Diane Sutton
Amity H. S., Amity, Arkansas

QUICK ROLLS

2 c. flour
1 tsp. baking powder
2 tbsp. sugar
1/2 tsp. salt
1/4 tsp. soda
1/3 c. shortening
1 pkg. yeast
3/4 c. buttermilk
Melted butter

Sift . . . . . . dry ingredients together into bowl.

Cut . . . . . . in shortening until crumbly.

Dissolve . . yeast in 1/4 cup warm water.

Add . . . . . buttermilk.

Stir . . . . . . into dry ingredients, mixing well.

Knead . . . lightly on floured surface.

Roll . . . . . to 1/4-inch thickness and cut with biscuit cutter.

Dip . . . . . . in butter.

Fold . . . . . in half and place on greased cookie sheet.

Let . . . . . . rise for 1 hour.

Bake . . . . . at 425 degrees for 12 minutes.

Rebecca Drone
Page H. S., Franklin, Tennessee

SPOON ROLLS

1 pkg. dry yeast
4 c. self-rising flour
4 tsp. sugar
4 tbsp. dried milk
1 egg, beaten
3/4 to 1 c. oil

Dissolve . . yeast in 2 cups warm water in large bowl.

Add . . . . . remaining ingredients, beating well.

Chill . . . . . covered, until ready to use, up to 10 days.

Beat . . . . . batter well.

Fill . . . . . . muffin cups 3/4 full.

Bake . . . . . at 400 degrees for 15 to 20 minutes.

Kay Hepler
Pine Tree H. S., Longview, Texas

Desserts

You're now entering the creative world of desserts — captured here for you in these idea-filled pages. But remember, careful planning is the key to real enjoyment!

For a full meal, select a lighter dessert from this section. Save those layered masterpieces for entertaining, or to finish a light meal. That way, you're assured every morsel is appreciated. Here are cakes with surprise fillings . . . delicious fruit desserts . . . flavorful pies and more. But before you turn the page, this is the world where calories don't count.

TRICKS OF THE TRADE

- For beautifully-topped pie crusts, brush with milk and sprinkle with sugar just before placing in the oven.
- When using prepared pie crust mix, use a little less liquid than the package directs. The crust will be more tender.
- Substitute slightly sweetened sour cream for whipped cream as a dessert topping. It has an unusually good flavor and saves calories.
- Cream will whip faster and stiffer if the bowl and beaters have been chilled.
- To make a lacy decoration on a sponge or angel food cake, place a paper doily on the top; sift confectioners' sugar over it; then carefully lift off the doily.
- When making cakes or cookies using extract and/or ground spices, add to the shortening *before* creaming with sugar to enhance the flavors.
- Substitute cereal for nuts in cookies. Unsweetened varieties, such as puffed rice and puffed wheat, are the best choices.

APPLE GOODIE

1 can apples
1 c. sugar
1 tsp. cinnamon
1 c. flour
1/4 tsp. each soda, baking powder
1/2 c. margarine, softened
1 c. oatmeal
1 c. packed brown sugar
1/2 c. chopped pecans

Place .... apples in 9 x 13-inch baking pan.
Top ..... with sugar and cinnamon.
Combine . remaining ingredients in bowl, mixing well.
Spread ... evenly over apples.
Bake ..... at 300 degrees for 40 minutes.

Mariann Bielke
Marion H. S., Marion, Texas

APPLE-NUT PUDDING

2 sticks margarine, softened
3 c. sugar
2 eggs
4 tsp. vanilla extract
Flour
2 tsp. each soda, cinnamon
Salt
4 apples, diced
1 c. chopped nuts
2 tsp. rum flavoring

Cream ... 1 stick margarine, 2 cups sugar, eggs and 2 teaspoons vanilla together in bowl.
Sift ...... 2 cups flour, soda, cinnamon and 1/2 teaspoon salt together.
Add ..... with 1 tablespoon water to creamed mixture.
Beat ..... for 2 minutes.
Add ..... apples and nuts, mixing well.
Pour ..... into greased and floured bundt pan.
Bake ..... at 350 degrees for 1 hour.
Bring .... 1 cup water and remaining 1 stick margarine to a boil in saucepan.
Sift ...... 2 tablespoons flour, 1/8 teaspoon salt and remaining 1 cup sugar together in bowl.
Add ..... to margarine mixture.
Cook .... over low heat until slightly thickened, stirring constantly.

Add ..... remaining 2 teaspoons vanilla and rum flavoring.
Serve .... over cooled cake.

Sister Julie Budai
Providence H. S., San Antonio, Texas

APPLE STRUDEL SQUARES

2 1/2 c. flour
Sugar
1 tsp. salt
1 c. shortening
Milk
2 eggs, separated
1 1/2 c. crushed corn flakes
8 or 10 apples, pared, thinly sliced
1/2 c. white seedless raisins (opt.)
1 tsp. cinnamon

Sift ...... flour, 1 tablespoon sugar and salt together.
Cut ...... in shortening until crumbly.
Add ..... enough milk to beaten egg yolks to measure 2/3 cup.
Stir ...... into flour mixture to make smooth dough.
Roll ..... out half the dough on floured surface to fit jelly roll pan.
Place .... the dough in pan.
Sprinkle .. with corn flake crumbs.
Combine . apples, 1 1/2 cups sugar, raisins and cinnamon in bowl, mixing well.
Arrange .. over corn flakes.
Cover .... with remaining dough, pinching to seal edges.
Brush .... with beaten egg whites.
Bake ..... at 400 degrees for 10 minutes; reduce heat.
Bake ..... at 350 degrees for 45 minutes.
Ice ...... with confectioners' sugar frosting while hot and garnish with chopped nuts.

Diane L. Stelten-Dane
Blair Public Schools, Blair, Wisconsin

BANANA SPLIT CAKE

2 c. graham cracker crumbs
2 sticks margarine, softened
2 1/2 c. confectioners' sugar
2 egg whites

1 lg. can crushed pineapple, drained well
3 lg. bananas, sliced lengthwise
1 lg. carton Cool Whip
Chopped nuts
Chopped cherries

Combine . graham cracker crumbs, 1 stick melted margarine and 1/2 cup confectioners' sugar in bowl.
Press . . . . . into bottom of 9 x 13-inch pan.
Beat . . . . . egg whites, remaining 2 cups confectioners' sugar and remaining stick of softened margarine in mixing bowl on high speed for 10 minutes.
Pour . . . . . over crumb crust.
Spoon . . . pineapple over cream layer.
Arrange . . bananas on top.
Spread . . . Cool Whip over bananas.
Sprinkle . . with nuts and cherries.
Chill . . . . . for 15 minutes.

Zane Townsend
Pelahatchie H. S., Pelahatchie, Mississippi

BANANA SPLIT DESSERT

Margarine, softened
2 c. graham cracker crumbs
3 eggs
3 c. confectioners' sugar
1 1/2 tsp. vanilla extract
5 or 6 bananas, sliced lengthwise
1 8-oz. can crushed pineapple, drained
9 oz. Cool Whip

Combine . 6 tablespoons melted margarine with crumbs in bowl, mixing well.
Spread . . . in 9 x 13-inch baking pan.
Bake . . . . . at 350 degrees for 10 minutes and set aside to cool.
Combine . next 3 ingredients with 1 1/2 sticks margarine in bowl, beating until fluffy.
Spread . . . over cooled crust.
Layer . . . . remaining ingredients in order given over egg mixture.
Garnish . . with chopped nuts and maraschino cherries.
Chill . . . . . for 3 hours or longer.

Margaret Landers
Bradford H. S., Bradford, Ohio

DUTCH PEACH KUCHEN

1/2 c. butter, softened
1 c. sugar
1 1/2 c. sifted all-purpose flour
1 tsp. cinnamon
1/2 tsp. each baking powder, salt
1/4 tsp. nutmeg
3 c. sliced fresh peaches
1/4 c. raisins, chopped

Cream . . . butter and sugar together in small mixing bowl.
Sift . . . . . . dry ingredients together.
Add . . . . . to creamed mixture gradually.
Press . . . . . into 8-inch baking pan to cover bottom and 1/2 inch of sides, reserving 1 cup.
Combine . half the reserved crumb mixture with peaches.
Spoon . . . into crust.
Mix . . . . . raisins and remaining mixture.
Sprinkle . . over peaches.
Bake . . . . . in preheated 375-degree oven for 40 to 45 minutes.

Photograph for this recipe below.

BLUEBERRY CRUNCH

1 c. self-rising flour
1/4 c. packed brown sugar
1 stick butter, softened
1/2 c. chopped pecans
1 3-oz. package cream cheese, softened
1 sm. carton Cool Whip
1 3/4 c. sugar
1 tsp. vanilla extract
2 cans blueberry pie filling

Combine . first 4 ingredients in bowl, mixing well.
Spread ... evenly in 9 x 13-inch baking pan.
Bake ..... at 350 degrees until firm.
Beat ..... cream cheese, Cool Whip, 3/4 cup sugar and vanilla together in bowl until smooth.
Pour ..... over cooled crust.
Combine . remaining 1 cup sugar with pie filling in bowl, mixing well.
Pour ..... over creamed mixture.
Chill ..... in refrigerator.

Deborah E. Foust
Southeast H. S., Greensboro, North Carolina

CARAMEL GLAZE

1 c. sugar
1/2 c. buttermilk
1/2 tsp. soda
1 tsp. corn syrup
1/2 c. margarine
1/2 tsp. vanilla extract

Combine . all ingredients in saucepan.
Boil ..... for 10 minutes, stirring frequently.
Serve .... warm over ice cream or cake.

Becki Scott
Wheeler H. S., Wheeler, Mississippi

QUICK CHERRY COBBLER

1 stick margarine
1 1-lb. can unsweetened cherries
1 c. flour
1 c. sugar
1 tsp. baking powder
3/4 c. milk

Melt ..... margarine in 8 x 12-inch baking dish.
Spoon ... in cherries.

Combine . remaining ingredients in bowl, stirring until smooth.
Pour ..... over cherries.
Bake ..... at 350 degrees for 30 to 40 minutes.
Serve .... warm with ice cream.

Mildred M. Mason
Fort Morgan H. S., Fort Morgan, Colorado

MICROWAVE CHERRY CRUNCH

1 can cherry pie filling
1 can crushed pineapple
1 1-layer yellow cake mix
1/2 to 3/4 c. chopped pecans
1/2 c. melted butter

Mix ..... pie filling and pineapple in square glass microwave cake pan.
Sprinkle .. cake mix evenly over top.
Sprinkle .. with pecans.
Drizzle ... butter over pecans.
Microwave on High for 15 minutes, turning at least once.

Lynne Winborn
Springfield H. S., Springfield, Louisiana

CHOCOLATE MOUSSE

2 sq. semisweet chocolate
2 tbsp. strong coffee
3 tsp. sugar
4 egg yolks
5 egg whites, stiffly beaten

Melt ..... chocolate in coffee in small saucepan.
Blend .... in sugar.
Stir ...... in egg yolks, one at a time, beating well after each addition.
Place .... chocolate mixture in serving bowl.
Fold ..... in beaten egg whites.
Chill ..... thoroughly.

N. M. Juk
Kosciuszko Middle School, St. Clair Shores, Michigan

HEAVENLY CHOCOLATE PUDDING DESSERT

1 stick butter, melted
1 c. flour
1 c. chopped nuts
1 c. confectioners' sugar
1 8-oz. package cream cheese, softened
9 oz. Cool Whip

2 c. milk
1 3 1/2-oz. package instant chocolate
    pudding mix
1 3 1/2-oz. package instant vanilla pudding mix
Crushed Heath bars

Combine . first 3 ingredients in bowl, mixing
well.
Press . . . . . into 9 x 13-inch pan.
Bake . . . . . at 350 degrees for 20 minutes.
Cream . . . confectioners' sugar and cream
cheese together in bowl.
Fold . . . . . in half the Cool Whip.
Spread . . . over cooled crust.
Beat . . . . . milk and pudding mixes together in
bowl until thick.
Spread . . . over cheese layer.
Top . . . . . with remaining Cool Whip.
Sprinkle . . Heath bars on top.
Chill . . . . . until serving time.

Imogene Halcomb
Williamsburg City School, Williamsburg, Kentucky
Elaine Young
Pasadena H. S., Pasadena, Texas
Beth Hale
Tom Bean H. S., Tom Bean, Texas

CLOUD OF CHOCOLATE

1 env. unflavored gelatin
2 squares unsweetened chocolate, melted
1/2 c. confectioners' sugar
1 c. milk, heated
3/4 c. sugar

1/4 tsp. salt
1 tsp. vanilla extract
2 c. heavy cream, whipped
1/2 c. finely chopped pecans
1/2 c. flaked coconut

Soften . . . gelatin in 1/4 cup cold water.
Combine . chocolate and confectioners' sugar
in saucepan.
Stir . . . . . . in milk gradually.
Heat . . . . . to boiling point over low heat, stir-
ring constantly. Do not boil.
Remove . . from heat.
Add . . . . . gelatin, stirring until dissolved.
Stir . . . . . . in sugar, salt and vanilla.
Chill . . . . . until thick.
Beat . . . . . until light and fluffy.
Fold . . . . . in remaining ingredients.
Pour . . . . . into 2-quart serving bowl.
Chill . . . . . for 2 to 3 hours.
Garnish . . with whipped cream and chopped
pecans.

Photograph for this recipe on this page.

BLUE RIBBON CREAMY CHEESECAKE

12 to 14 graham crackers, crushed
1/2 c. butter, melted
4 3-oz. packages cream cheese, softened
2 eggs, beaten
Sugar
3 tsp. vanilla extract
1/2 tsp. lemon juice
1 c. sour cream

Combine . graham cracker crumbs and butter,
mixing well.
Press . . . . . into pie pan to form crust.
Combine . cream cheese, eggs, 3/4 cup sugar, 2
teaspoons vanilla and lemon juice in
bowl, mixing well.
Pour . . . . . into prepared crust.
Bake . . . . . at 350 degrees for 15 to 20
minutes.
Cool . . . . . for 10 minutes.
Mix . . . . . sour cream, 3 1/2 tablespoons sugar
and 1 teaspoon vanilla in bowl.
Spread . . . evenly over top.
Bake . . . . . for 10 minutes longer.
Chill . . . . . for 5 hours.

Judy Ann Marlin
Evergreen Jr. H. S., Salt Lake City, Utah

BEST-EVER DATE PUDDING

1 c. sugar
1 c. flour
1 tsp. baking powder
1/8 tsp. salt
3/4 c. milk
1 c. diced dates
1 c. chopped nuts
1 c. packed brown sugar
1 tbsp. butter

Combine . first 7 ingredients in bowl, mixing well.
Pour . . . . . into buttered 8-inch square baking pan.
Combine . brown sugar, butter and 2 cups boiling water.
Pour . . . . . over date mixture.
Bake . . . . . at 325 degrees for 30 minutes.

Cynthia Singley
West Fork Schools, West Fork, Arkansas

LEMON CAKE-TOP PUDDING

3 tbsp. flour
3/4 c. sugar
2 tbsp. margarine, softened
2 egg yolks, beaten
1 c. milk
1/3 c. lemon juice
2 egg whites, stiffly beaten

Cream . . . flour, sugar and margarine together in bowl.
Add . . . . . egg yolks, milk and lemon juice, mixing well.
Fold . . . . . in egg whites.
Pour . . . . . into 8-inch baking dish.
Place . . . . in large pan of hot water.
Bake . . . . . at 375 degrees for 40 minutes.
Yields . . . . 4 servings/about 200 calories each.

Marilyn Gornto
Perry Jr. H. S., Perry, Georgia

STRAWBERRY TRIFLE

1 lg. angel food cake, thinly sliced
1 lg. package strawberry Jell-O
2 10-oz. packages frozen strawberries
1 lg. box instant vanilla pudding mix
1 lg. carton Cool Whip

Cut . . . . . . cake slices into 3 pieces each; set aside.

Dissolve . . Jell-O in 2 cups boiling water in large bowl.
Add . . . . . frozen strawberries, stirring to mix.
Set . . . . . . aside to cool slightly.
Prepare . . . pudding using package directions.
Arrange . . layers of cake slices, Jell-O mixture, pudding and Cool Whip in order given in large punch bowl.
Repeat . . . until all ingredients are used.
Chill . . . . . for several hours or overnight.

Patsy S. Coble
Arab H. S., Arab, Alabama

STRAWBERRY SHORTCAKE BOWL

2 pt. fresh California strawberries, sliced
Sugar
1 1/2 tsp. ground cinnamon
1 pkg. refrigerated flaky biscuits
1/4 c. butter, melted
1/2 c. chopped pecans
1 pt. vanilla ice cream

Combine . strawberries and sugar to taste in bowl, mixing well.
Chill . . . . . for 30 minutes.
Combine . cinnamon with 1/4 cup sugar in small bowl; set aside.
Separate . . each biscuit into 2 thinner biscuits by pulling layers apart.
Brush . . . . both sides with butter.
Dip . . . . . . in sugar mixture.
Place . . . . 1 inch apart on buttered baking sheet.
Press . . . . . pecans into tops of biscuits.
Bake . . . . at 400 degrees for 10 to 12 minutes.
Line . . . . . large serving bowl with several biscuits.
Spoon . . . half the strawberries over biscuits.
Spoon . . . in ice cream and remaining strawberries.
Top . . . . . with remaining biscuits.

Photograph for this recipe on page 120.

FRUITSICLES

1 ripe banana, mashed
1/2 10-oz. package frozen strawberries, thawed
1 c. crushed pineapple
1/3 c. evaporated milk

Combine . banana and strawberries in bowl, mixing well.
Add ..... pineapple, beating well.
Add ..... milk, beating well.
Pour ..... into four 5-ounce paper cups.
Insert .... small plastic spoons, handle up, in each cup.
Freeze ... until firm.
Peel ..... off paper cup to serve.
Yields .... 4 servings/about 165 calories each.

Maureen Marconi
Westminster H. S., Westminster, California

FROZEN CHERRY DESSERT

1 lg. carton Cool Whip
1 lg. can crushed pineapple, well drained
1 can sweetened condensed milk
1 lg. can cherry pie filling
1/2 c. chopped pecans (opt.)

Combine . all ingredients in large bowl, mixing well.
Pour ..... into large pan.
Freeze ... until firm.

Mary Cain
Thrall H. S., Thrall, Texas

YOGURT AMBROSIA

2 lg. ripe bananas, sliced
1 red Delicious apple, diced
1 pear, peeled, diced

Lemon juice
2 navel oranges, sectioned
1 1/3 c. flaked coconut
1 c. pineapple yogurt

Dip ...... bananas, apple and pear in lemon juice; drain.
Combine . with orange sections in glass bowl.
Chill ..... for 1 hour.
Fold ..... in coconut and yogurt.

Photograph for this recipe on this page.

OREO DESSERT

46 Oreo cookies, crushed
1/2 c. butter, softened
1/2 gal. ice cream
1 8-oz. carton Cool Whip
1 sm. can chocolate syrup
1/2 c. chopped pecans

Combine . cookie crumbs and butter in bowl, mixing well.
Press ..... into 9 x 14-inch pan.
Slice ..... ice cream and press over cookie mixture.
Spread ... with Cool Whip.
Drizzle ... with chocolate syrup and top with pecans.
Freeze ... until firm.

Eveline C. Kennedy
Elmore City H. S., Elmore City, Oklahoma

SUSAN'S CHOCOLATE DELIGHT

1 pkg. chocolate chip Snackin Cake mix
1/2 gal. chocolate ice cream, softened
1 c. peanut butter
Pecans, chopped
Chocolate syrup

Prepare ... cake mix using package directions.
Crumble .. cake and set aside.
Blend .... ice cream and peanut butter in bowl until smooth.
Stir ...... in cake and 1 cup pecans.
Pour ..... into 9 x 13-inch pan.
Freeze ... covered, until firm.
Remove .. from freezer 10 minutes before serving.
Cut ...... into squares.
Drizzle ... with chocolate syrup and top with additional pecans.

Susan Walton
Woodford County H. S., Versailles, Kentucky

CHOCOLATE MOUSSE CAKE

1 pkg. chocolate sandwich cookies with fudge
filling, finely crushed
1 c. sugar
1 12-oz. package semisweet chocolate chips
1 tsp. instant coffee
4 eggs, separated
3 c. heavy cream, whipped

Press . . . . . cookie crumbs over bottom and side of greased 9-inch spring form pan.
Bake . . . . . at 325 degrees for 10 minutes.
Combine . 1/2 cup sugar, 1/2 cup water, chocolate chips and coffee in top of double boiler.
Cook . . . . until chocolate melts, stirring to blend thoroughly.
Stir . . . . . . a small amount of hot mixture into beaten egg yolks.
Add . . . . . egg yolks to hot mixture, mixing well; set aside to cool.
Beat . . . . . egg whites until soft peaks form.
Add . . . . . remaining 1/2 cup sugar gradually, beating until stiff.
Fold . . . . . gently into whipped cream.
Fold . . . . . egg white mixture into chocolate mixture.
Pour . . . . . into cooled chocolate crust.
Freeze . . . covered, at least overnight.
Thaw . . . . in refrigerator for 8 hours before serving.

Judy Touby
Scottsdale H. S., Scottsdale, Arizona

Cook . . . . over low heat, stirring constantly, until thick.
Blend . . . . in peanut butter, beating until smooth.
Stir . . . . . . in rice.
Chill . . . . . until partially set.
Fold . . . . . in nuts and 2/3 of the whipped cream.
Spoon . . . into wafer cups.
Chill . . . . . until set.
Garnish . . with remaining whipped cream and additional nuts.

Photograph for this recipe above.

CHOCO-NUT RICE CONES

1 3 1/4-oz. package chocolate pudding mix
1 env. unflavored gelatin
1/4 c. sugar
1 1/2 c. milk
1/2 c. peanut butter
1 1/2 c. cooked rice
1 c. chopped nuts
1/2 pt. heavy cream, whipped
8 wafer ice cream cups

Combine . first 3 ingredients in saucepan, mixing well.
Blend . . . . in milk.

FROSTY STRAWBERRY SQUARES

1 c. flour
1/4 c. packed brown sugar
1/4 c. chopped nuts
1/2 c. margarine, melted
2 egg whites
2/3 c. sugar
1 10-oz. package frozen strawberries,
partially thawed
2 tbsp. lemon juice
1 c. whipped cream

Combine . first 4 ingredients in bowl, mixing well.
Spread . . . in 9 x 13-inch baking pan.

Bake . . . . . at 350 degrees for 20 minutes, stirring to crumble.

Combine . egg whites, sugar, strawberries and lemon juice in large mixing bowl.

Beat . . . . . with electric mixer at high speed for 15 minutes.

Fold . . . . . in whipped cream.

Place . . . . 2/3 of the crumbs in bottom of large pan.

Pour . . . . . in strawberry mixture.

Top . . . . . with remaining crumbs.

Freeze . . . until firm.

Barbara Elliott
Liberty Union H. S., Baltimore, Ohio

BASIC ICE CREAM

2 qt. milk
1 c. flour
1/2 tsp. salt
3 c. sugar
10 egg yolks, well beaten
3 lg. cans evaporated milk
3 tbsp. vanilla extract
1 tsp. lemon extract

Combine . 1 quart milk and next 3 ingredients in double boiler.

Cook . . . . until thick, stirring constantly.

Stir . . . . . . a small amount of hot mixture into egg yolks.

Add . . . . . hot mixture to egg yolks gradually, beating constantly.

Chill . . . . . in refrigerator until cool.

Pour . . . . . into 6-quart ice cream freezer container.

Add . . . . . remaining 1 quart milk, evaporated milk, vanilla and lemon.

Freeze . . . using freezer directions.

Note . . . . . Dissolve 2 cups caramelized sugar or 12 ounces semisweet chocolate chips in sugar mixture before adding eggs to vary flavor.

Florence H. Wendel
Spanish Fork Jr. H. S., Spanish Fork, Utah

HOMEMADE CHOCOLATE ICE CREAM

3 eggs, beaten
2 cans evaporated milk
3 c. sugar
3 c. heavy cream
1 can chocolate syrup
1 lg. package instant chocolate pudding mix
Milk
Dash of salt
2 tbsp. vanilla extract
1/2 to 1 c. chopped pecans (opt.)

Combine . first 3 ingredients in large bowl, mixing well.

Add . . . . . cream and chocolate syrup.

Combine . pudding mix with 2 to 3 cups milk in bowl.

Add . . . . . to cream mixture.

Pour . . . . . into 1 1/2-gallon ice cream freezer container.

Add . . . . . salt, vanilla and pecans.

Add . . . . . milk to within 4 inches of top of container.

Freeze . . . using freezer directions.

Remove . . dasher, repacking with additional ice and salt.

Let . . . . . . stand to harden until serving time.

Sue Pew
Chandler H. S., Chandler, Arizona

STRAW-BA-NUT ICE CREAM

2 c. sugar
6 eggs, beaten
1 can sweetened condensed milk
1/2 tsp. vanilla extract
1 pt. fresh strawberries
2 bananas, mashed
1 c. chopped pecans
1 8-oz. carton frozen whipped topping, thawed
Red food coloring

Beat . . . . . sugar with eggs in large bowl until thick.

Add . . . . . remaining ingredients, mixing well.

Pour . . . . . into electric ice cream freezer container.

Freeze . . . using freezer directions.

Remove . . dasher, covering top with foil.

Let . . . . . . stand for 1 to 3 hours in ice and salt to harden.

Peggy O. Munter
Moore Sr. H. S., Moore, Oklahoma

RAISIN ROCKY ROAD REFRIGERATOR CAKE

1 1-lb. package fudge brownie mix
3/4 c. California seedless raisins, coarsely
*   chopped*
1 tsp. instant coffee powder
1 1/2 tsp. rum extract
1 c. whipping cream
2 tbsp. cocoa
1/3 tsp. salt
3 tbsp. sugar
1/4 c. chopped walnuts
8 to 10 marshmallows, chopped

Prepare . . . brownie batter using package directions.
Stir . . . . . . in 1/2 cup raisins, coffee powder and 1 teaspoon rum flavoring.
Pour . . . . . into greased 9-inch square pan.
Bake . . . . . using package directions. Do not overbake.
Cool . . . . . completely and cut into three 3 x 9-inch strips.

Beat . . . . . whipping cream until soft peaks form.
Add . . . . . cocoa, salt and sugar, beating until stiff.
Fold . . . . . in walnuts, marshmallows and remaining 1/4 cup raisins and 1/2 teaspoon flavoring.
Spread . . . between layers and over top.
Chill . . . . . for 4 to 5 hours or overnight.
Yields . . . . 8 servings/about 545 calories each.

Photograph for this recipe above.

ICE CREAM CAKE ROLL

3/4 c. flour
1/4 c. cocoa
1 tsp. baking powder
1/4 tsp. salt
3 eggs
1 c. sugar
1 tsp. vanilla extract
Confectioners' sugar
1 pt. peppermint ice cream

Combine . first 4 ingredients; set aside.

Beat . . . . . eggs in bowl until very thick and lemon colored.

Add . . . . . sugar gradually, beating constantly.

Beat . . . . . in 1/3 cup water and vanilla.

Add . . . . . flour mixture gradually, beating until smooth.

Pour . . . . . into jelly roll pan lined with waxed paper, spreading batter into corners.

Bake . . . . . at 375 degrees for 12 to 15 minutes.

Invert . . . . onto towel sprinkled with confectioners' sugar.

Roll . . . . . hot cake and towel from narrow end.

Cool . . . . . on wire rack.

Unroll . . . cake, removing towel.

Spread . . . with ice cream and reroll.

Wrap . . . . in plastic wrap.

Freeze . . . for 6 hours or until firm.

Becky Hankins
Martinsville H. S., Martinsville, Indiana

GREAT GRANDMOTHER'S JELLY ROLL

4 eggs
1 c. sugar
1 c. flour
1 1/2 tsp. baking powder
1 tsp. vanilla extract
1 jar jelly, desired flavor

Beat . . . . . eggs in small mixing bowl.

Add . . . . . sugar gradually and continue beating.

Sift . . . . . . flour with baking powder.

Fold . . . . . into egg mixture with vanilla until smooth.

Line . . . . . greased jelly roll pan with waxed paper.

Pour . . . . . batter into pan.

Bake . . . . . at 350 degrees for 12 to 15 minutes or until cake tests done.

Invert . . . . onto towel sprinkled with powdered sugar.

Remove . . paper.

Roll . . . . . up jelly roll fashion.

Unroll . . . and cover with jelly.

Roll . . . . . up again.

Wrap . . . . in towel.

Serve . . . . warm.

Kathie Y. Perkinson
Bowling Green Jr.-Sr. H. S., Bowling Green, Kentucky

STRAWBERRY DELIGHT ROLL

1 c. sifted cake flour
1 tsp. baking powder
1/4 tsp. salt
3 eggs
3/4 c. sugar
1 tbsp. frozen concentrated orange juice, thawed
Confectioners' sugar
1/2 tsp. almond extract
2 c. whipping cream, whipped
2 pt. sliced fresh strawberries, sweetened to taste

Line . . . . . greased 10 x 15 x 1-inch jelly roll pan with greased and floured waxed paper.

Sift . . . . . . first 3 ingredients together.

Beat . . . . . eggs in bowl until thick.

Add . . . . . sugar gradually, beating until very thick and creamy.

Beat . . . . . in orange juice and 2 tablespoons water.

Add . . . . . flour mixture gradually, beating until smooth.

Pour . . . . . batter into prepared pan, spreading into corners.

Bake . . . . . at 375 degrees for 12 minutes.

Invert . . . . cake onto towel dusted with confectioners' sugar.

Roll . . . . . up and cool completely.

Blend . . . . 1/2 cup confectioners' sugar and almond extract with whipped cream.

Unroll . . . cake.

Trim . . . . . crust from edges.

Spread . . . with half the whipped cream mixture.

Spoon . . . 3/4 of the strawberries over whipped cream.

Reroll . . . . cake and place seam side down on serving plate.

Top . . . . . with remaining whipped cream and strawberries.

Nancy Pinkston
D. A. Hulcy Middle School, Dallas, Texas

APPLE BUNDT CAKE

3 c. flour
2 1/2 c. sugar
1 tsp. soda
2 tsp. baking powder
1 tsp. salt
4 eggs
2 c. oil
1/3 c. orange juice
2 tsp. vanilla extract
1 1/2 tsp. cinnamon
5 apples, pared, thinly sliced

Place .... flour, 2 cups sugar and next 7 ingredients in order given in large mixer bowl.
Beat ..... at medium speed until blended.
Combine . remaining 1/2 cup sugar and cinnamon in bowl.
Add ..... apples, tossing lightly.
Place .... 3 layers batter and 2 layers apples alternately in greased 10-inch tube pan, beginning and ending with batter.
Bake ..... at 350 degrees for 1 1/2 hours.

Ms. K. Hinks
Webster H. S., Webster, Wisconsin

FRESH APPLE HARVEST CAKE

3 tart apples, peeled, thinly sliced
1 tbsp. ground cinnamon
Sugar
2 3/4 c. sifted cake flour
3 tsp. baking powder
1/4 tsp. salt
4 eggs
1 c. oil
1/3 c. orange juice

Sprinkle .. apples in bowl with cinnamon and 6 tablespoons sugar, tossing lightly to coat.
Sift ...... next 3 ingredients together.
Beat ..... eggs in large bowl until frothy.
Add ..... 2 cups sugar gradually, beating constantly until thick and fluffy.
Add ..... oil in a thin stream, beating constantly until well blended.
Add ..... dry ingredients and orange juice alternately, stirring until smooth.

Spoon ... 1/3 of the batter into greased bundt pan.
Drain .... apples and arrange half over the batter.
Repeat ... layers ending with batter.
Bake ..... at 350 degrees for 30 minutes or until cake tests done.
Cool ..... thoroughly on wire rack before removing from pan.

Marilyn Odeh
Holmes H. S., San Antonio, Texas

OLD-FASHIONED DRIED APPLE CAKE

1 c. butter
2 c. sugar
2 c. blackberry jam
2 1/2 c. cooked dried apples
4 c. flour
3 tsp. soda
2 tsp. each nutmeg, allspice and cinnamon
1 lb. raisins
1 1/2 c. chopped nuts
1 c. chopped dates

Cream ... butter and sugar together in large bowl.
Add ..... jam and apples, beating well.
Sift ...... dry ingredients together.
Combine . 1 cup flour mixture with raisins, nuts and dates, tossing to coat.
Add ..... remaining flour mixture to creamed mixture, mixing well.
Fold ..... floured fruits into batter.
Pour ..... into large greased and floured tube pan.
Bake ..... at 300 degrees for 2 1/2 hours.
Place .... pan of hot water in oven during last 1 hour.
Store .... in airtight container with sliced fresh apples for 1 week before serving.

Nancy J. Bledsoe
Fordsville H. S., Fordsville, Kentucky

BANANA CRUNCH CAKE

5 tbsp. margarine, melted
1 pkg. coconut-pecan frosting mix
1 c. rolled oats

1 c. sour cream
4 eggs
2 lg. bananas, chopped
1 pkg. yellow cake mix

Combine . margarine, frosting mix and oats in bowl, stirring until crumbly; set aside.
Mix ..... next 3 ingredients in large bowl until smooth.
Add ..... cake mix.
Beat ..... for 2 minutes at medium speed of electric mixer.
Pour ..... 2 cups batter into greased and floured 10-inch tube pan.
Sprinkle .. with 1 cup crumb mixture.
Repeat ... layers twice.
Bake ..... in preheated 350-degree oven for 50 to 60 minutes or until cake tests done.

Rosemary Gasper
Shawnee Mission East H. S., Shawnee Mission, Kansas

A GOOD BASIC CAKE

2 c. sugar
1 c. shortening
2 tsp. vanilla extract
4 eggs
3 c. flour
2 tsp. baking powder
1/4 tsp. salt
1/3 c. dry milk

Cream ... first 3 ingredients together in mixing bowl.
Add ..... eggs, 1 at a time, mixing well after each addition.
Sift ...... remaining ingredients together.
Add ..... to creamed mixture alternately with 1 cup water, beginning and ending with flour.
Pour ..... into greased and floured bundt pan.
Bake ..... at 325 degrees for 1 hour.
Note ..... may be baked in 3 layer pans or cupcake pans at 350 degrees for 20 to 30 minutes.

Doris S. Hartman
Mexia H. S., Mexia, Texas

BUTTER-PECAN CAKE

2 1/4 c. sifted flour
2/3 c. sugar
3 tsp. baking powder
1 tsp. salt
1 c. packed brown sugar
3/4 c. shortening
1 c. milk
3 eggs
1 tsp. vanilla extract
Finely chopped pecans

Sift ...... first 4 ingredients together into bowl.
Stir ...... in brown sugar.
Add ..... shortening and 3/4 cup milk.
Beat ..... for 2 minutes.
Add ..... eggs, remaining 1/4 cup milk and vanilla.
Beat ..... for 2 minutes longer.
Stir ...... in 3/4 cup pecans.
Pour ..... into greased and floured 9 x 13-inch baking pan.
Bake ..... at 375 degrees for 45 to 50 minutes.
Frost .... with seafoam frosting.
Sprinkle .. with additional pecans.

Marjean Hofmeister
Allison-Bristow, Allison, Iowa

CARROT CAKE

2 c. sugar
1 1/2 c. oil
4 eggs
2 c. flour
2 tsp. soda
1 tsp. salt
2 tsp. cinnamon
2 sm. jars baby food carrots

Beat ..... sugar and oil together in bowl.
Add ..... eggs, beating well.
Sift ...... dry ingredients together.
Fold ..... into egg mixture alternately with carrots, blending well.
Pour ..... into 3 prepared layer pans.
Bake ..... at 300 degrees for 40 minutes.
Frost .... with Cream Cheese Icing.

Peggy Nash
Hatley H. S., Amory, Mississippi

FRAN'S CARROT CAKE

2 eggs
1 c. sugar
3/4 c. oil
Salt
1 c. flour
1 1/2 tsp. cinnamon
1 tsp. soda
2 tbsp. vanilla extract
1 1/2 c. carrots, grated
1   3-oz. package cream cheese, softened
1/2 stick margarine, softened
2 c. confectioners' sugar
1 c. chopped nuts

Combine . first 3 ingredients in bowl, mixing
             well.
Blend . . . . 1/2 teaspoon salt and dry ingredi-
             ents together in bowl.
Add . . . . . to egg mixture, stirring to combine
             thoroughly.
Fold in . . . 1 tablespoon vanilla and carrots.
Pour . . . . . into greased square baking pan.
Bake . . . . . at 325 degrees for 30 minutes.
Beat . . . . . 1 tablespoon vanilla, remaining in-
             gredients except nuts and pinch of
             salt in mixing bowl on high speed
             until light and fluffy.
Add . . . . . nuts and frost cooled cake.

Fran Gildon
Velma-Alma H. S., Velma, Oklahoma

MICROWAVE-BLENDER CARROT CAKE

1 3/4 c. sifted flour
1 tsp. each baking powder, soda
1/2 tsp. each salt, cinnamon and nutmeg
1 c. oil
1 c. sliced carrots
1 c. sugar
2 eggs
1/2 c. orange juice
1 tsp. vanilla extract
1/2 c. raisins

Sift . . . . . . first 6 dry ingredients together into
             large mixing bowl.
Place . . . . oil and carrots in blender container.
Process . . . on grate for 30 seconds.
Add . . . . . sugar, eggs, orange juice and vanilla.
Blend . . . . for 10 to 15 seconds.

Add . . . . . raisins.
Process . . . on grate for 10 seconds.
Stir . . . . . . b l e n d e d   m i x t u r e   into   dry
             ingredients.
Pour . . . . . into ungreased microwave tube pan.
Microwave on Bake for 10 minutes, turning
             1/4 turn every 3 minutes.
Microwave on High for 3 minutes or until cake
             tests done.
Frost . . . . with Cream Cheese Icing if desired.

Ruth L. Metcalf
Oviedo H. S., Oviedo, Florida

CHOCOLATE ANGEL FOOD CAKE

1 c. (scant) sifted cake flour
3 tbsp. cocoa
1 3/4 c. sifted sugar
1 2/3 c. egg whites at room temperature
1/2 tsp. salt
1 1/2 tsp. cream of tartar
1 tsp. vanilla extract
1 tsp. almond extract

Sift . . . . . . flour, cocoa and 3/4 cup sugar to-
             gether 4 times; set aside.
Combine . egg whites with next 4 ingredients
             in large bowl.
Beat . . . . . at high speed of electric mixer until
             whites are stiff but not dry.
Add . . . . . remaining 1 cup sugar gradually,
             beating constantly.
Sprinkle . . fl our mixture quickly over egg
             whites, beating constantly at low
             speed.
Spoon . . . into ungreased tube pan.
Cut . . . . . . through batter with spatula 6 times.
Bake . . . . . at 375 degrees for 35 minutes.
Cool . . . . . completely, inverted.

Linda Phillips Smith
Martins Ferry H. S., Martins Ferry, Ohio

CHOCOLATE SHEET CAKE

2 sticks margarine
1/2 c. cocoa
1/2 c. oil
2 c. sifted flour
2 c. sugar
1 tsp. soda
1 1/2 tsp. vanilla extract
Buttermilk
2 eggs, beaten

1 lb. confectioners' sugar
1/2 tsp. salt
1 c. chopped nuts

Combine . 1 stick margarine, 1/4 cup cocoa, 1 cup water and oil in saucepan.
Boil ..... for 1 minute.
Mix ..... flour, sugar and soda together in large bowl.
Pour ..... cocoa mixture over dry ingredients, mixing well.
Add ..... 1 teaspoon vanilla, 1/2 cup buttermilk and eggs, mixing well.
Pour ..... into large greased baking pan.
Bake ..... at 400 degrees for 20 minutes.
Combine . remaining 1 stick margarine, 1/4 cup cocoa and 1/3 cup buttermilk in large saucepan.
Bring .... mixture to a boil.
Add ..... confectioners' sugar, salt, 1/2 teaspoon vanilla and nuts, mixing well.
Frost .... cake and cut into squares.

Constance Lebel
Mascenic Regional School
New Ipswich, New Hampshire

FUNNY CAKE

3 c. flour
2 c. sugar
1/2 c. cocoa
2 tsp. soda
1 tsp. salt
2 tbsp. vinegar
2 tsp. vanilla extract
2/3 c. oil

Combine . all ingredients with 2 cups cold water in bowl, mixing well.
Pour ..... into greased and floured 9 x 13-inch baking pan.
Bake ..... at 350 degrees for 40 to 45 minutes or until cake tests done.

Denise Winn-Bower
Cary-Grove H. S., Cary, Illinois

CHOCOLATE SYRUP CAKE

1 box white cake mix
1 sm. box instant vanilla pudding mix
4 eggs
3/4 c. oil
1 sm. can Hershey's chocolate syrup
1 6-oz. package chocolate chips

Combine . first 4 ingredients and 1 cup water in mixing bowl, beating until well mixed.
Pour ..... 2/3 of the batter into greased and floured bundt pan.
Add ..... chocolate syrup to remaining batter, mixing well.
Pour ..... into cake pan, swirling with knife to marble.
Sprinkle .. chocolate chips on top.
Bake ..... at 350 degrees for 45 to 60 minutes or until cake tests done.

Mrs. Sara J. Kendrick
Raymondville H. S., Raymondville, Texas

MIRACLE WHIP CHOCOLATE CAKE

1 c. Miracle Whip salad dressing
1 c. sugar
1 tsp. vanilla extract
2 1/4 c. sifted cake flour
1/2 c. cocoa
1 tsp. baking powder
1 tsp. soda
Dash of salt

Combine . salad dressing and sugar in bowl, blending until smooth.
Add ..... vanilla, mixing well.
Combine . dry ingredients.
Add ..... alternately with 3/4 cup cold water, mixing well after each addition.
Pour ..... into 2 greased and floured 8-inch layer pans.
Bake ..... at 350 degrees for 25 to 30 minutes or until cake tests done.
Cool ..... for 10 minutes before removing from pan.
Frost .... with Chocolate-Cream Cheese Frosting.

Chocolate-Cream Cheese Frosting

1 8-oz. package cream cheese, softened
1 tbsp. milk
1 tsp. vanilla extract
Dash of salt
1 box confectioners' sugar
3 1-oz. squares unsweetened chocolate, melted

Combine . all ingredients in bowl, beating until of spreading consistency.

Levonn Bohnstedt
Welch H. S., Welch, Oklahoma

WALNUT-COCOA CAKE

1/2 c. shortening
3/4 c. sugar
2 eggs
1/2 c. honey
2 1/2 tsp. grated orange peel
Cocoa
2 c. sifted cake flour
1 tsp. soda
1/2 tsp. salt
1/4 tsp. each cinnamon, nutmeg
2/3 c. buttermilk
1 1/4 c. finely chopped California walnuts
1/2 c. butter, melted
1 lb. confectioners' sugar
1/4 c. light cream
1/2 tsp. vanilla extract

Cream ... shortening and sugar together in bowl until light.

Add ..... eggs 1 at a time, beating well after each addition.

Add ..... honey and 2 teaspoons orange peel, beating until light and creamy.

Sift ...... 1/3 cup cocoa and next 5 dry ingredients together.

Add ..... dry ingredients to creamed mixture alternately with buttermilk, beating well after each addition.

Stir ...... in 3/4 cup walnuts.

Pour ..... into 2 greased and floured 9-inch layer pans.

Bake ..... at 350 degrees for 25 to 30 minutes or until cake tests done.

Let ...... stand for 5 minutes.

Turn ..... onto wire racks to cool.

Combine . 1/4 cup cocoa and butter in mixer bowl.

Add ..... confectioners' sugar and cream, beating until smooth.

Stir . . . . . . in vanilla and 1/2 teaspoon orange peel, mixing well.
Spread . . . between layers and over top and side of cake.
Pat . . . . . . remaining 1/2 cup walnuts around side.

Photograph for this recipe on page 136.

MISSISSIPPI MUD CAKE

1 1/2 c. butter
4 tsp. vanilla extract
3/4 c. cocoa
2 c. chopped nuts
2 c. sugar
1/2 c. shortening
4 eggs
1 1/2 c. flour
1 lg. bag marshmallows
6 tbsp. milk

Combine . 1 cup butter, 3 teaspoons vanilla, 1/4 cup cocoa, 1 cup nuts and next 4 ingredients in bowl, mixing well.
Pour . . . . . into large greased and floured baking pan.
Bake . . . . . at 350 degrees for 40 minutes or until cake tests done.
Melt . . . . . marshmallows and spread over cake.
Combine . remaining 1/2 cup butter, 1 cup nuts, 1/2 cup cocoa and milk in saucepan until melted.
Add . . . . . remaining vanilla, mixing well.
Frost . . . . cake.
Chill . . . . . for 1/2 hour.

Ms. K. Hinks
Webster Jr.-Sr. H. S., Webster, Wisconsin

TURTLE CAKE

1 box German chocolate cake mix
1 14-oz. bag caramels
1/2 c. evaporated milk
3/4 c. melted butter
2 c. nuts
1 c. chocolate chips

Prepare . . . cake mix using package directions.
Pour . . . . . half the batter into greased 9 x 13-inch baking pan.
Bake . . . . . at 350 degrees for 15 minutes.

Melt . . . . . caramels with milk and butter in saucepan over low heat, stirring constantly.
Pour . . . . . over cake.
Sprinkle . . with 1 cup nuts and chocolate chips.
Pour . . . . . remaining batter over filling.
Sprinkle . . with remaining nuts.
Bake . . . . . for 20 minutes longer.

Nancy Conway
Washington H. S., Washington, Missouri

COCONUT DREAM CAKE

1 butter cake mix
1 16-oz. can cream of coconut
1 can sweetened condensed milk
1 9-oz. carton whipped topping
1 can flaked coconut

Prepare . . . cake using package directions for oblong cake.
Pierce . . . . top of hot cake.
Pour . . . . . next 2 ingredients over top.
Let . . . . . . stand for 2 hours.
Spread . . . with whipped topping.
Sprinkle . . with coconut.

Deanna Reeves
Granite H. S., Granite, Oklahoma

COCONUT-SOUR CREAM CAKE

1 pkg. white cake mix
1/4 c. oil
3 eggs
1 8-oz. carton sour cream
1 8 1/2-oz. can cream of coconut
1 8-oz. package cream cheese, softened
1 tsp. vanilla extract
2 tbsp. milk
1 box confectioners' sugar
1 c. coconut

Combine . first 5 ingredients in bowl, mixing well.
Pour . . . . . into greased 9 x 13-inch cake pan.
Bake . . . . . at 350 degrees for 30 to 50 minutes or until cake tests done.
Combine . next 4 ingredients in bowl, blending well.
Stir . . . . . . in coconut.
Frost . . . . cake with coconut icing.

Betty Copas
Northwest H. S., McDermott, Ohio

COCONUT LAYER CAKE

2 sticks margarine, softened
2 c. sugar
1 tsp. vanilla extract
1 tsp. lemon extract
4 eggs, separated
3 c. all-purpose sifted flour
1 tbsp. baking powder
1/4 tsp. salt
1 c. milk

Cream ... margarine and sugar in bowl until smooth.
Add ..... vanilla and lemon flavoring, beating until fluffy.
Beat ..... in egg yolks.
Sift ...... dry ingredients together.
Add ..... dry ingredients and milk alternately, beating well after each addition.
Beat ..... egg whites until stiff but not dry.
Fold ..... into batter.
Pour ..... into 3 greased and floured 9-inch cake pans.
Bake ..... at 375 degrees for 30 minutes or until cake tests done.
Frost .... with Never-Fail Frosting.

Never-Fail Frosting

1 1/2 c. sugar
1/4 tsp. salt
1/2 tsp. cream of tartar
3 egg whites
1 1/2 tsp. vanilla extract
1 14-oz. package flaked coconut

Combine . first 3 ingredients with 7 tablespoons water in small saucepan.
Bring .... to a boil over moderate heat.
Pour ..... syrup slowly into egg whites in mixer bowl, beating constantly at high speed.
Reduce ... speed; add vanilla and continue beating until of spreading consistency.
Sprinkle .. frosted cake with coconut.

Mae Zona Sears
Forest H. S., Ocala, Florida

EGGLESS CAKE

2 c. flour
2 tsp. soda

2 c. sugar
1 No. 2 can crushed pineapple
1/2 c. chopped pecans
1 sm. can evaporated milk
1 stick margarine

Sift ...... flour and soda together into bowl.
Stir ...... in 1 1/2 cups sugar and pineapple, mixing well.
Pour ..... into 9 x 13-inch cake pan.
Sprinkle .. with pecans.
Bake ..... at 350 degrees for 30 minutes.
Combine . remaining ingredients with 1/2 cup sugar in saucepan.
Bring .... to a boil.
Pour ..... over cake.

B. J. Adams
Mechanicsburg H. S., Mechanicsburg, Ohio

FRUIT PECAN FRUITCAKE

1 3/4 c. cake flour
3/4 lb. candied cherries
1/2 lb. candied citron, chopped
1/2 lb. candied pineapple, chopped
4 c. pecans, chopped
1 c. butter, softened
1/2 c. sugar
1/2 c. packed light brown sugar
5 lg. eggs
1/4 tsp. each baking powder, soda
1/2 tsp. vanilla extract
1 tsp. rum flavoring

Combine . half the flour with fruits and pecans, tossing to coat well.
Cream ... next 3 ingredients together in large mixing bowl until light and fluffy.
Add ..... eggs 1 at a time, beating well after each addition.
Mix ..... baking powder and soda with remaining flour.
Stir ...... into creamed mixture, blending well.
Add ..... flavorings, mixing well.
Fold ..... in fruits and pecans.
Pour ..... into greased and lined 10-inch tube pan.
Place .... cake in cold oven.
Bake ..... at 250 degrees for 3 hours.

Thelma L. Lucas
DeLand Jr. H. S., DeLand, Florida

HAWAIIAN CAKE

1 box yellow cake mix
1 11-oz. can mandarin oranges
2 sm. packages instant vanilla pudding mix
2 c. canned crushed pineapple
4 eggs
1 lg. carton Cool Whip

Combine . cake mix, oranges, 1 package pudding mix, 1 cup pineapple and 4 eggs in large mixing bowl.
Beat . . . . . for 4 minutes.
Pour . . . . . into greased 9 x 13-inch pan.
Bake . . . . . at 350 degrees for 30 to 40 minutes or until cake tests done.
Combine . remaining 1 cup pineapple, 1 package pudding mix and Cool Whip in bowl, mixing well.
Spread . . . over cooled cake.
Chill . . . . . in refrigerator until serving time.

Airs Crawford
Liberty Jr. H. S., Hutchinson, Kansas

HAWAIIAN DREAM CAKE

1 c. oil
2 c. sugar
3 eggs
1 8-oz. can crushed pineapple, undrained
1 1/2 tsp. vanilla extract
2 c. flour
1 c. whole wheat flour
1 tsp. each soda, baking powder and cinnamon
2 c. finely diced bananas
1 3/4 c. sifted confectioners' sugar
2 to 3 tbsp. orange juice

Combine . oil and sugar in large mixing bowl, beating well.
Add . . . . . eggs, 1 at a time, beating well after each addition.
Fold . . . . . in pineapple and vanilla.
Mix . . . . . dry ingredients together.
Add . . . . . to pineapple mixture, blending well.
Stir . . . . . . in bananas.
Pour . . . . . into greased 10-inch bundt pan.
Bake . . . . . at 350 degrees for 60 to 70 minutes or until cake tests done.
Cool . . . . . for 10 minutes before removing from pan to rack.

Combine . remaining ingredients in bowl to make thin glaze.
Drizzle . . . over cooled cake.

Emily Lewis
Capitol Hill H. S., Oklahoma City, Oklahoma

ITALIAN CREAM CAKE

1 c. buttermilk
1 tsp. soda
5 eggs, separated
1/2 c. butter
1/2 c. shortening
2 c. sugar
2 c. flour
1 tsp. vanilla extract
1 c. pecans, chopped
1 sm. can coconut

Combine . buttermilk and soda in small bowl; let stand for a few minutes.
Beat . . . . . egg whites until stiff in small bowl; set aside.
Cream . . . butter, shortening and sugar in large bowl until fluffy.
Add . . . . . egg yolks, one at a time, beating well after each addition.
Add . . . . . flour and buttermilk alternately, beating well after each addition.
Stir . . . . . . in vanilla.
Fold . . . . . in egg whites.
Stir . . . . . . in pecans and coconut gently.
Pour . . . . . into three 9-inch layer pans.
Bake . . . . . at 350 degrees for 25 to 30 minutes until cake tests done.

Cream Cheese Icing

1 8-oz. package cream cheese, softened
1/2 c. butter, softened
1 tsp. vanilla extract
1 lb. confectioners' sugar

Cream . . . cream cheese and butter in bowl until well blended.
Beat . . . . . in vanilla and add confectioners' sugar gradually until of spreading consistency.
Spread . . . between layers and over top of cake.

Bonnie Hire
Del City H. S., Del City, Oklahoma

JAM CAKE

2 c. flour
1 tsp. salt
1 1/4 tsp. soda
1 tsp. each nutmeg, cinnamon and allspice
1 c. oil
2 c. sugar
1 tsp. vanilla extract
3 eggs
1 1/4 c. buttermilk
1 c. jam
1/2 c. chopped nuts
1 1/2 tsp. light corn syrup
2 tbsp. butter

Combine . flour, salt and 1 teaspoon soda with spices in bowl, stirring to mix; set aside.
Mix . . . . . oil and 1 1/2 cups sugar in large bowl.
Add . . . . . vanilla and eggs, one at a time, beating well after each addition.
Stir . . . . . . in dry ingredients alternately with 1 cup buttermilk.
Add . . . . . jam and nuts, stirring until just blended.
Spoon . . . into greased 10-inch tube pan.
Bake . . . . . at 325 degrees for 60 minutes.
Remove . . from pan and cool on wire rack.
Combine . 1/2 cup sugar, 1/4 cup buttermilk, 1/4 teaspoon soda and remaining ingredients in saucepan.
Cook . . . . over medium heat for several minutes, stirring constantly.
Spoon . . . over warm or cool cake allowing topping to soak into cake.

Lorraine Ptacek
Fort Collins H. S., Fort Collins, Colorado

LEMON-NUT CAKE

2 c. butter
2 c. sugar
2 oz. lemon extract
6 eggs, beaten
4 c. flour
1 1/2 tsp. baking powder
1 1/2 tsp. salt
1 lb. white raisins
1 lb. shelled pecans, chopped

Cream . . . butter and sugar in bowl until fluffy.
Add . . . . . lemon flavoring and eggs, beating well.
Sift . . . . . . dry ingredients together.
Mix . . . . . raisins and pecans with flour.
Add . . . . . to creamed mixture.
Spoon . . . into greased and floured tube pan.
Bake . . . . . at 275 degrees for 2 hours.

Gail M. Skelton
Biggersville H. S., Corinth, Mississippi

ORA'S OATMEAL CAKE

1 c. oatmeal
Margarine, softened
1 c. packed brown sugar
1 1/2 c. all-purpose flour
2 eggs
1 tsp. each soda, cinnamon
1/2 tsp. each salt, nutmeg
1 1/2 c. sugar
2 tbsp. corn syrup
1 tsp. vanilla extract
1/4 c. evaporated milk
1 c. coconut
1 c. chopped pecans

Combine . oatmeal with 1 1/2 cups boiling water and 1 stick margarine in large bowl.
Let . . . . . . stand, covered, for 20 minutes, stirring occasionally.
Combine . next 7 ingredients with 1 cup sugar in bowl, mixing well.
Add . . . . . to oatmeal mixture blending thoroughly.
Pour . . . . . into 8 x 16 x 2-inch baking pan.
Bake . . . . . at 350 degrees for 40 minutes or until cake tests done.
Blend . . . . 6 tablespoons margarine with 1/2 cup sugar and remaining ingredients in bowl.
Spread . . . over cake.
Broil . . . . . until brown.

Brenda Broaddus
Berea Community School, Berea, Kentucky

ORANGE JUICE CAKE

1 pkg. yellow cake mix
1 pkg. instant coconut pudding mix
1/2 c. coconut

3/4 c. oil
4 eggs
2 c. confectioners' sugar
1/2 c. orange juice
2 tbsp. melted butter

Beat ..... first 5 ingredients and 3/4 cup water together in mixing bowl for 6 to 10 minutes.
Pour ..... into 9 x 12-inch pan.
Bake ..... at 350 degrees for 30 to 40 minutes.
Pierce .... surface with fork.
Combine . remaining ingredients in bowl, mixing well.
Pour ..... over hot cake.

Christine Anders
New Haven H. S., New Haven, Indiana

PINEAPPLE CAKE

2 eggs
2 c. sugar
2 c. flour
2 tsp. soda
1 15 1/2-oz. can crushed pineapple
1 c. chopped nuts
2 tsp. vanilla extract
1/2 stick margarine, softened
1 8-oz. package cream cheese, softened
1 3/4 c. confectioners' sugar

Combine . first 5 ingredients with 1/2 cup nuts and 1 teaspoon vanilla in bowl, mixing well.
Pour ..... into greased and floured 9 x 13-inch baking pan.
Bake ..... at 350 degrees for 45 minutes.
Combine . 1 teaspoon vanilla, 1/2 cup nuts and remaining ingredients in bowl, mixing well.
Spread ... on hot cake.

Wanda Sextro
Flinthills H. S., Rosalia, Kansas

PEACH GLOW ANGEL CAKE

1 pkg. angel food cake mix
1 4-oz. package vanilla pudding mix
2 c. milk
1 No. 2 can peach pie filling
1 c. whipping cream, whipped

Bake ..... cake, using package directions for 10-inch tube pan.

Cool ..... and remove from pan.
Slice ..... 1-inch layer from top.
Scoop ... out center to within 1 inch of side and bottom.
Prepare ... pudding and milk, using package directions.
Mix ..... half the pudding with pie filling in bowl.
Spoon ... into cavity of cake.
Replace .. top layer.
Chill ..... until filling is firm.
Fold ..... remaining pudding into whipped cream.
Frost .... top and side of cake.
Chill ..... until serving time.

Photograph for this recipe above.

MOIST POUND CAKE

2 sticks butter, softened
2 c. sugar
6 eggs
2 c. flour, sifted 4 times
1 tsp. vanilla extract

Cream ... butter and sugar until smooth.
Add ..... eggs, one at a time, beating well after each addition.
Add ..... flour, beating until creamy.
Beat ..... in vanilla.
Spoon ... into greased and floured tube pan.
Bake ..... at 300 degrees for 1 hour or until cake tests done.

Mrs. David Crawford
Myrtle H. S., Myrtle, Mississippi

BANANA POUND CAKE

1 1/2 c. shortening
2 1/2 c. sugar
4 eggs
6 bananas, mashed
2 tsp. soda
Pinch of salt
3 c. flour
1 tsp. vanilla extract

Cream ... shortening and sugar together in bowl.
Add ..... eggs, 1 at a time, beating well after each addition.
Add ..... bananas, mixing well.
Add ..... remaining ingredients, mixing well.
Pour ..... into large greased and floured bundt pan.
Bake ..... at 300 degrees for 1 1/2 hours.

Myrtle Chapman
El Reno H. S., El Reno, Oklahoma

WILMA'S POUND CAKE

1 c. shortening
1 3/4 c. sugar
3 eggs
3 c. flour
1 c. milk
1 tsp. baking powder
1/4 tsp. salt
1 tsp. desired flavoring

Cream ... shortening in bowl until light and fluffy.
Add ..... sugar, 2 tablespoons at a time, beating continuously.
Add ..... eggs, one at a time, beating until light and fluffy.
Add ..... flour and milk alternately, beating well after each addition and adding baking powder and salt with last flour addition.
Beat ..... in flavoring and continue beating for 3 minutes.
Pour ..... batter into greased, waxed paper-lined tube pan.
Bake ..... at 350 degrees for 1 hour or until cake tests done.
Cool ..... for 10 minutes and remove from pan to cooling rack.

Wilma E. Fortenberry
Jones Jr. H. S., Laurel, Mississippi

GERMAN CHOCOLATE POUND CAKE

1 c. butter
2 c. sugar
4 eggs
2 tsp. each vanilla extract, butter flavoring
1 c. buttermilk
3 c. sifted all-purpose flour
1/2 tsp. soda
1 tsp. salt
1 4-oz. package German's sweet chocolate
Sifted confectioners' sugar

Cream ... butter and sugar together in mixing bowl.
Add ..... eggs, flavoring and buttermilk.
Sift ...... next 3 dry ingredients together.
Add ..... to creamed mixture, mixing well.
Melt ..... chocolate in top of double boiler.
Stir ...... into batter, blending well.
Pour ..... into greased and floured bundt pan.
Bake ..... at 300 degrees for 1 1/2 hours.
Wrap .... in aluminum foil until cool.
Sprinkle .. with confectioners' sugar.

Micki Jeffery
Center Jr. H. S., Kansas City, Missouri

SOCK-IT-TO-ME CAKE

1 pkg. Duncan Hines yellow butter recipe cake mix
1 c. sour cream
3/4 c. Wesson buttery oil
Sugar
4 eggs
1 tbsp. cinnamon

Combine . first 3 ingredients with 1/2 cup sugar in bowl.
Beat ..... until fluffy.
Add ..... eggs, one at a time, beating well after each addition.
Pour ..... half of batter into greased and floured bundt pan.
Combine . 3 tablespoons sugar with cinnamon in small bowl, mixing well.
Sprinkle .. half of mixture over batter in pan, cutting in with a knife.
Add ..... remaining batter and cinnamon mixture, cutting in as before.
Bake ..... at 350 degrees for 1 hour or until cake tests done.

Lori Ellen Walker
Northwestern H. S., Springfield, Ohio

STRAWBERRY CAKE

1 pkg. white cake mix
1 sm. package strawberry Jell-O
3/4 c. Wesson oil
3/4 c. milk
4 eggs, separated
1 c. shredded coconut
1 c. chopped pecans
2 c. halved strawberries
1/2 stick margarine, softened
1 box confectioners' sugar

Combine . cake mix and jello in large bowl.
Add ..... oil, milk and egg yolks, stirring just to mix.
Combine . coconut, pecans and strawberries in bowl, mixing well.
Add ..... half the strawberry mixture to batter, reserving half for frosting.
Beat ..... egg whites in small bowl until stiff but not dry.
Fold ..... into batter.
Pour ..... into 3 greased and floured 8-inch cake pans.
Bake ..... at 350 degrees for 20 to 25 minutes or until cake tests done.
Cream ... margarine in bowl.
Blend .... in confectioners' sugar and remaining strawberry mixture.
Frost .... cooled cake.

Anna Lois Hinton
John Shaw School, Mobile, Alabama

SWEDISH NUT CAKE

1 c. chopped nuts
2 tsp. vanilla extract
1 3/4 c. sugar
2 c. flour
2 tsp. soda
2 eggs
1 10-oz. can crushed pineapple
1 8-oz. package cream cheese, softened
1 3/4 c. confectioners' sugar
1 stick margarine, softened

Combine . 1/2 cup nuts, 1 teaspoon vanilla and next 5 ingredients in large bowl, mixing well.
Pour ..... into greased and floured 9 x 13-inch pan.

Bake ..... at 350 degrees for 40 to 45 minutes.
Combine . remaining 1 teaspoon vanilla and next 3 ingredients in bowl, beating until creamy.
Frost .... cooled cake.
Sprinkle .. with remaining 1/2 cup nuts.

Carol Huffstetler
Boca Raton H. S., Boca Raton, Florida

WINE CAKE

1 pkg. yellow cake mix
1 pkg. instant vanilla pudding mix
1 tsp. nutmeg
3/4 c. oil
3/4 c. Sherry
4 eggs, beaten

Combine . cake mix, pudding mix and nutmeg in bowl.
Add ..... remaining ingredients, mixing well.
Pour ..... into greased and floured bundt pan.
Bake ..... at 350 degrees for 35 to 45 minutes or until cake tests done.
Cool ..... on rack for 20 minutes before removing from pan.

Julie Frye
Jarman Jr. H. S., Midwest City, Oklahoma

DEBORAH'S MARSHMALLOWS

1 c. sugar
1 tbsp. corn syrup
1 tbsp. unflavored gelatin
Confectioners' sugar

Combine . first 2 ingredients and 1/2 cup water in saucepan.
Cook .... to hard-ball stage, 260 degrees on candy thermometer.
Soften ... gelatin in 1/4 cup cold water.
Add ..... to syrup.
Cool ..... until thick.
Beat ..... until soft peaks form.
Pour ..... into 8 x 8-inch pan.
Sprinkle .. with confectioners' sugar.
Let ...... stand until set.
Cut ...... into 2-inch squares.
Roll ..... in confectioners' sugar.

Deborah J. Risch
Beaufort Jr. H. S., Beaufort, South Carolina

CARAMEL MARSHMALLOWS

1 c. margarine
1 lb. light caramels
1 can sweetened condensed milk
1 pkg. large marshmallows, frozen
1 sm. box Rice Krispies

Melt . . . . . first 3 ingredients together in double boiler.
Dip . . . . . . marshmallows in caramel, coating well.
Roll . . . . . in Rice Krispies.
Chill . . . . . until set.

Barbara Johnson
Ord Jr.-Sr. H. S., Ord, Nebraska

QUICK CARAMEL CORN

1/4 c. unpopped popcorn
2 tbsp. light corn syrup
4 tbsp. margarine, melted
1/4 c. packed brown sugar

Pop . . . . . popcorn using package directions.
Add . . . . . corn syrup to margarine in saucepan.
Stir . . . . . . in sugar, mixing well.
Bring . . . . to a boil.
Pour . . . . . over popcorn.
Stir . . . . . . until thoroughly mixed.

Beth A. Archer
Grover Cleveland Jr. H. S., Zanesville, Ohio

NO-FAIL MICROWAVE DIVINITY

4 c. sugar
1 c. light corn syrup
Dash of salt
3 egg whites, stiffly beaten
1 tsp. vanilla extract
1/2 c. chopped nuts

Combine . first 3 ingredients with 3/4 cup water in 2-quart casserole.
Microwave on High for 19 to 20 minutes or to 260 degrees on candy thermometer, stirring every 5 minutes.
Pour . . . . . hot syrup gradually over egg whites, beating constantly at high speed until candy thickens and loses its gloss.
Stir . . . . . . in vanilla and nuts.
Drop . . . . by teaspoonfuls onto waxed paper.

Sharon Nelsen
Cameron H. S., Cameron, Wisconsin

MINT STICKS

Margarine
4 sq. semisweet chocolate
4 eggs
2 c. sugar
1 1/4 c. flour
1 1/4 tsp. peppermint extract
1/2 c. chopped nuts (opt.)
3 c. confectioners' sugar
Dash of salt
2 to 4 tbsp. milk

Melt . . . . . 1 cup margarine and 2 squares chocolate together in small saucepan; cool.
Beat . . . . . eggs and sugar in bowl until foamy.
Add . . . . . melted chocolate, mixing well.
Add . . . . . flour, 3/4 teaspoon peppermint and nuts, mixing well.
Pour . . . . . into 9 x 13-inch baking pan.
Bake . . . . . at 350 degrees for 25 to 35 minutes; cool.
Cream . . . 1/4 cup softened margarine, confectioners' sugar, salt and 1/2 teaspoon peppermint extract together in bowl.
Add . . . . . milk to spreading consistency.
Spread . . . over chocolate layer.
Let . . . . . . stand until set.
Melt . . . . . remaining 2 squares chocolate with 2 tablespoons butter in small saucepan.
Spread . . . over frosting.
Chill . . . . . and cut into squares.

Jan Moeller
Thomas Jefferson Sr. H. S., Cedar Rapids, Iowa

MINT PUFFS

3 egg whites
1/2 tsp. cream of tartar
1/3 tsp. salt
3/4 c. sugar
2 oz. green Creme de Menthe
2 to 3 drops green food coloring (opt.)

Beat . . . . . first 3 ingredients together in bowl until stiff peaks form.
Add . . . . . sugar gradually, beating constantly.
Add . . . . . remaining ingredients gradually, beating until glossy.
Press . . . . . through pastry tube into desired shapes onto greased cookie sheet.

Bake . . . . . at 250 degrees for 30 minutes or until completely dry.

Karen Overstreet
Groves School, Savannah, Georgia

PEPPERMINT BARK

1 lb. white chocolate
1/2 c. crushed peppermint candies
4 to 7 drops of food coloring

Melt . . . . . chocolate in saucepan over low heat.
Stir . . . . . . in candies and food coloring.
Spread . . . in foil-covered 12 x 15-inch baking sheet.
Let . . . . . . stand until firm.

Pat Duncan
Haltom Jr. H. S., Fort Worth, Texas

MINT PUFF CANDY SQUARES

5 c. puffed rice
1/2 c. crushed hard mint candies
3 c. miniature marshmallows
2 tbsp. butter
1 6-oz. package semisweet chocolate pieces

Spread . . . puffed rice in shallow baking dish.
Bake . . . . . at 350 degrees for 10 minutes.
Pour . . . . . into large greased bowl.
Add . . . . . crushed candies.
Melt . . . . . marshmallows and butter over low heat in saucepan, stirring occasionally.
Pour . . . . over puffed rice, stirring to coat evenly.
Press . . . . . into greased 9 x 13-inch pan.
Melt . . . . . chocolate pieces in top of double boiler over hot water, stirring occasionally.
Spread . . . over puffed rice.
Chill . . . . . for several hours.
Serve . . . . cut in squares.

Photograph for this recipe above.

SPEARMINT WALNUTS

1 c. sugar
1/4 tsp. salt
1 tbsp. light corn syrup
6 marshmallows
3/4 tsp. mint extract
Food coloring (opt.)
4 1/2 c. walnut halves

Combine . first 3 ingredients with 1/3 cup water in saucepan.
Cook .... to soft-ball stage, 240 degrees on candy thermometer.
Remove .. from heat.
Blend .... in marshmallows and mint until melted.
Stir ...... in food coloring and walnuts until coated.
Pour ..... onto waxed paper and separate.

Carolyn Freeman
Alta H. S., Sandy, Utah

PEANUT BRITTLE

1 c. sugar
1 c. light corn syrup
2 c. raw peanuts
1 tsp. vanilla extract
2 tbsp. butter
1 tsp. soda

Combine . sugar, syrup and 1/4 cup water in saucepan.
Cook .... to soft-ball stage, 240 degrees on candy thermometer.
Add ..... peanuts.
Cook .... until light brown.
Add ..... vanilla and butter, stirring to blend.
Add ..... soda and stir briskly until thoroughly dissolved.
Pour ..... onto foil-lined baking sheet.
Cool ..... and break into pieces.

Mary Garnett Richey
Allen County-Scottsville H. S., Scottsville, Kentucky

FAST FUDGE

2 c. sugar
1 c. peanut butter
1 tsp. vanilla extract

Mix ..... sugar and 1/2 cup water in saucepan.
Boil ..... rapidly for exactly 1 minute.

Pour ..... over peanut butter and vanilla in bowl.
Beat ..... until thick.
Pour ..... into buttered pan.
Cut ...... into squares when cool.
Note ..... may add 3 tablespoons cocoa with sugar to make chocolate fudge.

G. Sue Lacy
Kermit H. S., Kermit, West Virginia

PEANUT BUTTER FUDGE

3/4 c. peanut butter
1 c. ground peanuts
1/2 c. corn syrup
1/2 c. butter
4 c. confectioners' sugar

Combine . all ingredients in large bowl, kneading to mix well.
Spread ... in 8 x 8-inch pan.
Chill ..... until firm.
Yields .... 64 one-inch squares/about 80 calories each.

Patricia Taylor
Western Middle School, Louisville, Kentucky

QUICK PEANUT BUTTER FUDGE

2 c. sugar
1 c. evaporated milk
3 tbsp. butter
1 12-oz. jar peanut butter
1 c. miniature marshmallows
1 tsp. vanilla extract

Combine . first 3 ingredients in electric skillet.
Cook .... at 280 degrees, bringing to a boil.
Boil ..... for 5 minutes, stirring constantly.
Turn ..... off heat.
Add ..... remaining ingredients, stirring to blend well.
Pour ..... into buttered 9-inch square pan.
Cool ..... and cut into squares.

Norma P. Dabney
Liberty Jr. H. S., Orlando, Florida

PEANUT BUTTER ROLL

1 c. light corn syrup
4 c. sugar

3 egg whites, stiffly beaten
Confectioners' sugar
Peanut butter

Combine . syrup, sugar and 1 cup water in saucepan.
Cook .... to hard-ball stage, 260 degrees on candy thermometer.
Pour ..... slowly over egg whites, beating constantly.
Beat ..... until thick and doughy.
Stir ...... until cool enough to handle.
Roll ..... out on waxed paper sprinkled with confectioners' sugar to form a rectangle 1/8 inch thick.
Spread ... with peanut butter.
Roll ..... as for jelly roll and slice.

Shirley Slemp
Dryden H. S., Dryden, Virginia

REESE-TYPE BARS

1 c. peanut butter
1/2 c. butter, melted
1 3/4 c. confectioners' sugar
3 tbsp. brown sugar
1/2 tsp. vanilla extract
1/4 tsp. salt
1 6-oz. bag chocolate chips
2 tbsp. oil

Combine . first 6 ingredients with 2 tablespoons water in large bowl, beating until well blended and mixture forms a ball.
Pat ...... into 7 x 11-inch pan, smoothing top.
Melt ..... and blend remaining ingredients together in double boiler.
Spread ... smoothly over peanut butter mixture.
Cut ...... into squares when cooled.

Audrey Smith
Wheaton North H. S., Wheaton, Illinois

NUT GOODIE BARS

2 c. creamy peanut butter
1 12-oz. package chocolate chips
1 12-oz. package butterscotch chips
1 lb. salted peanuts

1 pkg. vanilla pudding mix
1/2 c. evaporated milk
1 c. butter
1 tsp. maple flavoring
2 lb. confectioners' sugar

Melt ..... first 3 ingredients together in double boiler pan.
Pour ..... half the chocolate mixture into greased jelly roll pan, spreading evenly.
Chill ..... until cooled.
Add ..... peanuts to remaining half, stirring well.
Keep .... warm over hot water.
Heat ..... pudding mix, evaporated milk and butter in saucepan.
Boil ..... for 1 minute; remove from heat.
Add ..... remaining ingredients, beating until smooth.
Spread ... over chilled layer.
Cover .... with peanut mixture.
Chill ..... until firm.
Yields .... 10 dozen/about 115 calories each.

Doris Kirk
St. Croix Falls H. S., St. Croix Falls, Wisconsin

CHEWY PRALINES

1 6 1/2-oz. can evaporated milk
2 c. light corn syrup
3/4 c. sugar
1 can sweetened condensed milk
1/2 stick margarine
1 tsp. salt
3 c. broken pecans

Combine . first 3 ingredients in saucepan, mixing well.
Cook .... over medium heat, stirring constantly, to 248 degrees on candy thermometer. Mixture will curdle.
Add ..... next 2 ingredients.
Cook .... stirring constantly, to 238 degrees on candy thermometer.
Remove .. from heat and stir in salt and pecans.
Drop .... by tablespoonfuls onto foil.
Wrap .... pieces individually in plastic wrap after cooling.

Robin Weynand
Bangs H. S., Bangs, Texas

BUTTERMILK BROWNIES

2 sticks margarine
1/2 c. cocoa
2 c. flour
2 c. sugar
1/2 tsp. salt
Buttermilk
2 eggs
1 tsp. soda
2 tsp. vanilla extract
1 box confectioners' sugar
1 c. chopped nuts (opt.)

Combine . 1 stick margarine, 1/4 cup cocoa and 1 cup water in saucepan.
Bring . . . . to a boil, mixing well.
Pour . . . . . over mixture of flour, sugar and 1/2 teaspoon salt in bowl.
Add . . . . . 1/2 cup buttermilk, eggs, soda and 1 teaspoon vanilla, mixing well.
Pour . . . . . into greased and floured jelly roll pan.
Bake . . . . . at 400 degrees for 20 minutes.
Combine . remaining 1 stick margarine with 1/4 cup cocoa and 1/3 cup buttermilk in saucepan.
Bring . . . . to a boil, blending well.
Remove . . from heat and add remaining ingredients, mixing until creamy.
Frost . . . . brownies immediately upon removing from oven.
Cut . . . . . . into squares when cooled.

Lana J. Crawford
Tarkington H. S., Cleveland, Texas

CHIPPEROO BARS

2/3 c. shortening, melted
1   1-lb. box brown sugar
2 3/4 c. all-purpose flour
2 1/2 tsp. baking powder
1/2 tsp. salt
3 eggs, beaten
1   6-oz. package chocolate chips
1 c. chopped pecans

Combine . first 2 ingredients in bowl; set aside.
Sift . . . . . . dry ingredients together; set aside.
Beat . . . . . eggs into brown sugar mixture.
Add . . . . . flour mixture slowly, mixing well.
Stir . . . . . . in remaining ingredients.
Spread . . . in greased 9 x 13-inch baking pan.

Bake . . . . . at 350 degrees for 25 to 30 minutes.
Cool . . . . . and cut into bars.

Linda Evans
New Caney H. S., Porter, Texas

CHOCOLATE MELTAWAYS

1 pkg. devil's food cake mix
2 eggs
1/4 c. butter, softened
1/4 c. packed brown sugar
1/2 c. chopped nuts
1 pkg. creamy white frosting mix
3 sq. unsweetened chocolate

Combine . half the dry cake mix with 1/4 cup water and next 3 ingredients in bowl, mixing thoroughly.
Add . . . . . remaining cake mix and nuts, blending well.
Spread . . . in greased and floured 10 1/2 x 15 1/2 x 1-inch baking pan.
Bake . . . . . at 375 degrees for 20 to 25 minutes.
Prepare . . . frosting mix using package directions.
Spread . . . over cake.
Melt . . . . . chocolate and spread evenly over frosting.
Cut . . . . . . into 1 1/2-inch squares before chocolate is completely firm.
Yields . . . . 70 cookies/about 85 calories each.

Bonnie N. Prewitt
Swartz Jr. H. S., Swartz, Louisiana

FORTY-NINER SQUARES

1   1-lb. box light brown sugar
2 c. biscuit mix
4 eggs, beaten
2 c. chopped pecans
2 tbsp. vanilla extract

Combine . all ingredients in large bowl, mixing well.
Pour . . . . . into greased and floured 9 x 13-inch baking pan.
Bake . . . . . at 325 degrees for 35 minutes.
Cool . . . . . completely before cutting.
Dust . . . . . with confectioners' sugar.

Mareen Strange
Walker H. S., Walker, Louisiana

HONEYSNAPS

1 1/2 c. shortening
Sugar
2 eggs
1/2 c. honey
4 c. sifted flour
2 tsp. soda
2 tsp. cinnamon
1 tsp. vanilla extract

Cream ... shortening and 2 cups sugar in bowl until smooth.
Beat ..... in eggs and honey.
Add ..... dry ingredients and vanilla, mixing well.
Shape .... into 1-inch balls.
Roll ..... in sugar.
Place .... 2 inches apart on baking sheet.
Bake ..... at 375 degrees for 15 to 18 minutes.
Yields .... 5 dozen/about 110 calories each.

Judy Gebhardt
J. L. Williams Jr. H. S., Copperas Cove, Texas

GINGERSNAPS

1 c. shortening
Sugar
2 eggs
1 c. molasses
4 c. flour
1 tsp. cinnamon
2 tsp. ginger
1/2 tsp. cloves
1/2 tsp. salt
1 tbsp. soda

Cream ... shortening and 2 cups sugar together in bowl until light and fluffy.
Add ..... eggs, mixing well.
Add ..... molasses, mixing well.
Sift ...... remaining ingredients together.
Add ..... to creamed mixture, mixing well.
Shape .... into tablespoon-sized balls.
Place .... on cookie sheet and flatten slightly.
Sprinkle .. with sugar.
Bake ..... at 375 degrees for 8 to 10 minutes.

Lois Pagnette
Chippewa Falls Sr. H. S., Chippewa Falls, Wisconsin

LEMON SQUARES

1 c. flour
Margarine, softened
1 c. confectioners' sugar
2 eggs
1 c. sugar
1/2 tsp. baking powder
1/4 tsp. salt
2 tbsp. lemon juice
1/2 tsp. vanilla extract
1 1/2 tsp. milk

Combine . flour, 1/2 cup margarine and 1/4 cup confectioners' sugar in bowl, mixing well.
Press ..... into bottom of 9-inch square baking dish.
Bake ..... at 325 degrees for 30 minutes.
Combine . next 5 ingredients in bowl, beating until fluffy.
Pour ..... over first layer.
Bake ..... for 25 minutes longer.
Cool ..... thoroughly.
Combine . remaining 3/4 cup confectioners' sugar with 1 tablespoon margarine, vanilla and milk in small bowl, blending until smooth.
Spread ... glaze over lemon layer and cut into squares.

Linda Beth Hardin
Houston H. S., Houston, Mississippi

MELTAWAYS

1/2 lb. margarine, softened
3/4 c. cornstarch
1 c. flour
1 1/3 c. confectioners' sugar
1 3-oz. package cream cheese, softened
1 tsp. vanilla extract

Cream ... margarine in bowl until fluffy.
Blend .... in cornstarch, flour and 1/3 cup confectioners' sugar, mixing well.
Drop .... by teaspoonfuls onto cookie sheet.
Bake ..... at 350 degrees for 12 minutes.
Cream ... remaining ingredients together in bowl.
Frost .... cookies.

Betty Ambrose
Robert E. Lee Sr. H. S., Midland, Texas

NO-NAME COOKIES

1 pkg. (about) saltine crackers
1 c. margarine
1 c. packed brown sugar
1   12-oz. package chocolate chips
1/2 to 1 c. chopped pecans (opt.)

Line . . . . . jelly roll pan with buttered foil.
Cover . . . . bottom of pan with crackers.
Combine . margarine and brown sugar in saucepan.
Bring . . . . to a boil.
Boil . . . . . for 3 minutes, stirring constantly. Do not overcook.
Pour . . . . . over crackers, spreading to cover completely.
Bake . . . . . at 375 degrees for 5 minutes.
Remove . . from oven.
Sprinkle . . with chocolate chips, spreading to cover as chips melt.
Top . . . . . with pecans.
Break . . . . into pieces when cooled.

Johnsie Walker Reglin
Marengo Community H. S., Marengo, Illinois

OATMEAL COOKIES

2 c. flour
2 c. oats
1 c. sugar
1 tsp. cinnamon
1/8 tsp. salt
1 c. shortening
3 eggs
1 tsp. vanilla extract
1 tsp. soda
4 tbsp. milk
1 c. raisins
1 c. chopped nuts

Combine . all dry ingredients in bowl.
Add . . . . . shortening, mixing well.
Add . . . . . eggs, mixing well.
Add . . . . . vanilla.
Mix . . . . . soda and milk together.
Stir . . . . . . into egg mixture, blending thoroughly.
Fold . . . . . in raisins and nuts, mixing well.
Drop . . . . by teaspoonfuls onto greased cookie sheet.
Bake . . . . . at 350 degrees for 10 minutes or until golden brown.

Cool . . . . . on cake rack.
Yields . . . . 5 dozen/about 90 calories each.

Teresa Schultz
Fairdale H. S., Fairdale, Kentucky

CHOCOLATE-OATMEAL COOKIES

1/2 c. shortening
1 c. sugar
2 eggs
1 1/2 c. flour
1/2 tsp. salt
2 tsp. cinnamon
1/2 tsp. soda
1 1/2 c. quick-cooking oatmeal
1/2 c. milk
1 c. ground raisins
1 c. chocolate chips (opt.)
1/2 c. chopped walnuts (opt.)
1 tsp. vanilla extract

Cream . . . shortening and sugar together in bowl.
Add . . . . . eggs, beating well.
Sift . . . . . . flour, salt and cinnamon together.
Dissolve . . soda in 2 tablespoons water.
Add . . . . . oatmeal and flour mixture alternately with milk and soda mixture, beating after each addition.
Stir . . . . . . in raisins, chocolate chips and nuts.
Add . . . . . vanilla, mixing well.
Drop . . . . onto lightly greased cookie sheet.
Bake . . . . . at 375 degrees for 10 minutes.
Yields . . . . 3 dozen/about 135 calories each.

Margaret A. Allen
Kaysville Jr. H. S., Kaysville, Utah

ORANGE SLICE COOKIES

2 c. packed light brown sugar
1 c. sugar
2 c. shortening
1 1/2 tsp. soda
3 eggs
20 candy orange slices, chopped
1 1/2 c. chopped pecans
1 can Angel Flake coconut
3 c. flour
1 1/2 tsp. baking powder
3 c. oatmeal

Cream . . . brown sugar, sugar and shortening together in bowl.

Dissolve . . soda in 3 tablespoons water.

Add . . . . . soda, eggs, candy, pecans and coconut to creamed ingredients, mixing well.

Sift . . . . . . flour and baking powder together.

Add . . . . . to batter, mixing well.

Stir . . . . . . in oatmeal.

Shape . . . . into roll.

Chill . . . . . wraped, for several hours.

Slice . . . . . to desired thickness.

Bake . . . . . at 325 degrees for 10 to 15 minutes.

Note . . . . . may be frozen.

Sue B. Gentry
Copperas Cove H. S., Copperas Cove, Texas

PEANUT BUTTER BARS

1 c. packed brown sugar
1/2 c. shortening
1 egg
1 tsp. vanilla extract
Peanut butter
1 1/2 c. flour
1 tsp. soda
1/2 tsp. salt
1/2 c. quick oats
2 tbsp. butter
1 1/2 c. confectioners' sugar
2 1/2 tbsp. milk

Cream . . . first 4 ingredients and 1/2 cup peanut butter together in bowl.

Sift . . . . . . next 3 ingredients together.

Add . . . . . to creamed mixture, mixing well.

Stir . . . . . . in oats.

Pat . . . . . . firmly into greased 10 x 15-inch baking pan.

Bake . . . . . at 375 degrees for 12 to 15 minutes until brown.

Cool . . . . . completely.

Combine . remaining ingredients with 2 tablespoons peanut butter and a dash of salt, blending well.

Frost . . . . and cut into bars.

Debbie Fair
Emerson Jr. H. S., Enid, Oklahoma

CRUNCHY PEANUT BUTTER BARS

1 sm. box yellow cake mix
1 egg

7 tsp. oil
1/4 c. peanut butter
1/4 c. chopped peanuts

Combine . all ingredients except peanuts with 1 tablespoon water in bowl, mixing well.

Spread . . . in 7 1/2 x 11 1/2-inch baking pan.

Sprinkle . . peanuts evenly over top.

Bake . . . . . at 375 degrees for 13 to 15 minutes.

Cool . . . . . slightly and cut into bars.

DeAnn Pence
Chandler H. S., Chandler, Oklahoma

PECAN PIE BARS

1 box yellow cake mix
4 eggs
1/2 c. margarine, melted
1 c. packed brown sugar
1 1/2 c. dark corn syrup
1 tsp. vanilla extract
1 c. chopped pecans

Combine . 1/3 of the cake mix with 1 egg and margarine in bowl, mixing well.

Press . . . . . into greased 9 x 13-inch pan.

Bake . . . . . at 350 degrees for 15 minutes.

Combine . remaining cake mix, 3 eggs, brown sugar, corn syrup and vanilla in bowl.

Beat . . . . . for 2 minutes with electric mixer at medium speed.

Pour . . . . . over crust.

Sprinkle . . with pecans.

Bake . . . . . for 30 to 35 minutes longer or until light brown.

Cool . . . . . and cut into bars.

Carol Brandt
Alburnett Community School, Alburnett, Iowa

SHAPED SCOTCH SHORTBREAD

1 c. sugar
2 c. butter
4 c. flour

Cream . . . sugar into butter.

Knead . . . in flour gradually until smooth.

Roll . . . . . out 1/2 inch thick.

Cut . . . . . . into desired shapes.

Bake . . . . . at 325 degrees for 15 to 20 minutes.

Florence Hart
Hants West Rural H. S., Newport, Nova Scotia, Canada

PINEAPPLE COOKIES

1 c. shortening
1 c. packed brown sugar
1 c. sugar
4 c. flour
2 tsp. baking powder
1/2 tsp. soda
1/2 tsp. salt
2 eggs
1 c. crushed pineapple
1 tsp. vanilla extract
1 c. chopped nuts

Cream ... shortening and sugars together in bowl.
Sift ...... dry ingredients together.
Add ..... 1 egg, half the pineapple and half the dry ingredients, beating well after each addition.
Repeat ... and add all remaining ingredients.
Drop .... by teaspoonfuls onto greased cookie sheet.
Bake ..... at 400 degrees for 10 minutes or until brown.

Janet K. Francis
Savoy H. S., Savoy, Texas

SNICKERDOODLES

Sugar
1/2 c. shortening
1/2 c. margarine, softened
2 eggs
1 tsp. vanilla extract
2 3/4 c. flour
1 tsp. soda
1/4 tsp. salt
2 tsp. cream of tartar
2 tsp. cinnamon

Cream ... 1 1/2 cups sugar, shortening and margarine together in bowl.
Add ..... eggs and vanilla, mixing well.
Combine . next 4 ingredients in bowl.
Stir ...... into creamed mixture.
Chill ..... overnight.
Shape .... into walnut-sized balls.
Mix ..... cinnamon and 2 tablespoons sugar in small bowl.
Roll ..... cookies in sugar mixture.
Place .... 2 inches apart on cookie sheet.
Bake ..... at 375 degrees for 8 to 10 minutes.

Esther L. Moorhead
Berryhill H. S., Tulsa, Oklahoma

ANGEL PIE

1 c. crushed pineapple
Sugar
3/4 tsp. salt
6 tbsp. cornstarch
3 egg whites
1 8-in. baked pie shell
1/2 pt. whipping cream, whipped
1/4 c. finely chopped pecans

Combine . pineapple with 1 cup sugar and salt in saucepan.
Bring .... to a boil, stirring constantly.
Blend .... cornstarch with 1/2 cup cold water in small bowl.
Add ..... to pineapple mixture.
Cook .... until clear and glossy, stirring constantly.
Set ...... aside to cool.
Beat ..... egg whites until stiff.
Fold ..... in 2 tablespoons sugar.
Fold ..... egg whites into pineapple mixture.
Spoon ... into pie shell.
Top ..... with whipped cream and pecans.
Chill ..... before serving.

Janet Chapman
Woodstock H. S., Woodstock, Illinois

BASIC APPLE PIE

1 recipe 2-crust pie pastry
1/2 c. sugar
2 tbsp. cornstarch
1/2 tsp. ground cinnamon
1/4 tsp. ground nutmeg
1/2 tsp. grated lemon rind
6 apples, peeled, cored, sliced
1 tbsp. lemon juice
2 tbsp. margarine

Line ..... 9-inch pie plate with half the pastry, allowing 1-inch overhang.
Combine . next 5 ingredients in bowl.
Add ..... apples, tossing to coat.
Sprinkle .. with lemon juice.
Turn ..... into pastry-lined pie plate.
Dot ..... with margarine.
Cover .... with remaining pastry, sealing and fluting edges.
Make .... several slits in top crust.
Bake ..... at 425 degrees for 50 minutes or until crust is brown.

Photograph for this recipe on cover.

MARY'S APPLE PIE

4 c. peeled sliced apples
1 c. sugar
3 tbsp. flour
1/2 tsp. nutmeg
1/3 c. orange juice
1/3 c. melted butter
2 unbaked pie shells

Combine . apples with remaining ingredients except pie shells in large bowl, tossing lightly to mix well.
Pour . . . . . into 1 pie shell.
Top . . . . . pie with top crust or strips of pastry as desired, sprinkling lightly with sugar.
Bake . . . . . at 450 degrees for 15 minutes.
Reduce . . . temperature to 325 degrees.
Bake . . . . . for 45 minutes longer.

Mary E. Roddam
Clio H. S., Clio, Alabama

FROZEN CHERRY CHEESE PIE

2 3-oz. packages cream cheese, softened
1/2 c. sugar
Dash of salt
2 egg yolks
1 tbsp. vanilla extract
1 env. Dream Whip
7/8 c. cold milk
2 egg whites, stiffly beaten
1 unbaked 9-in. graham cracker crust, chilled
1 can cherry pie filling (opt.)

Combine . first 3 ingredients in bowl, blending well.
Add . . . . . egg yolks and vanilla, beating until smooth.
Prepare . . . Dream Whip with milk using package directions.
Add . . . . . 2 cups Dream Whip to cream cheese mixture.
Fold . . . . . in egg whites.
Pour . . . . . into crust.
Freeze . . . for 3 to 4 hours.
Let . . . . . . stand at room temperature for a few minutes before serving.
Top . . . . . with pie filling and remaining Dream Whip.

Kathleen Ann McConkie
Southwest Jr. H. S., Hot Springs, Arkansas

CANDY CRUST ICE CREAM PIE

2/3 c. semisweet chocolate bits
1/4 c. butter
1/4 c. milk
2 cans flaked coconut
1 qt. cherry-vanilla ice cream

Combine . first 3 ingredients in small saucepan.
Cook . . . . over low heat until chocolate melts, stirring to blend.
Fold . . . . . in coconut.
Spread . . . on bottom and side of greased 9-inch pie plate.
Chill . . . . . until firm.
Fill . . . . . . shell with ice cream.
Freeze . . . until serving time.
Thaw . . . . in refrigerator for 20 minutes before slicing.
Garnish . . with sweetened whipped cream.

Photograph for this recipe on page 6.

BLUEBERRY DESSERT PIE

16 graham crackers, crushed
3/4 c. butter, softened
6 tbsp. sugar
2 boxes wild raspberry gelatin
1 15-oz. can crushed pineapple
1 can wild blueberries
1 c. chopped black walnuts
2 pkg. Dream Whip

Combine . graham cracker crumbs, butter and sugar·in bowl, mixing well.
Press . . . . . into two 8-inch pie pans.
Bake . . . . . at 350 degrees for 8 minutes.
Dissolve . . gelatin in 2 cups boiling water in bowl.
Drain . . . . pineapple and blueberries, reserving juice.
Add . . . . . enough water to combined juices to measure 2 cups.
Stir . . . . . . into gelatin, mixing well.
Chill . . . . . until partially congealed.
Remove . . 3/4 cup gelatin; set aside.
Add . . . . . fruits and nuts to remaining gelatin.
Pour . . . . . into prepared crusts.
Prepare . . . Dream Whip, using package directions.
Fold . . . . . into reserved 3/4 cup gelatin.
Spread . . . over fruit layer.
Chill . . . . . for several hours.

Marie Jones
Osage City H. S., Osage City, Kansas

POPCORN AND APPLE PIE

5 c. popped popcorn
3 egg whites
1 c. sugar
1/2 c. finely chopped nuts
2 c. chunky applesauce
2 c. nondairy whipped topping

Place .... popcorn, 1 cup at a time, in electric blender container.
Process ... to crush.
Beat ..... egg whites until soft peaks form.
Add ..... sugar gradually, beating until stiff.
Fold ..... in nuts and crushed popcorn.
Spread ... in buttered pie pan.
Bake ..... at 350 degrees for 15 minutes.
Fold ..... applesauce into whipped topping in bowl.
Pour ..... into cooled crust.
Chill ..... until serving time.
Yields .... 8 servings.

Ralpha Richie
Hoover Middle School, Oklahoma City, Oklahoma

BUTTER TARTS

Sifted flour
3/4 tsp. salt
10 tbsp. shortening
1/2 c. packed brown sugar
1/4 c. sugar
1 egg, beaten
1 tbsp. milk
1/2 tsp. vanilla extract
1/4 c. melted butter
1/2 c. chopped nuts

Combine . 1 1/2 cups flour and salt in bowl.
Cut ...... in shortening until crumbly.
Add ..... 3 tablespoons water, mixing well.
Divide ... dough into 24 portions.
Roll ..... out and line tart or muffin cups.
Combine . 1 1/2 teaspoons flour with sugars in bowl.
Beat ..... egg, milk and vanilla together in small bowl.
Add ..... to sugar mixture, mixing well.
Stir ...... in butter and nuts.
Fill ...... pastry shells.
Bake ..... at 425 degrees for 15 to 20 minutes or until set.

Renee R. Porter
American Fork H. S., American Fork, Utah

NO-ROLL CHERRY PIE

1/2 c. butter
Sugar
1 1/4 c. flour
1 can cherry pie filling
1 egg
1/4 c. milk

Melt ..... butter with 1 tablespoon sugar in saucepan.
Add ..... 1 cup flour and stir until mixture forms a ball.
Press ..... into bottom and side of 9-inch pie plate, forming an edge.
Pour ..... in filling.
Combine . egg and milk with remaining 1/4 cup flour and 1/2 cup sugar in small bowl, mixing well.
Spoon ... over filling.
Bake ..... at 350 degrees for 50 to 60 minutes until brown.

Lee Helzer
Fort Calhoun Community Schools
Fort Calhoun, Nebraska

GRAPEFRUIT CHIFFON PIE

1 1/3 c. gingersnap cookie crumbs
1/4 c. butter, melted
1 c. sugar
1 env. unflavored gelatin
1/2 tsp. finely chopped candied ginger
1/4 tsp. grated grapefruit rind
3 eggs, separated
1 c. fresh Florida grapefruit juice
1/2 c. heavy cream, whipped
Fresh grapefruit sections

Combine . crumbs, butter and 1/4 cup sugar in bowl, mixing well.
Press ..... into 9-inch pie plate.
Combine . gelatin, 1/2 cup sugar, ginger and rind in saucepan.
Beat ..... egg yolks with grapefruit juice and stir into gelatin mixture.
Cook .... over low heat until gelatin dissolves and mixture thickens slightly, stirring constantly.
Chill ..... until mixture mounds when dropped from spoon.
Beat ..... egg whites until stiff but not dry.

Add ..... remaining 1/4 cup sugar gradually, beating until stiff peaks form.

Fold ..... into cooled gelatin mixture.

Fold ..... in whipped cream.

Pour ..... into prepared crust.

Chill ..... until set.

Garnish .. with additional whipped cream and grapefruit sections.

Photograph for this recipe on page 1.

GRASSHOPPER PIE

1 1/2 c. chocolate wafer crumbs
1/4 c. melted butter
25 lg. marshmallows
2/3 c. light cream
3 or 4 tbsp. green Creme de Menthe
3 or 4 tbsp. white Creme de Cacao
1 c. heavy cream, whipped

Combine . chocolate crumbs and butter in bowl, reserving 2 tablespoons crumbs.

Press ..... over bottom and side of 9-inch pie pan.

Chill ..... in refrigerator until needed.

Combine . marshmallows and light cream in saucepan.

Heat ..... until marshmallows are melted; set aside.

Fold ..... liquers and whipped cream into cooled mixture.

Pour ..... into chilled crust.

Sprinkle .. with reserved crumbs.

Freeze ... until firm.

Sandra J. Bennett
Kimball Jr. H. S., Elgin, Illinois

LEMON PIE

1   14-oz. can sweetened condensed milk
8 oz. cream cheese, softened
2 egg yolks, beaten
1/3 to 1/2 c. lemon juice
6 prepared graham cracker tart shells
1   8-oz. carton Cool Whip
6 maraschino cherries

Combine . first 4 ingredients in medium bowl, mixing well.

Pour ..... into tart shells.

Chill ..... for 3 hours or until firm.

Top ..... with Cool Whip and cherries.

Lurene J. Traynham
Caldwell H. S., Columbus, Mississippi

LEMON CHEESECAKE PIE

1   3 1/2-oz. can flaked coconut
1/4 c. chopped pecans
2 tbsp. butter, melted
2 c. cottage cheese
2   3 3/4-oz. packages lemon instant pudding mix
1 3/4 c. milk
2 tbsp. grated lemon peel
1/2 c. sour cream

Combine . first 3 ingredients in small bowl, mixing well.

Press ..... into bottom and side of 9-inch pie plate.

Bake ..... at 325 degrees for 15 to 20 minutes or until golden; set aside to cool.

Beat ..... cottage cheese in bowl until smooth.

Prepare ... pudding mix using package directions with 1 3/4 cups milk.

Combine . pudding, cottage cheese and lemon peel, blending well.

Spoon ... into pie shell.

Top ..... with sour cream and additional pecans.

Chill ..... for several hours.

Photograph for this recipe below.

PINK GRAPEFRUIT PARFAIT PIE

1 env. unflavored gelatin
1/2 c. Florida pink grapefruit juice
1 pt. vanilla ice cream, melted
2 egg whites
1 tbsp. sugar
2 c. Florida pink grapefruit sections, cut up
1 baked 9-in. pie shell

Combine . gelatin and juice in small saucepan; let stand for 1 minute.
Stir . . . . . . over low heat until gelatin dissolves, stirring constantly.
Remove . . from heat.
Stir . . . . . . in ice cream.
Chill . . . . . until thick, stirring occasionally.
Beat . . . . . egg whites in medium bowl until soft peaks form.
Add . . . . . sugar gradually, beating until stiff peaks form.
Fold . . . . . into gelatin mixture.
Fold . . . . . in grapefruit sections.
Pour . . . . . in baked pie shell.
Chill . . . . . until firm.
Garnish . . with whipped cream and additional grapefruit sections.

Photograph for this recipe on page 104.

PUMPKIN CHIFFON PIE

3 egg yolks, beaten
3/4 c. packed brown sugar
1 1/2 c. cooked pumpkin
1/2 c. milk
1/2 tsp. salt
1 tsp. cinnamon
1/2 tsp. nutmeg
1 env. unflavored gelatin
3 egg whites
1/4 c. sugar
1 baked pie shell

Combine . first 7 ingredients in top half of double boiler.
Cook . . . . until thick, stirring constantly.
Soften . . . gelatin in 1/4 cup cold water.
Stir . . . . . . into hot mixture, stirring to dissolve.
Beat . . . . . egg whites until soft peaks form.
Add . . . . . sugar gradually, beating until stiff.
Fold . . . . . into pumpkin mixture.

Pour . . . . . into pie shell.
Chill . . . . . until set.
Garnish . . with whipped cream.

Joan S. Walker
Scott H. S., Huntsville, Tennessee

FRESH STRAWBERRY PIE

1 c. sugar
3 tbsp. cornstarch
2 tbsp. light corn syrup
Pinch of salt
2 tsp. strawberry gelatin
Red food coloring
3 c. fresh strawberries, washed, drained
1 8-in. baked pie shell
Whipped cream

Combine . first 4 ingredients and 1 cup water in saucepan.
Cook . . . . over low heat until thick and clear, stirring constantly.
Cool . . . . . slightly and add gelatin and food coloring, stirring to dissolve.
Arrange . . strawberries in baked pie shell.
Pour . . . . . glaze over top.
Top . . . . . with whipped cream and additional strawberries, if desired.

Marilyn Frisbee
Cabool Middle School, Cabool, Missouri

EASY FRIED PIES

1/4 c. butter
1 c. flour
3 tbsp. hot milk
1 egg yolk
Pie filling of choice
Oil for deep frying

Cut . . . . . . butter into flour with pastry blender.
Combine . milk and egg yolk.
Pour . . . . . over flour mixture, stirring to mix well.
Roll . . . . . out small portions on floured surface.
Place . . . . pie filling in center.
Fold . . . . . over and seal edges.
Fry . . . . . . in deep hot fat until golden brown.

Judy Adler
Snyder H. S., Snyder, Oklahoma

Count-Your-Calories Chart

Almonds, shelled, 1/4 cup .213
Apples: 1 med. 70
  chopped, 1/2 cup 30
Apple juice, 1 cup 117
Applesauce: sweetened 1/2 cup 115
  unsweetened, 1/2 cup 50
Apricots: fresh, 3 55
  canned, 1/2 cup 110
  dried, 10 halves 100
Apricot nectar, 1 cup 140
Asparagus: fresh, 6 spears 19
  canned, 1/2 cup 18
Avocado, 1 med. 265
Bacon, 2 sl. crisp-cooked, drained 90
Banana, 1 med. 100
Beans: baked, 1/2 cup 160
  dry, 1/2 cup 350
  green, 1/2 cup 20
  lima, 1/2 cup 95
  soy, 1/2 cup 95
Bean sprouts, 1/2 cup 18
Beef, cooked, 3 oz. serving:
  roast, rib 375
  roast, heel of round 165
  steak, sirloin 330
Beer, 12 oz. 150
Beets, cooked, 1/2 cup 40
Biscuit, from mix, 1 90
Bologna, all meat, 3 oz. .235
Bread: roll, 1 85
  white, 1 slice 65
  whole wheat, 1 slice 65
Bread crumbs, dry, 1 cup 390
Broccoli, cooked, 1/2 cup 20
Butter: 1/2 cup 800
  1 tbsp. 100
Buttermilk, 1 cup 90
Cabbage: cooked, 1/2 cup 15
  fresh, shredded, 1/2 cup 10
Cake: angel food, 1/12 pkg. prepared 140
  devil's food, 1/12 pkg. prepared 195
  yellow, 1/12 pkg. prepared 200
Candy: caramel, 1 oz. 115
  chocolate, sweet, 1 oz. 145
  hard candy, 1 oz. 110
Marshmallows, 1 oz. 90
Cantaloupe, 1/2 med. 60
Carrots, cooked, 1/2 cup 23
  fresh, 1 med. 20
Catsup, 1 tbsp. 18
Cauliflower: cooked, 1/2 cup 13
  fresh, 1/2 lb. 60
Celery, chopped, 1/2 cup 8
Cereals: bran flakes, 1/2 cup 53
  corn flakes, 1/2 cup 50
  oatmeal, cooked, 1/2 cup 65

Cheese: American, 1 oz. 105
  Cheddar: 1 oz. 113
    shredded, 1 cup 452
  Cottage: creamed, 1/2 cup 130
    uncreamed, 1/2 cup 85
  Cream, 1 oz. 107
  Mozzarella, 1 oz. 80
    shredded, 1 cup 320
  Parmesan, 1 oz. 110
  Velveeta, 1 oz. 84
Cherries: canned, sour in water, 1/2 cup 53
  fresh, sweet, 1/2 cup 40
Chicken, meat only, 4 oz. serving:
  boned, chopped 1/2 cup 170
  broiled 155
  canned, boned 230
  roast, dark meat 210
  roast, light meat 207
Chili peppers: green, fresh, 1/2 lb. 62
  red, fresh, 1/2 lb. 108
Chili powder with seasonings, 1 tbsp. 51
Chocolate, baking, 1 oz. 143
Cocoa mix, 1 oz. package 115
Cocoa powder, baking, 1/3 cup 120
Coconut, dried, shredded, 1/4 cup 166
Coffee 0
Corn: canned, cream-style, 1/2 cup 100
  canned, whole kernal, 1/2 cup 85
Cornbread, mix, prepared, 1 x 4 in. piece 125
Corn chips, 1 oz. 130
Cornmeal, 1/2 cup 264
Cornstarch, 1 tbsp. 29
Crab, fresh, meat only, 3 oz. 80
  canned, 3 oz. 85
Crackers: graham, 2 1/2-in. square 28
  Ritz, each 17
  saltine, 2-in. square 13
Cracker crumbs, 1/2 cup 281
Cranberries: fresh, 1/2 lb. 100
  juice, cocktail, 1 cup .163
  sauce, 1/2 cup 190
Cream: half-and-half, 1 tbsp. 20
  heavy, 1 tbsp. 55
  light, 1 tbsp. 30
Creamer, imitation powdered, 1 tsp. 10
Cucumber, 1 med. 30
Dates, dried, chopped, 1/2 cup 244
Eggs: 1 whole, large 80
  1 white 17
  1 yolk 59
Eggplant, cooked, 1/2 cup 19
Fish sticks, 5 200
Flour: rye, 1 cup 286
  white: 1 cup 420
    1 tbsp. 28
  whole wheat, 1 cup 400

COUNT-YOUR-CALORIES CHART

Fruit cocktail, canned, 1/2 cup 98
Garlic, 1 clove 2
Gelatin, unflavored 1 env. 25
Grapes: fresh, 1/2 cup 35-50
    juice, 1 cup 170
Grapefruit: fresh, 1/2 med. 60
    juice, unsweetened, 1 cup 100
Ground beef, patty, lean 185
    regular 245
Haddock, fried, 3 oz. 140
Ham, 3 oz. servings:
    boiled 200
    fresh, roast 320
    country-style 335
    cured, lean 160
Honey, 1 tbsp. 65
Ice cream, 1/2 cup 135
Ice milk, 1/2 cup 96
Jams and preserves, 1 tbsp. 54
Jellies, 1 tbsp. 55
Jell-O, 1/2 cup. 80
Lamb, 3 oz. serving, leg roast 185
    1 1/2 oz., rib chop 175
Lemon juice, 1 tbsp. 4
Lemonade, sweetened, 1 cup 110
Lentils, cooked, 1/2 cup 168
Lettuce, 1 head 40
Liver, 2 oz. serving: beef, fried 130
    chicken, simmered 88
Lobster, 2 oz. 55
Macaroni, cooked, 1/2 cup 90
Mango, 1 fresh 134
Margarine: 1/2 cup 800
    1 tbsp. 100
Mayonnaise: 1 tbsp. 100
Milk: whole, 1 cup 160
    skim, 1 cup 89
    condensed, 1 cup 982
    evaporated, 1 cup 345
    dry nonfat, 1 cup 251
Muffin, plain 120
Mushrooms: canned, 1/2 cup 20
    fresh, 1 lb. 123
Mustard: prepared, brown, 1 tbsp. 13
    prepared, yellow, 1 tbsp. 10
Nectarine, 1 fresh 30
Noodles: egg, cooked, 1/2 cup 100
    fried, chow mein, 2 oz. 275
Oil, cooking, salad, 1 tbsp. 120
Okra, cooked, 8 pods 25
Olives: green, 3 lg. 15
    ripe, 2 lg. 15
Onion: chopped, 1/2 cup 32
    dehydrated flakes, 1 tbsp. 17
    green, 6 20
    whole, 1 40
Orange: 1 whole 65
    juice, 1 cup 115
Oysters, meat only, 1/2 cup 80

Pancakes, 4-in. diameter, 1 60
Peaches: fresh, 1 med. 35
    canned, 1/2 cup 100
    dried, 1/2 cup 210
Peanuts, shelled, roasted, 1 cup 420
Peanut butter, 1 tbsp. 100
Pears: fresh, 1 med. 100
    canned, 1/2 cup 97
    dried, 1/2 cup 214
Peas: black-eyed, 1/2 cup 70
    green, canned, 1/2 cup 83
    green, frozen, 1/2 cup 69
Pecans, chopped, 1/2 cup 400
Peppers: sweet green, 1 med. 14
    sweet red, 1 med. 19
Perch, white, 4 oz. 50
Pickles: dill, 1 lg. 15
    sweet, 1 average 30
Pie crust, mix, 1 crust 626
Pie, 8-in. frozen, 1/6 serving
    apple 234
    cherry 300
    peach 280
Pimento, canned, 1 avg. 10
Pineapple: fresh, diced, 1/2 cup 36
    canned, 1/2 cup 90
    juice, 1 cup 135
Plums: fresh, 1 med. 30
    canned, 3 101
Popcorn, plain, popped, 1 cup 54
Pork, cooked, lean:
    Boston butt, roasted, 4 oz. 280
    chop, broiled, 3.5 oz. 260
    loin, roasted, 4 oz 290
Potato chips, 1 oz. 322
Potatoes, white:
    baked, 1 sm. with skin 93
    boiled, 1 sm. 70
    French-fried, 10 pieces 155
    hashed brown, 1/2 cup 225
    mashed, with milk and butter, 1/2 cup 90
Potatoes, sweet:
    baked, 1 avg. 155
    candied, 1 avg 295
    canned, 1/2 cup 110
Prune: 1 lg. 19
    dried, cooked, 1/2 cup 137
    juice, 1 cup 197
Puddings and pie fillings, prepared:
    banana, 1/2 cup 165
    butterscotch, 1/2 cup 190
    chocolate, 1/2 cup 190
    lemon, 1/2 cup 125
Puddings, instant, prepared:
    banana, 1/2 cup 175
    butterscotch, 1/2 cup 175
    chocolate, 1/2 cup 200
    lemon, 1/2 cup 180
Pumpkin, canned, 1/2 cup 38

COUNT-YOUR-CALORIES CHART

Raisins, dried, 1/2 cup 231
Rice: cooked, white, 1/2 cup 90
   cooked, brown, 1/2 cup 100
   precooked, 1/2 cup .105
Salad dressings, commercial:
   blue cheese, 1 tbsp. 75
   French, 1 tbsp. 70
   Italian, 1 tbsp. 83
   mayonnaise, 1 tbsp. 100
   mayonnaise-type, 1 tbsp. 65
   Russian, 1 tbsp. 75
   Thousand Island, 1 tbsp. 80
Salami, cooked, 2 oz. 180
Salmon: canned, 4 oz. .180
   steak, 4 oz. 220
Sardines, canned, 3 oz. 175
Sauces: barbecue, 1 tbsp. 17
   hot pepper, 1 tbsp. 3
   soy, 1 tbsp. 9
   white, med. 1/2 cup 215
   Worcestershire, 1 tbsp. 15
Sauerkraut, 1/2 cup 21
Sausage, cooked, 2 oz. 260
Sherbet, 1/2 cup 130
Shrimp: cooked, 3 oz. 50
   canned, 4 oz. 130
Soft drinks, 1 cup 100
Soup, 1 can, condensed:
   chicken with rice 116
   cream of celery 215
   cream of chicken 235
   cream of mushroom 331
   tomato 220
   vegetable-beef 198
Sour cream, 1/2 cup 240
Spaghetti, cooked, 1/2 cup 80
Spinach: fresh, 1/2 lb. 60
   cooked, 1/2 cup 20
Squash: summer, cooked, 1/2 cup 15
   winter, cooked, 1/2 cup 65
Strawberries, fresh, 1/2 cup 23

Sugar: brown, packed, 1/2 cup 410
   confectioners', sifted, 1/2 cup 240
   granulated: 1/2 cup .385
    1 tbsp. 48
Syrups: chocolate, 1 tbsp. 50
   corn, 1 tbsp. 58
   maple, 1 tbsp. 50
Taco shell, 1 shell 50
Tea, 1 cup 0
Tomatoes: fresh, 1 med. 40
   canned, 1/2 cup 25
   juice, 1 cup 45
   paste, 6-oz. can 150
   sauce, 8-oz. can 34
Toppings: caramel, 1 tbsp. 70
   chocolate fudge, 1 tbsp. 65
   Cool Whip, 1 tbsp. 14
   Dream Whip, prepared, 1 tbsp. 8
   Strawberry, 1 tbsp. 60
Tortilla, corn, 1 65
Tuna: canned in oil, drained, 4 oz. 230
   canned in water, 4 oz. 144
Turkey: dark meat, roasted, 4 oz. 230
   light meat, roasted, 4 oz. 200
Veal; cutlet, broiled, 3 oz. 185
   roast, 3 oz. 230
Vegetable juice cocktail, 1 cup 43
Vinegar, 1 tbsp. 2
Waffles, 1 130
Walnuts, chopped, 1/2 cup 410
Water chestnuts, sliced, 1/2 cup 25
Watermelon, fresh, cubed, 1/2 cup 26
Wheat germ, 1 tbsp. 29
Wine: dessert, 1/2 cup .140
   table, 1/2 cup 85
Yeast: compressed, 1 oz. 24
   dry, 1 oz. 80
Yogurt: plain, w/whole milk, 1 cup 153
   plain, w/skim milk, 1 cup 123
   with fruit, 1 cup 260

Equivalent Chart

	WHEN RECIPE CALLS FOR:	YOU NEED:
BREAD & CEREAL	1 c. soft bread crumbs	2 slices
	1 c. fine dry bread crumbs	4-5 slices
	1 c. small bread cubes	2 slices
	1 c. fine cracker crumbs	24 saltines
	1 c. fine graham cracker crumbs	14 crackers
	1 c. vanilla wafer crumbs	22 wafers
	1 c. crushed corn flakes	3 c. uncrushed
	4 c. cooked macaroni	1 8-oz. package
	3 1/2 c. cooked rice	1 c. uncooked
DAIRY	1 c. freshly grated cheese	1/4 lb.
	1 c. cottage cheese or sour cream	1 8-oz. carton
	2/3 c. evaporated milk	1 sm. can
	1 2/3 c. evaporated milk	1 tall can
	1 c. whipped cream	1/2 c. heavy cream
SWEET	1 c. semisweet chocolate pieces	1 6-oz. package
	2 c. granulated sugar	1 lb.
	4 c. sifted confectioners' sugar	1 lb.
	2 1/4 c. packed brown sugar	1 lb.
MEAT	3 c. diced cooked meat	1 lb., cooked
	2 c. ground cooked meat	1 lb., cooked
	4 c. diced cooked chicken	1 5-lb. chicken
NUTS	1 c. chopped nuts	4 oz. shelled
		1 lb. unshelled
VEGETABLES	4 c. sliced or diced raw potatoes	4 medium
	2 c. cooked green beans	1/2 lb. fresh or 1 16-oz. can
	1 c. chopped onion	1 large
	4 c. shredded cabbage	1 lb.
	2 c. canned tomatoes	1 16-oz. can
	1 c. grated carrot	1 large
	2 1/2 c. lima beans or red beans	1 c. dried, cooked
	1 4-oz. can mushrooms	1/2 lb. fresh

WHEN RECIPE CALLS FOR:	YOU NEED:
4 c. sliced or chopped apples	4 medium
2 c. pitted cherries	4 c. unpitted
3 to 4 tbsp. lemon juice plus 1 tsp. grated peel	1 lemon
1/3 c. orange juice plus 2 tsp. grated peel	1 orange
1 c. mashed banana	3 medium
4 c. cranberries	1 lb.
3 c. shredded coconut	1/2 lb.
4 c. sliced peaches	8 medium
1 c. pitted dates or candied fruit	1 8-oz. package
2 c. pitted prunes	1 12-oz. package
3 c. raisins	1 15-oz. package

(FRUIT)

COMMON EQUIVALENTS

1 tbsp. = 3 tsp.	4 qt. = 1 gal.
2 tbsp. = 1 oz.	6 1/2 to 8-oz. can = 1 c.
4 tbsp. = 1/4 c.	10 1/2 to 12-oz. can = 1 1/4 c.
5 tbsp. + 1 tsp. = 1/3 c.	14 to 16-oz. can (No. 300) = 1 3/4 c.
8 tbsp. = 1/2 c.	16 to 17-oz. can (No. 303) = 2 c.
12 tbsp. = 3/4 c.	1-lb. 4-oz. can or 1-pt. 2-oz. can (No. 2) = 2 1/2 c.
16 tbsp. = 1 c.	1-lb. 13-oz. can (No. 2 1/2) = 3 1/2 c.
1 c. = 8 oz. or 1/2 pt.	3-lb. 3-oz. can or 46-oz. can or 1-qt. 14-oz. can = 5 3/4 c.
4 c. = 1 qt.	6 1/2-lb. or 7-lb. 5-oz. can (No. 10) = 12 to 13 c.

Metric Conversion Chart

VOLUME

1 tsp.	=	4.9 cc
1 tbsp.	=	14.7 cc
1/3 c.	=	28.9 cc
1/8 c.	=	29.5 cc
1/4 c.	=	59.1 cc
1/2 c.	=	118.3 cc
3/4 c.	=	177.5 cc
1 c.	=	236.7 cc
2 c.	=	473.4 cc
1 fl. oz.	=	29.5 cc
4 oz.	=	118.3 cc
8 oz.	=	236.7 cc

1 pt.	=	473.4 cc
1 qt.	=	.946 liters
1 gal.	=	3.7 liters

CONVERSION FACTORS:

Liters	X	1.056	=	Liquid quarts
Quarts	X	0.946	=	Liters
Liters	X	0.264	=	Gallons
Gallons	X	3.785	=	Liters
Fluid ounces	X	29.563	=	Cubic centimeters
Cubic centimeters	X	0.034	=	Fluid ounces
Cups	X	236.575	=	Cubic centimeters
Tablespoons	X	14.797	=	Cubic centimeters
Teaspoons	X	4.932	=	Cubic centimeters
Bushels	X	0.352	=	Hectoliters
Hectoliters	X	2.837	=	Bushels

WEIGHT

1 dry oz.	=	28.3 Grams
1 lb.	=	.454 Kilograms

CONVERSION FACTORS:

Ounces (Avoir.)	X	28.349	=	Grams
Grams	X	0.035	=	Ounces
Pounds	X	0.454	=	Kilograms
Kilograms	X	2.205	=	Pounds

Substitutions Chart

	INSTEAD OF:	USE:
BAKING	1 tsp. baking powder	1/4 tsp. soda plus 1/2 tsp. cream of tartar
	1 c. sifted all-purpose flour	1 c. plus 2 tbsp. sifted cake flour
	1 c. sifted cake flour	1 c. minus 2 tbsp. sifted all-purpose flour
	1 tsp. cornstarch (for thickening)	2 tbsp. flour or 1 tbsp. tapioca
SWEET	1 1-oz. square chocolate	3 to 4 tbsp. cocoa plus 1 tsp. shortening
	1 2/3 oz. semisweet chocolate	1 oz. unsweetened chocolate plus 4 tsp. sugar
	1 c. granulated sugar	1 c. packed brown sugar or 1 c. corn syrup, molasses, honey minus 1/4 c. liquid
	1 c. honey	1 to 1 1/4 c. sugar plus 1/4 c. liquid or 1 c. molasses or corn syrup
DAIRY	1 c. sweet milk	1 c. sour milk or buttermilk plus 1/2 tsp. soda
	1 c. sour milk	1 c. sweet milk plus 1 tbsp. vinegar or lemon juice or 1 c. buttermilk
	1 c. buttermilk	1 c. sour milk or 1 c. yogurt
	1 c. light cream	7/8 c. skim milk plus 3 tbsp. butter
	1 c. heavy cream	3/4 c. skim milk plus 1/3 c. butter
	1 c. sour cream	7/8 c. sour milk plus 3 tbsp. butter
	1 c. bread crumbs	3/4 c. cracker crumbs
SEASONINGS	1 c. catsup	1 c. tomato sauce plus 1/2 c. sugar plus 2 tbsp. vinegar
	1 tbsp. prepared mustard	1 tsp. dry mustard
	1 tsp. Italian spice	1/4 tsp. each oregano, basil, thyme, rosemary plus dash of cayenne
	1 tsp. allspice	1/2 tsp. cinnamon plus 1/8 tsp. cloves
	1 medium onion	1 tbsp. dried minced onion or 1 tsp. onion powder
	1 clove of garlic	1/8 tsp. garlic powder or 1/8 tsp. instant minced garlic or 3/4 tsp. garlic salt or 5 drops of liquid garlic
	1 tsp. lemon juice	1/2 tsp. vinegar

Index

PHOTOGRAPHY CREDITS

Cover Design: Jessica Jenkins, Goodgraphiks; Best Foods, a Unit of CPC North America; Florida Citrus Commission; Idaho Potato Commission; United Fresh Fruit and Vegetable Association; The McIlhenny Company (Tabasco); Tuna Research Foundation; Fleischmann's Yeast; Spanish Green Olive Commission; R. C. Bigelow, Inc.; Knox Gelatin, Inc.; Western Growers Association; The Pillsbury Company; Campbell Soup Company; American Dairy Association; United Dairy Industry Association; National Livestock and Meat Board; The Rice Council; Pickle Packers International, Inc; Western Research Kitchens, a Division of Life and Associates, Inc.; Angostura-Wupperman Corporation; California Avocado Advisory Board; The Pie Filling Institute; Pineapple Growers Association; California Strawberry Advisory Board; California Raisin Advisory Board; Diamond Walnut Kitchen; Borden Company; and The Quaker Oats Company.

Favorite Recipes®
of Home Economics Teachers
COOKBOOKS

Add to
Your Cookbook Collection
Select from These ALL-TIME
Favorites

BOOK TITLE	ITEM NUMBER
Today's All-Purpose Cookbook (1982) 168 Pages	15717
Holiday Season Cookbook (1981) 160 Pages	15040
Breads (1981) 128 Pages	15032
Meats (1981) 128 Pages	14958
*Salads * Vegetables* (1979) 200 Pages	05576
Desserts—Revised Edition (1962) 304 Pages	01422
Quick and Easy Dishes—Revised Edition (1968) 256 Pages	00043
Dieting To Stay Fit (1978) 200 Pages	01449
Foods From Foreign Nations (1977) 200 Pages	01279
Life-Saver Cookbook (1976) 200 Pages	70335
Canning, Preserving and Freezing (1975) 200 Pages	70084
New Holiday (1974) 200 Pages	70343
Americana Cooking (1972) 192 Pages	70351

FOR ORDERING INFORMATION

Write to: Favorite Recipes Press
P. O. Box 77
Nashville, Tennessee 37202

BOOKS OFFERED SUBJECT TO AVAILABILITY.